The Theatre in Leicestershire

A history of entertainment in the county from the 15th century to the 1960s.

Helen and Richard Leacroft

Leicestershire
Libraries & Information Service

The authors dedicate this book to the memory of the Theatre Royal where they first met; and to all those playgoers and performers who helped to bring the Theatre to life.

BOOKS BY THE SAME AUTHORS
Theatre and Playhouse — An illustrated survey of Theatre Building from Ancient Greece to the Present Day, Methuen, 1984.
Development of the English Playhouse, Methuen, 1973.

First published 1986. Leicestershire Libraries and Information Service, Thames Tower, Navigation Street, Leicester, LE1 3TZ.

ISBN 0 8502220 2 8

Designed by Clare Johnson

Typeset in Palacio and printed by AB Printers Limited, Leicester.

The authors and publishers have made every effort to trace the owners of copyright material that appears in this book and wish to acknowledge the copyright of any material where its source has not been traced.

Author's drawing of part of the ornamentation in the Theatre Royal, Leicester.

Contents

Preface

The history of the theatre in Leicestershire as depicted and told in this book could well be a general history of the theatre. Leicestershire shows us a microcosm of theatrical development in the rest of the country; the assembly rooms, theatres, amphitheatres, fairs and music hall buildings follow similar patterns to those seen elsewhere. The same is true of the performances which took place, with a range of players varying from the stars and variety turns of the London scene, to tight-rope walkers and performing dogs, or the charlatans who were ever ready to take advantage of the more gullible members of the public.

In the last decade since the opening of the Phoenix and the Haymarket Theatres, Leicester has been fortunate in being in the forefront of the professional drama scene, many shows being 'tried out' here and later transferred to the West End. It is, however, fascinating to research the local newspapers and records of the 18th, 19th and 20th centuries, and discover that this is by no means a new feature of the dramatic activity that has been seen here. From the 15th century entertainment, often of a high standard, has been performed in our county in its varying forms, presented by both professional and amateur players.

When in April 1983, the travelling exhibition *Curtains* was presented at the Kimberlin Hall of the Leicester Polytechnic, it was augmented by a special exhibit on Leicester Theatres, and it was this local feature which was to become the starting point for the preparation of this book, in which the theatre buildings shown in the exhibition, plus many others in Leicester and the County are brought to life by the actors, managers and scenic artists who worked in them. Reading back over the centuries, it is found that there is nothing new, for the theatre was often blamed for outbreaks of violence and other social ills, just as today television is now the culprit. But the pleasure which patrons took in going to the theatre, and the ways in which plays helped to form social conscience and fashions are clearly to be seen. Strikes, recessions and epidemics all played a part in the ups and downs of theatrical life, as did also the coming of the railways, and the many other innovations and inventions of the times. The theatres catered for all classes, and even the poorest of the population could enjoy an evening out at the circus or one of the music halls for as little as 3d.

The authors wish to acknowledge a debt of gratitude to the many people who have so generously loaned material or given their help during the preparation of this book. These include Kate Bishop, Tony Bond, Ted Bottle, Robert Buist, Dennis A. Calow, David Campton, Dr E.C. Cawte, Bernard Collin, E. Arthur Crane, Paul Davies, Cyril and Percy Dawkins, David Duxbury, J. Percy Fletcher, Dr James Fowler, Mark Gamble, David Garratt, Mrs Gilbert, Frederick Glover, Douglas Goodlad, Kenneth Hillier, Drs Howell and Ford, Irene Hubbard, C.G. Johnson, Robert Jones, C. Wilkins-Jones, Gilbert King, Sean McCarthy, Thomas Roy Miller, Mrs G. Mowsley, George Pearce, Mrs Gladys Petty, Rev. George W. Punshon, Terence Rees, Mrs A. Robinson, Sybil Rosenfeld, H. Shuttleworth, Leslie Simpson, Douglas Smith, Ron Smith, Sherri Steel, Eric Swift, John Tampin, Stanley H. Veasey. Particular acknowledgement must be made to Aubrey Stevenson and the Staffs of the Leicestershire Libraries and Information Service for their energetic help, and also to our son, Robert, for printing the majority of the photographs used in this book. Thanks are also due to those people who have supplied us with information since we first started our investigations while working at the Theatre Royal, but whose names have unfortunately been mislaid over the many years that have passed since then.

The exhibition mentioned above, together with the theatre models illustrated in this book are available on loan from the Leicestershire Museum Education Service, who also have further panels and models illustrating the history of entertainment in Leicester, and theatre history in general. The models illustrated were made by students of the Leicester School of Architecture from reconstructions in *The Development of the English Playhouse*. The settings illustrated in figs. 77, 147-153 and the adaptations of the Pork Pie Chapel and the Corn Exchange, figs.160-1, were designed by Richard Leacroft, and the setting illustrated in figs.152-3 was constructed by the resident stage manager, Percy Dawkins, from the existing stock of theatre scenery.

Helen and Richard Leacroft,
March 1986.

Chapter One

Medieval, Elizabethan & Jacobean Leicestershire

In Europe drama in the Middle Ages began in the churches. The earliest plays, known as Mysteries, were simple performances of extracts from the life and Passion of Jesus, and stories from the Old Testament; while Miracle plays dealt with the lives of the saints. At first these were performed by the priests, but as they developed and more performers were required, they were found from among the townsmen who belonged to the religious and craft guilds.

The Church Wardens' accounts of the parishes of St Mary de Castro and St Martin's in Leicester show evidence of such performances. At St Mary's in 1491, the sum of 6d was paid to the players on New Year's Day, and 2d was 'paid for a play' at Epiphany. At St Martin's in 1560 the players were paid 7d 'for ther paynes' and 11d was paid out for three gallons of ale and 2d for cakes to entertain them. There were also several entries relating to costumes and properties, for example, at St Mary's in 1504, 1s 3d was paid for mending Jesus' garment and painting the cross; the St Martin's accounts in 1546-7 showed payment for making and painting a sword for Herod. In 1561 the same church received 6d for 'serten stufe lent to the players of Fosson'. [1.1]

There is no direct evidence as to how these plays were presented in Leicester; but the plans of a 12th-13th century French play about the Resurrection show that scenes were performed at different places in the church. At each place, or 'mansion', some form of platform was set up as an acting area, representing such places as Paradise or Hell's mouth (fig.1), and the same pattern would have been followed here. Later, the plays moved outside, and were performed in different parts of the town on wheeled mansions, known as 'pageants' (fig.2). A pageant used in Chester is described as

'a high scafolde with two rowmes, a higher and a lower, upon four wheeles. In the lower they apparelled them selves, and in the higher rowme they played, beinge all open on the tope, that all beholders mighte heare and see them. The places where they played them was in every streete....to se which playes was great resorte, and also scafoldes and stages made in the streetes in those places where they determined to playe their pagiantes'. [1.2]

As plays became more secular in outlook an 'Act' of Common Hall held in Leicester on March 26th 1478, laid down that in future all such performances should be undertaken only by the Craft guilds, and that all money and costumes held by the players should be handed over to the 'pachents'. [1.3] It is difficult to trace the exact meaning of pageant in this instance; the word being used to describe both the movable platform on which the actors performed or the actual performance. In 1495 there is a note in the Borough Records of a pageant being stored in the Saturday Market.

As well as plays, religious processions, such as may still be seen in some Catholic countries, also took place in Leicester. Each year on Whit-Monday there was a procession from St Mary de Castro to St

1   *Hell's Mouth, Doom painting from the church of S. Peter and S. Paul, Gt. Bowden. (photo: R L)*

Margaret's church, outside the city wall (fig.3). The richly dressed and crowned figure of the Virgin Mary, standing in a shrine beneath a canopy, with a lighted candle before it, was carried by four men through the streets. Minstrels went in front of the statue, and twelve men, representing the Apostles, followed it, each man having the name of the apostle he represented on a piece of parchment attached to his bonnet. The young women of the parish also took part, and a 'great streamer of silk' carried by fourteen men, and many banners followed behind. The procession wound its way by the castle to the High Cross, and then proceeded out of the town by the North Gate to St Margaret's where gifts were presented.

On the same day a procession of vicars, priests and clerks left St Martin's church bearing a statue of their saint, and with twelve attendants again representing the apostles, but carrying their names on scrolls.[1:4] The two processions converged at the High Cross and continued together to St Margaret's; afterwards the participants returned to St Mary's where they were feasted. The most spectacular procession, which all the townspeople turned out to watch, was given by the religious Guild of St George. Known as the 'Riding of the George', this took place on the day appointed by the Guild Master sometime between the saint's day April 23rd and Whitsuntide.

The Guild, although not wealthy, had its own hall in what was known as Holy Roode Lane, now St Martin's, and also a chapel within the church where the statue of the saint, clad in armour and set beneath a canopy, was lodged. The town records show that the master and guildsmen were often unable to pay

2   *A Medieval Pageant wagon*

the expenses involved in the ceremonials, as at Common Hall on September 21st 1498, it was agreed that 'every of the forty-eight that had been chamberlains should pay to the upholding of St George's Guild by year 6d, and they that had not been

3   *Processional route from S. Mary's to S. Margaret's, after a map of 1741. (R O)*

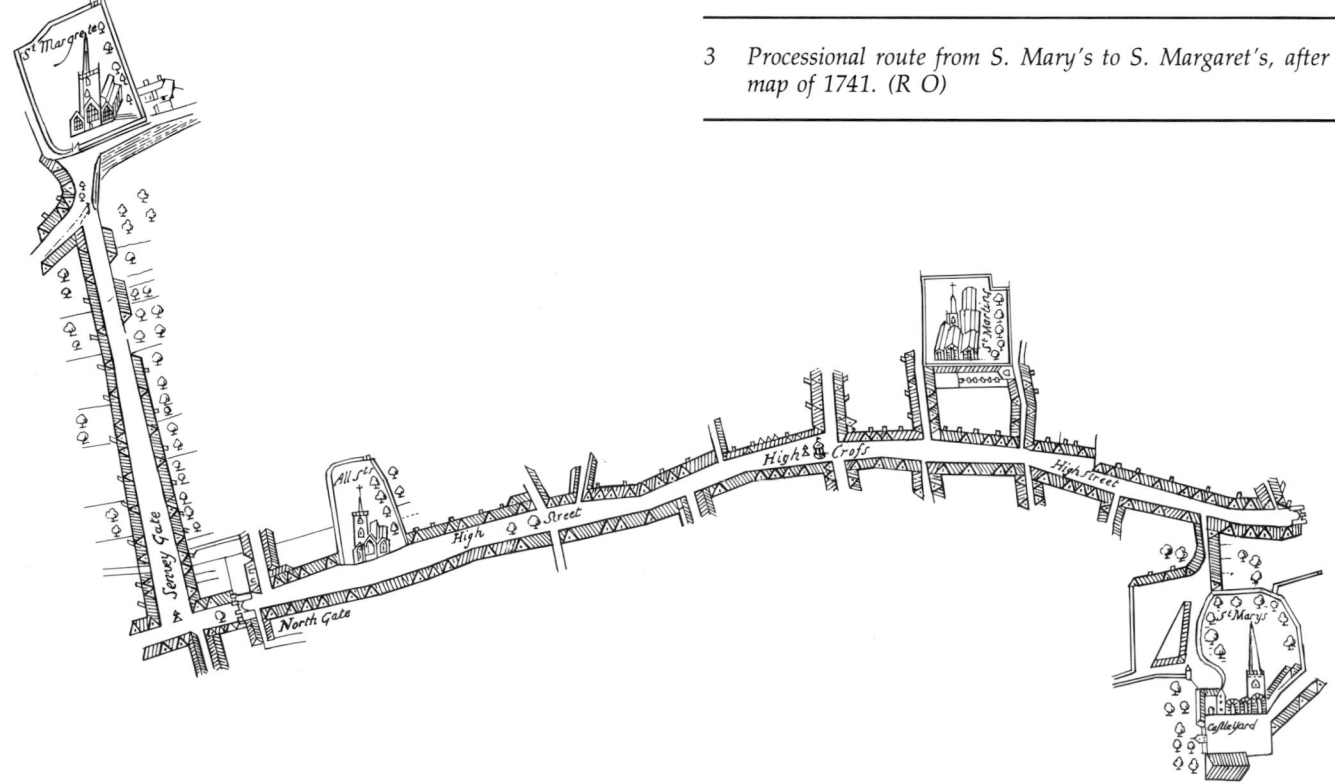

chamberlains, at least 4d, or more if they pleased'. Today the forty eight would be town councillors, the chamberlains being the town treasurers.

By 1523 the 'Riding' had been missed on several occasions and the records state that if it did not take place in any year the master was to be fined £5, and the mayor and chamberlains were to supervise the event. If they failed in their duties the mayor had to forfeit 26s 8d and the chamberlains 6s 8d.[1:5] So the procession of the patron saint of England became part of the activities of the town.

The purpose of the 'Riding' was to stir up patriotic feeling and show civic pride by retelling the legend of St George and his fight against evil, as represented by the dragon. The Princess was portrayed by one of the fairest youths of the town, as it was not the custom for women to take part in plays. The dragon was worked by one or two men from inside a cloth skin which had a head, no doubt with ferocious snapping red jaws (fig.4). All the important people from the town and surrounding countryside were commanded to watch, so much importance being attached to the event that anyone who was so summoned but did not attend, was fined.

The documents of the Guild of St George in Leicester are lost, so evidence as to the method of performance must be taken from the records of other cities, such as Norwich, where the 'Riding' continued until 1835. The proceedings started with a service in the church, attended by the Guild members and town dignitaries. St George, mounted on a horse, was accompanied by the Princess (also known as 'The Maiden' or 'The Margaret') and, preceded by 'St George's standard supported by very tall stout men who had dresses suitable and proper for them', it processed through the decorated streets of the town, stopping several times to hear speeches. Following behind St George came the dragon carried by a bearer and his man inside the body which was 'so constructed as to spread and clap his wings, distend or contract its head, it was made of basket work, and painted cloath over it.' The crowds lining the streets and leaning from the windows of the houses were highly amused by the antics of the creature, 'they always seemed very much to fear it when it was near them, but always looked upon it with pleasure when it was any little distance from them'.[1:6]

In 1343 the Guild of Corpus Christi had been formed by influential men of the borough. By 1489 the guild undertook the building of a hall on the western side of St Martin's church, which is now the Guild Hall in Guildhall Lane (fig.5); after 1495 the meetings of the town's officials were held here. In 1535 Henry VIII broke away from the Roman Catholic Church and guilds were no longer permitted to have their chantry chapels, or undertake the religious processions or plays which had been connected with the Roman Church.

From earliest times the ordinary people had celebrated the changes in the seasons with dramatic

4   *The Norwich Snap-dragon. (Muskett, Norfolk County Library)*

representations, games, songs and dances. Ballads of the outlaw, Robin Hood, were sung by minstrels in the manor houses or at open gatherings of towns-people and villagers. Plays about Robin, in which his band of followers and Maid Marian appeared, were performed at May festivals. An entry in a book of copies of Wills in the Archdeaconry Court of Leicester records that in 1534 William Biller paid 16d 'for a yarde and a halfe of Kendaull', which was the green cloth worn by foresters, and the next entry states that his costs and charges for giving attendance to 'Robyn Hode' cost him a further 16d. The accounts of the Church Wardens of Melton Mowbray for 1556 also record the receipt of money gathered at 'Robyn Hoods Playe', and Melton is mentioned again on July 12th 1562, when 30 shillings was received of 'Stevyne Shaw and hys co[m]pany ffor Robyne Hoode[s] play'. Morris or Moorish dances which are thought to have been brought to England from Spain by John of Gaunt, who resided at Leicester Castle, were also performed at the May games.[1:7]

Although religious pageants were finally suppress-ed under Elizabeth I, the May games and Robin Hood plays were still to be found in the country areas until the early 20th century. They were kept alive by the Mummers, dealing with subjects which had their origins in antiquity; such as fertility, the triumph of good over evil, and death and resurrection. The mummers were groups of men who went from house to house to present their plays (fig.6). Disguise was important, and varied according to the area in which the players lived; in Market Bosworth in the 1840s the Plough-bullockers performed on Plough Monday, when some wore white dresses and tall hats, others had masks and faces smeared with iron oxide; Beelzebub had a dress covered with strips of cloth. At Gilmorton the mummers, who performed at Christmas, blackened their faces and wore top hats and coats covered with coloured rug clippings. The character of St George lingered on as Prince George in the Gilmorton and Lutterworth plays, and as King George in the Caldecote play performed at Great Easton circa 1905.[1:8]

From the 14th century companies of professional players, under the patronage of noblemen or even the monarch, performed in the halls of manor houses and guilds. The first recorded visit of such a professional company to Leicester was in 1530, when 3s 4d was paid by the corporation to 'my lade prynces pleares' who performed in the Guild Hall. This company was under the patronage of the Princess — later Queen Mary I: they returned in the following year. Henry VIII's company also received 3s 4d in 1531. Other companies to play there were

5   *The Hall of Corpus Christi.*
     (Read)

those of the Earl of Derby, the Lord Secretary's and the Prince's — afterwards Edward VI — players. Henry Parker's players entertained the town in 1547, and my Lord Marquis' players of Northampton were paid 2s 8d for a performance in 1550. In 1555 the Queen's players were paid 3s 6d, 'ou and above that was gathered'. At a performance the players would pass round the hat or bag for the audience to show their appreciation, but on this occasion the mayor added to the sum. Many instances are noted in the Borough Records where the town authorities added to the amounts collected with payments from the public purse: an early form of subsidy.[1:9]

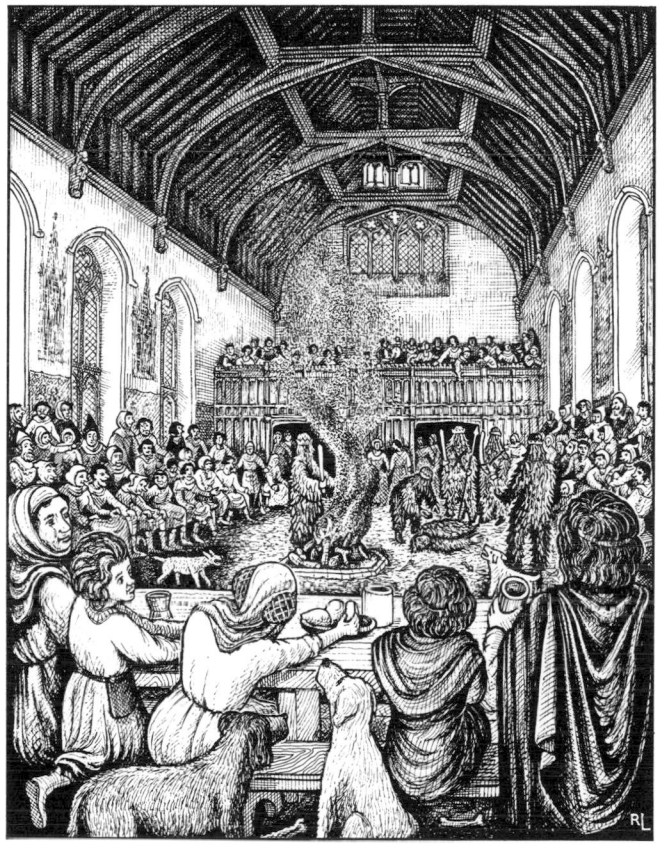

6   *Mummers performing in the Hall of a Manor House*

In 1556 an Act was passed to suppress all dramatic entertainments. However, when Elizabeth I came to the throne the records show regular entries of visiting companies. In 1572 Parliament decreed that all companies of players must be servants of the Queen or a noble lord, and be authorised to play under a licence. This was to restrain the many performers who were travelling around the country, and who might be a charge upon the Poor Law of the towns they visited. On arrival, all licensed players had to present themselves to the mayor, state whose servants they were and receive permission to perform. Players without a licence were deemed to be rogues, vagabonds and sturdy beggars and were turned out of town.

From 1563 to 1574 the company of players under the patronage of Robert Dudley, later the Earl of Leicester, often visited the town; their leading actor was James Burbage. In 1599 Burbage built the Globe Theatre in London where the plays of Shakespeare were performed. It is known that Shakespeare was a member of the Globe company, which also included James' son, Richard, as a patent or licence was granted under the Great Seal of James I to the King's Players: Lawrence Fletcher, William Shakespeare, Richard Burbage and others to perform either at the Globe in Surrey, or in any other part of the Country.[1:10] However, in spite of suggestions that he did, no firm evidence has come to light to show that Shakespeare ever played in the Leicester Guild Hall.

Among the many companies who visited the town were troupes of juvenile players. One was the company of the Children of the Chapel, which was under the protection of Elizabeth I. The company became the Children of the Revels when James I came to the throne, and they played here in 1608, when they were given 20 shillings. The boys were apprenticed whilst they learnt their craft, and provided with education and living accommodation. Some of them joined the professional companies when they were old enough, at first playing the female roles. A juvenile troupe from the Leicester Free School, under the Master, Mr Pott, played at the Guild Hall in 1564 and received 5 shillings.[1:11]

The players had to carry all their properties and costumes with them as they tramped from one town or lord's house to another. They had little time to prepare for their performances and had to make use of the existing fittings in the hall. These halls of guilds and manor houses were laid out in a similar manner, being entered through a passage called 'the screens'. On one side were the kitchens and pantries; on the other side the hall was entered through two doorways in the screen. At the far, or upper, end of the hall was a raised dais where the lord's table was set, with further tables and benches for the retainers set lengthwise down the hall. For a performance these tables and benches were drawn to the sides, leaving a clear open space for the performers, who made their entrances and exits through the screen doors (fig.7). If an upper acting area was needed the gallery above the screens passage, also used by the minstrels, could be pressed into service.

The permanent theatres being built in London (fig.8) followed the pattern with which the actors were familiar as far as the stage was concerned, but this was set within a 'circular' frame derived from the existing bull and bear baiting yards found in most cities, but not to our knowledge in Leicester.

7   *The Great Hall, Penshurst, Kent; with tables and benches arranged for a performance on the open floor before the screens. (Photo: R L)*

8   *The Swan Theatre, Bankside, London; with 'hall' type stage set within a circular frame. (Photo: R L)*

A popular form of entertainment at Court was the Masque, a mixture of drama, songs and dances in which the court took part. In 1606 the Countess of Derby was entertained in Ashby Castle, and a Masque was performed in the Great Hall for her pleasure. For this it is probable that a stage was erected before the 'screens' concealed by a 'travers'

or curtain which 'slyded away; presently a cloud was seen to move upp and downe, almost to the topp of the greate chamber, upon which Cynthia was discovered riding;' Ariadne also appeared riding on a cloud. The clouds descended and the curtain, having been closed, sank down to reveal a scene representing 'the syde of a steeply assending wood; on the top of which in a fayre oak, sat a golden eagle, under whose wings, satt in eight several throanes the eight masquers.' The place was 'full of shields, lights, and pages all in blewe satten robes, embroidered with starrs.' The masquers then descended, most probably advancing from the scene and descending to the hall floor where they danced.[1:12]

Such spectacular masques were developed at Court by Inigo Jones, who introduced the perspective scene from Italy, made up of side wings joined across the top by horizontal borders, the whole backed by sliding shutters, which could draw apart to reveal a further scene (fig.9).

In 1642 Parliament, under Cromwell, ordered the closing of all theatres and the public performance of plays was forbidden. The Leicester records show that it was not until 1722 that plays were once again considered acceptable in the town. However, the mayor and all future mayors were forbidden to let the Town Hall (as the Guild Hall was now known) to 'any players for any shows, whatever ... without the consent of a Common Hall.'[1:13]

9   *The Tudor Hall, Whitehall, London; arranged by Inigo Jones for a performance of* Florimene, *with raised stage and perspective scenery set before the screens. (Photo: R L)*

Assembly Rooms & Theatres

During the 18th century companies of comedians played in various venues. In Leicester one of these could have been a thatched tithe-barn, situated outside the town walls in Millstone Lane, reported [2:1] as having also been used as a riding school and as a store for coal. Similar buildings were adapted as theatres in the county (fig.10), and as late as 1767 a barn at Ashby, used for the storage of corn, was converted into 'a commodious theatre', and opened by a Mr Stanton on Monday, November 9th.[2:2] The Leicester barn was purchased in 1753 for use as a Methodist chapel, but by then more suitable accommodation for the drama had been provided.

In 1750 a Mr John Bass erected a first floor Assembly Room mainly on his own land situated on the Bare or Coal Hill outside the East Gates, but partly on land belonging to the Corporation, who permitted him 'to erect four or more columns' on their property. from a survey made in 1827 [2:3] it would seem that the building was some 77 feet long by 28 feet wide (figs.11-12). When advertised for sale in 1780 it was described as a

'large commodious Building situated upon the Coal-hill in LEICESTER, known by the name of the NEW ASSEMBLY ROOM. For which purpose it was built, and is constantly used upon all public, as well as private occasions. It is also in the season made use of as a THEATRE, and indeed is the only place in Leicester commodious and spacious enough to hold a large company. Underneath are tea rooms and other accommodation for the ladies, the whole vaulted.'

There is also mention at an earlier date of a communication being formed between a Dancing and a Card room.[2:4]

When used for concerts admission charges were 2s to the Room, and 1s to the Gallery.[2:5] The gallery is also mentioned by Joseph Cradock, who, when organising a concert in aid of the new Infirmary, tells us that

'our concert room was used in the winter as a theatre, and finding that I was hard pressed for accommodation ... some ladies of distinction, who particularly wished to benefit the charity ... insisted on my fitting up the upper gallery at full price, and they would occupy the front rows. I accordingly engaged my own people, for the whole preceding night, and had the honour to hand up and down those narrow stairs, some of the fairest ornaments of our county'.[2:6]

Cradock speaks of this as the 'upper gallery', and there are numerous occasions on which the Assembly Room is fitted up as a Theatre when the prices for the Pit are 2s but we read of the Gallery 1s: First Gallery 1s, Second Gallery 6d: First Gallery 1s, Upper Gallery

10 *A Country Barn Theatre of 1788.*
(British Library)

6d or Galleries 1s. The first gallery could well have been built up on the floor of the hall (fig.10) beneath the (second) structural gallery, or possibly a single gallery was sub-divided into front and rear seats, as was the case in 'The Theatre in the Riding' school at Northampton, to which Messrs Durravan's Company moved from Leicester in May 1762. Here the gallery was priced at 1s with Back Seats at 6d.[2:7]

Joseph Cradock also tells us that the Coal Hill gallery was 'weakly built',[2:8] and this was not unusual. The gallery in the Hinckley Theatre gave way in 1804 (fig.13), when it was 'crowded with people ... the greater part thereof fell into the pit, by which accident a few young ladies were bruised.' They did not have much luck at Hinckley as the same thing happened again during a performance of *Richard III* in September, 1835.[2:9]

Fitting up the Assembly Room as a Theatre must have been a considerable operation. On March 2nd 1771, we read that Mr Whitley 'purposes to open the theatre in a few days, and which is now actually fitting up', but it was not until Monday, April 8th that the first performance was given. Presumably the stage had to be built up, high enough to accommodate the 'sinkings' and at least one trap through which Harlequin could rise 'from the infernal regions'.[2:10] Provision also had to be made for the 'Machines and Flyings' which were an essential part of the performances.

William Gardiner, writing in 1853, says that 'The Assembly Room was fitted up with Boxes, pit and gallery', but in the fifty years of its use it is only in two seasons in 1791 and 1793, that we read of Boxes

12   *The Coal Hill Assembly Room, after the sale of 1805, when the building had been divided into lots. (R L C)*

13   *Collapse of a Gallery. (Egan)*

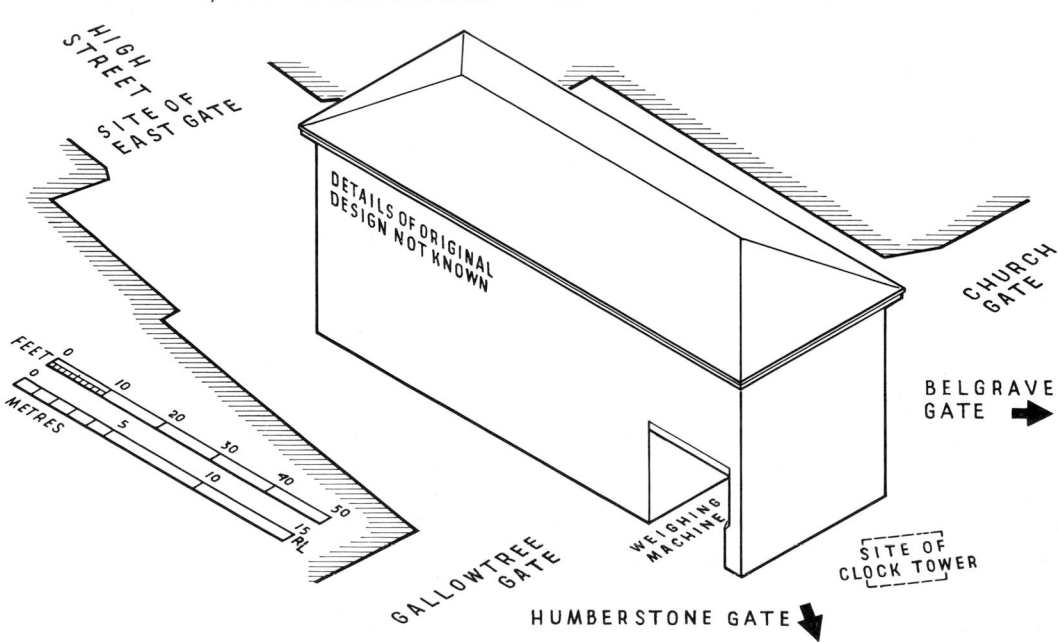

11   *The Coal Hill Assembly Room, 1750; based on a survey by Unicome. Details of original appearance not known.*

14   Travelling players on the move. (Egan)

3s, Pit 2s, Gallery 1s, when Mr Beynon claimed 'that he has this season fitted up the Theatre in a stile of elegance never yet attempted at Leicester'.[2:11] For the remaining seasons only Pit and Galleries are mentioned. Perhaps Gardiner was confusing the Coal Hill Theatre with its successor, which could rightly be described in this manner.

Without boxes the audience probably sat on benches on the hall floor, so that 'Persons of the *first quality,* and those of the *lowest Rank'* were 'seated on the same Bench together', a condition which was described as disagreeable in Bath in 1747.[2:12] On the occasion of the visit of Durravan's Company to Northampton in 1762, 'The pit was crowded with almost all the ladies and gentlemen in and about the town', so, here too, it would seem there were no boxes.

The Assembly Room Theatre was only open for seasons during the winter and spring months, playing usually for three days of the week. The company had a stock of plays and presented a different one each night. However, during the summer entertainment was also provided in the Bath or Vauxhall Gardens, situated in Bath Lane bordering the River Soar, and overlooking the Dane Hills. The gardens were illuminated with decorations, and concerts of music and singing took place, concluding with a display of fireworks. By 1777, however, we read that 'the New Theatre at the Bath Assembly Room will be open on Monday, 8th September next to entertain the ladies and gentlemen of this place with some select performances'.[2:13] The first performance was given by the Leicester Company of Comedians, under the management of Mrs Fisher, when the main item of the programme was the comedy of the *Provoked Husband or A Journey to London.* There were entertainments between the Acts and also a Farce. Mrs Fisher assured her patrons that 'no pains or expence has been spared to make the Theatre commodious'. Prices were Pit 2s, First Gallery 1s and Upper Gallery 6d.

After the Restoration, drama might be performed only at the Theatres Royal, Drury Lane and Covent Garden, which had been granted patents by Charles II, giving them a monopoly: from this came the term 'legitimate theatre'. In 1737, however, the Lord Chancellor was given powers to license any dramatic performances which took place within a twenty-five mile radius of London, or veto any play or entertainment which he did not consider suitable. This curtailed the activities of the minor London theatres and provincial houses, but they overcame the problem by presenting concerts of music with recitations from plays; a charge being made for the concert which was accompanied by a free showing of a play. Plays also masqueraded as 'burlettas', (dramas containing not less than five pieces of vocal music in each act) such as the 'Burlesque Burletta ... entitled OTHELLO, ACCORDING TO ACT OF PARLIAMENT' performed at the New Theatre, Leicester, in October 1836 (p.84).[2:14]

In 1766 magistrates in the areas outside the Lord Chamberlain's jurisdiction were empowered within strict limits to license seasons of plays. So it can be seen why the programmes presented at the early playhouses in Leicestershire were a mixture of plays, with songs (often comic) between the acts, musical interludes, farces and dances; a great favourite being the hornpipe.

Each manager established a company and toured around a circuit of theatres. Mr Whitley, as well as playing in the Coal Hill Theatre, took his performers to many other towns.[2:15] The playhouses were similar in size and layout, so that the scenery and performances could be easily transferred. If business was good the manager travelled from town to town on horseback, the players riding on waggons with the scenery (fig.14); if they had bad houses and could not pay the necessary hire charges, then they tramped the distance carrying their properties and wardrobe with them.

In July, 1772, a number of gentlemen associated themselves for the purpose of putting in execution the statute of George II 'against any Persons acting any PLAY, &c for hire, within the Town of LEICESTER.' They were moved to do this by 'the

15   *The Benefit Night. 'A Beggarly Account of Empty Boxes ... No joke in THEATRICALS.'* (Egan)

distress among all ranks' due to extravagance. They therefore wished 'to remove, as far as possible, all temptations to needless expense, all incentives to dissipation and idleness.' As a result of these threats Robert Chamberlain, who had applied for a licence, decided not to bring his company to Leicester in 1773. Later in the year he renewed his application for the following year, but the gentlemen again advertised their intention of carrying out their threat. They were, however, persuaded 'by the distressed circumstances' of Mr Chamberlain's company to permit them a six week season in the new year.[2:16]

The gentry of an area could usually be persuaded to give the players their patronage, and in this instance the performance on Monday, January 31st, was 'By Desire of Sir Charles and Lady Halford' of Wistow Hall. On this occasion the play to be given by Mr Chamberlain and Co's Company of Comedians at the 'Theatre in the Hay-Market' was *As You Like It, or Love in a Forest*, with a 2 Act Farce, *The Citizen*.[2:17] The cast list for both these pieces included Mr Siddons, husband of Sarah. The manager hoped that his patrons would bring a large party, so enhancing the sale of tickets. The Gentlemen of the Leicestershire Hunt bespoke many plays, as did the Officers and Men of the Militia, when they gathered for their exercises and also the Ladies and Gentlemen of the Leicester Assembly.

The leading players of the company might expect to be paid from a guinea to twenty-five shillings a week, and they had to provide boots, shoes, buckles, silk stockings, hats, feathers, gloves, swords, canes, wigs, modern dress, long hose and military costumes.[2:18] Singers were responsible for furnishing their own musical parts for the band. The other members of the company received proportionately less, but still had to provide certain items of wardrobe. During each season the players and the theatre staff, such as the prompter — who not only held the book, but was also the stage manager — and the box book-keeper, were allowed a 'benefit' to supplement their meagre wages; the manager also took a benefit for himself.

Benefits were arranged in several ways: the manager could make a charge for the theatre for one night, all takings above that amount going to the player concerned; or the takings could be shared by manager and performer after the deduction of expenses. A third method was for the manager to give performers a certain number of tickets which they had to sell for their own advantage. The minor members of the company shared a benefit. If the unfortunate actor did not cover the charges (fig.15) levied he was personally responsible for them. E.C. Everard who

> 'had scarcely been a month there [Leicester] ... wished to decline there being no partner to go with me, and a single benefit in this company, was on no account allowed. ... at last reluctantly I consented ... As I foresaw, so it fell out, there was hardly the bare nightly charges.'

The performance took place on March 29th 1783, the drama being *The Stratagem* by George Farquhar, together with an interlude and a farce. Mr and Mrs Siddons were given a benefit in 1774.[2:19]

In spite of being poor, actors have always been generous in giving their services for deserving causes. On February 9th 1778, a benefit was given for a Mr and Mrs Cooper. They had been in business in the town but by misfortune, sickness and a large family 'are reduced to the indispensible necessity of this only Resource for a Temporary Relief, and Totally rely on the Compassion and Generosity of the Public'. In 1796 the resident company gave a benefit in aid of the Infirmary and Lunatic Asylum, and on November 27th 1797, the performance was 'for the Widows and Orphans of those seamen who fell or were wounded in LORD DUNCAN'S late Engagement with, and glorious Victory over the Dutch'.[2:20]

One way in which managers attempted to fill the house was by the introduction of subscription seasons. In January 1778, Mr Whitley proposed a subscription of fourteen shillings for fourteen plays, each subscriber to receive a transferable silver token. In the following week he thanked the audiences for their support for as he said theatrical companies often had to compete with 'ITINERANTS accustomed to Bellow in Barns and Strut in Stables', by which he probably meant the company at the Bath Assembly Rooms.[2:21]

The companies playing at the Coal Hill Theatre were stock companies. The earliest available newspaper items and advertisements about the theatre date from c.1759, and from these we learn that from December of that year to March, 1766, Messrs Durravan and Co, and Mr Whitley's Company of Comedians played alternate seasons. The manager for the next four years was Mr Miller, after whom Mr Whitley and his Company returned; in 1771-2 joining in the management with Mr Herbert. In 1774-5 Mr Chamberlain, a basket-maker and his wife, who lived in Leicester, joined with Mr Crump to present a season. From December 1776 until January 1781 Mr Whitley reigned supreme. He also took his company to play in Loughborough in 1780. When Whitley died at Wolverhampton on September 13th 1781, the following was quoted in the *Leicester Journal* of September 22nd.

'Whitley! who thought this mortal life a jest,
O frail and transitory no more.
Of all the fancy'd grandeur he possessed,
Hath bore away — but the poor shirt he wore!'

The season at Leicester which began on Monday December 3rd 1781, was undertaken by the Leicester, Nottingham and Derby Company of Comedians, whose proprietors were Mr Gosli and his wife, Elizabeth, who was Whitley's daughter. One of their patrons was A. Hesilrige, Esq.[2:22] In 1785 Mr Stanton took over the Coal Hill Theatre for a season. Other managers for the later years of the theatre's life were Chamberlain and Baker, Messrs. Emery and Beynon, Mr Beynon, Myrton Hamilton and His Majesty's Servants from the Theatre Royal, Cheltenham.

The plays presented by these companies covered a wide range of types and subject matter. *The London Merchant, or The History of George Barnwell* written by George Lillo in 1731 has an important place in the history of drama, as it marked the beginning of a new movement to show ordinary people. This was a departure from the Restoration 'Comedy of Manners', in which the majority of the characters were from aristocratic circles and depended for their success upon witty and brilliant conversation; the lower social classes being depicted as servants, or buffoons for comic relief. After Lillo's play many authors chose themes which ordinary people could enjoy, identify and sympathise with, and which also started to arouse social conscience. On March 10th 1760 *Oroonoko, or The Royal Slave* was performed and here the leading character was a black slave; the play being used as a weapon against the slave trade.[2:23]

There were many performances of Shakespeare's plays, often with re-written texts. In 1785 *Lear* was presented as *'KING LEAR and his THREE DAUGHTERS'*, with a happy ending, the tragedy being felt too much for the audience to bear. *Macbeth* by Mr Parsons was announced in 1762 with

'singing witches by Mr and Mrs Blanchard. Speaking witches by MR COOPER, MR GOODHALL and MRS COOPER. In Act the 4th a *Dance of Witches* incidental to the Play. The Entire *New Scenes* proper to the Play. With all the Original Music both Vocal and Instrumental. Scenes, Machines, Sinkings, Flyings, and other necessary Decorations.'[2:24]

When *'THE TEMPEST, or, THE ENCHANTED ISLAND'* was performed, among the delights presented were

'the Ship, Sea, an Artificial Shower of Hail, and Fire, (as performed at the Theatres in London) and all incidentals to the *Tempest Scene*. The whole to conclude with a CALM SEA — *Neptune and Amphitrite*, drawn in a chariot by SEA HORSES — Ariel and Attendants *Descend* in THREE ARIEL CHARIOTS.'[2:25]

The local paper commented that the play was performed 'for four successive nights... to very crowded houses and with great applause ... The Machinery ... far exceeds any thing of the kind ever seen here.' Managers were not always so successful in getting the machinery into place as the *Journal* of March 12th 1763 records 'We are assur'd that tho' Mr Whitley could not get all his Machinery, ready for last night, that it will be in order for Monday ... and he humbly hopes that no Lady or Gentleman, will take it ill that they were disappointed.' Other Shakespearean plays performed included *Cymbeline*, *As You Like It*, *Henry VIII* and *Richard III*, always a great favourite with the audiences, due to its local connections.

The after-pieces included such farces as *The Lying Valet* by David Garrick, *Miss in her Teens*, *The Padlock*, *The Upholsterer, or, What News* and *Hob in the Well*. In addition, from 1763, pantomimes or harlequinades were introduced to round off the evening's entertainment. The pantomimes, which were accompanied by music, were performances in mime which had developed from the Italian Commedia dell'Arte (fig.16). After a time speaking pantomimes were introduced such as the 'HARLEQUIN MARINER: or A TRIP TO LEICESTER', produced by Mr Whitley's company on February 5th 1781.

'Among a variety of CAPITAL SCENERY, painted on purpose for the above piece, are the following A TEMPESTOUS SEA and SHIPWRECK.
The THREE CROWNS INN,
THE 'CHANGE.

16   *Pantomime characters. (Boz)*

The CONDUIT and part of the MARKET PLACE
And the INFIRMARY — all in LEICESTER.
Likewise will be introduced.'
A representation of Admiral Rodney's Victory over
the Spanish Fleet. A Review of the Ships and a view
of the Rock of Gibraltar with a Salute from the Grand
Battery. An elegant full-length Transparent Painting
of the BRAVE ADMIRAL RODNEY, accompanied by
BRITANNIA, FAME and LIBERTY. To conclude with
a full CHORUS and a Procession of FRENCH and
SPANISH PRISONERS, amidst a general discharge
of CANNON.

'On account of the vast expence attending the
above entertainment nothing under FULL PRICE can
possibly be taken.'[2:26] It was the accepted custom
that for most performances where plays were
followed by farces and other items, patrons might
pay half price to enter the theatre after the play itself
was finished.

When the theatre was not occupied by the resident
company, other entertainments were provided. The
Sadler's Wells Company from London played at the
Theatre for a week in 1769, presenting a programme
of equestrian items accompanied by 'Tight and Slack
Rope dancing. Tumbling, a la mode by a Gemini of
Dextrous Fellows from Lapland ... the whole to
conclude every evening with new Pantomimes.'
There were also many musical evenings and balls and
in 1793 Sieur Boaz presented a grand *Hurlophusicon
and Thaumaturgick Exhibition.*[2:27]

Opera was to become popular with Leicester
audiences ... 'on this day arrived here from London
the famous Mr Breslaw and his Italian Opera
performers'. *The Beggar's Opera* was performed in
1763, and twenty years later *The Beggar's Opera
Reversed* was presented

'The idea of reversing the characters [that is the
men playing the women's roles and vice versa]
was taken up last summer by Mr Coleman in the
Haymarket and was received with such
Approbation, that the papers inform us *no
Entertainment* ever received such loud applause.'
George Coleman's musical version of *Inkle and Yarico*
— another anti-slavery story — first performed at the
Haymarket, London, in 1787, was given in 1790 in
Leicester,[2:28] and repeated many times over the next
thirty years.

Just as the leading actors and actresses of today
learned their craft in the provincial theatres, this was
equally true of the players of earlier times. Sarah
Siddons, the sister of John Philip Kemble, played in
Leicester in *George Barnwell* in 1774. Kemble appeared
in the town with Messrs Chamberlain and Crump's
Companies of Comedians in 1776 in *The Gamester*,
and as Alonzo, King of Naples, in *The Tempest*, in
Barbarossa and *The Distrest Mother*. The comment on
his performance in the last play remarks

'the character of ORESTES performed by Mr
Kemble, was greatly supported;- that his figure
was manly, graceful and striking: majestic as
would become the Son of Agamemnon; bold yet
not tough; not beautiful but engaging: not easy but
expressive of the ungoverned heat of a brave
Prince, who knew no enterprize above his
courage, nor thought any woman fairer than he
merited. ... His last scene with Hermione, was
excellently performed on both sides, and gave the
house great expectations of satisfaction ... Nor
were they deceived — Love, Anger, Expectation,
Torture, Despair and Horror, spoke from his eye,
whilst his voice served only as an echo, to the
feelings of a judicious and polite audience.'
In 1790 Kemble and his wife were engaged to play for
three nights by Mr Beynon.[2:29]

When members of the London Companies were
not required for performances, they took engagements outside the capital. On Wednesday, February
19th 1777, the part of Richard III was played by Mr
Perry, 'who has had the honour of performing it
before some of the principal Nobility in England, at
the THEATRE ROYAL, COVENT-GARDEN.' In
December 1790, Mr Beynon brought Mr Lee Lewes
from Covent Garden to play Sir Peter Teazle in *The
School for Scandal*, Touchstone in *As You Like It* and
Marlow in *She Stoops to Conquer*.

The public were informed that Mr Lewes's benefit
would be on December 22nd,

...'and that as the nature of his engagement is not generally understood, it is necessary to say that, it ... rests entirely with the public, as the receipts of the house on the above night will be his only emolument.'

The young men of quality were always anxious to go behind the scenes, often hindering the movement of the machines; Mr Beynon announced before Mr Lewes's arrival, that he 'humbly begs that no gentleman will be offended at being refused admittance behind the scenes, as he can on no pretext whatever allow it.'[2:30]

In October 1795, Mr Myrton Hamilton advertised that he 'having obtained Permission of the Worshipful the Mayor, proposes opening the Theatre in November next.' His company performed until February 1796. The newspapers do not give any account of theatrical activity in that year. The 1797-8 season was provided by Their Majesty's Servants from the the Theatre Royal, Cheltenham, who ...'humbly hoped that the Theatre in Leicester will be honored with patronage and support.' There appear to be no records of a season in 1799, due, no doubt, to discussions regarding the provision of a new theatre. In 1805 we read of the Sale of 'All that substantial BUILDING upon the Coal-hill, lately used as an Assembly Room, &c to be divided into lots for the convenience of Retail Dealers.' It was finally removed in 1862.[2:31]

In the county towns there are numerous advertisements of various companies of players performing in 'The Theatre'. In 1768 Mr Stanton's Company was playing in the Town Hall at Loughborough, which was advertised as having a pit 2s, and gallery 1s. In 1771 the same company was appearing in the 'New Theatre', in 1774 at 'The Theatre' and in 1775 once again in the 'New Theatre'. The season for 1774 opened on November 21st with a performance of *The Merry Wives of Windsor*, to which was added a Pantomime, *The Magician of the Rocks, or, Harlequin's Progress to the Temple of Hymen*. All the machinery was new and had been painted especially for the entertainment, which was to finish with a 'Grand Transparent Scene of the Temple of Hymen and a Country Dance.'[2:32]

These scenes were made by painting on loosely woven cloth such as gauze or scrim, which, when lit from the front showed one picture, a magical effect being created when the scene was lit from behind. A description of such a scene is given in an advertisement for 1778, which states that the performance will conclude

'... with a grand Act of TRANSPARENT SCENES (painted by the celebrated Signior Columbus) which represent the God Apollo, delivering to the immortal Bard a Promethian Torch. Also TRANSPARENT FIGURES of LEAR, HAMLET,

SHYLOCK and FALSTAFF.'[2:33]

In 1777 Mr Stanton 'begs leave to inform' us, 'that the theatre will be fitted up in the most elegant Manner, and with all expedition for the Season.' So it would seem that in all these cases the venue is most probably the same, the theatre being fitted up for each season in the Town Hall; presumably the Court Leet Chamber built in 1688. In this season Mr Stanton presented amongst other performances, the Leicester Company of Comedians and Mr Astley's Company from Sadler's Wells, performing surprising feats of activity.[2:34]

At Ashby Mr Stanton has earlier been noted as appearing in 1767 in a converted barn. This venue was probably used again in 1769 by Mr Miller's company from Leicester; but when Mr Stretton visited the town some twenty-five years later the performance of *Castles in the Air* was in the Concert Room. The next mention of a Theatre is in a playbill of May 3rd 1810, when 'French Gentlemen Prisoners of War' gave a performance in aid of the poor in the Society Theatre, which they had erected in the Assembly Room.[2:35]

On April 7th 1812, twenty-seven 'principal inhabitants' of Ashby petitioned the Justices of the Peace to grant Mr Charles Stanton a theatrical licence, on the grounds that 'there hath been no regular periodical performances of Tragedies Comedies and other theatrical representations ... for a long period although repeated applications had lately been made by strolling Companies of Comedians.' They pointed out that the Earl of Moira had 'sanctioned the same and agreed to allow a reasonable sum towards the building of a theatre upon his land.' According to Scott 'a theatre was built in Vinrace's yard, behind what is now No 17, Market Street,' which was 'played in for the first time by Charles Stanton's Company' between May 8th and June 17th 1812, and although time is short it may well be that the two references relate to the same building. Scott also mentions a later theatre in Mill Lane, which may well be the same as that which he describes as 'a granary over some posting stables' in Cotton Mill Lane — later Bath Street. In 1822 'A young man belonging to Mr. Bennett's Company of Comedians, proceeding from Lichfield to Ashby ... on Mon. se'night, was mistaken' for a suspected murderer and apprehended, but later released.[2:36]

In 1774 Mr Chamberlain's company from the Theatre Royal, Cheltenham, were playing in Hinckley, and on May 2nd 1774, Mr Burton, a performer of low comedy died, the cost of the burial in St Mary's churchyard being defrayed by a subscription from the company, who also agreed to put up a stone to his memory. In 1793 Mr Beynon's company had a six weeks season at the 'Theatre', which is billed as having Pit 2s and Gallery 1s. The

17   *New Theatre, Hinckley. Playbill of 1800.*
      (R O)

theatre had been 'fitted up more eligible than heretofore.' Which suggests that it was a converted hall. However, in 1800 Mr Chamberlain's players are billed (fig.17) as appearing at the 'New Theatre': perhaps this was the 'small theatre' described by H.J. Francis as standing 'in a yard in the Borough.'[2:37]

In Melton Mowbray the Leicester Company of Comedians appeared at the Theatre in King Street in February 1778, where there was a Pit and a First and Upper Gallery. In May 1787, Mr Pero's Nottingham and Derby Company advertised that the Theatre had been 'considerably enlarged, and every method taken to make it as cool as possible.' In July of the following year *Inkle and Yarico* was advertised at the New Theatre, and in 1835 Mr Smedley's company performed a season at the Theatre, which was probably the building referred to in 1837 in an announcement of a sale[2:38] which described

'A LARGE and commodious BUILDING, situate in Melton Mowbray, which, for several years past, has been used as a THEATRE AND COCKPIT, it has been erected within the last ten years, is substantially built, and may, at a moderate expense, be converted into Warehouses or Dwelling Houses.'

Early Playhouses & Players

In 1799 it was resolved by a Committee of the recently formed 'Proprietors of the Leicestershire Hotel and Assembly Rooms' to build a new theatre 'upon part of the Ground adjoining the Hotel,' with an approximate site area of some 112 feet by 45 feet (fig.18).[3:1] This project was put in hand, but due to the 'extreme severity of the Season', it was necessary 'to postpone the opening', until Monday March 17th 1800, when their Majesties Servants from the Theatre Royal, Cheltenham, performed '*THE HEIR AT LAW* with *THE PURSE.*' Prices were Boxes 3s, Pit 2s and Gallery 1s. In his opening speech the manager, Mr Watson, described the theatre as being 'as handsome and complete a House, for its size as any in the country'. Curtis, however, described it as 'very small, built entirely of brick, and so extremely plain in its exterior that it nearly approaches to meanness. It holds about 70L [£] when well filled.' Nichols described it as 'a small Theatre, built ... by Mr Johnson, neatly and commodiously fitted up, nearly on the plan of the London houses.'[3:2]

A Prologue written by Mr Henry Carter described the interior

'We boast not here a wide extended plain,
Rome's Colosseum or New Drury Lane,'
[Henry Holland's colossal new theatre of 1794]
'But that our house is just of such a size
That it may please your ears as well as eyes.
Our skilfull Architect delights to grace
With art palladian this his native place,'[3:3]

In addition to the Boxes, Pit and Gallery, we know from evidence given at a court case [3:4] resulting from a disturbance in the theatre, that there were also slips or upper boxes approached from either side by their own stairs. This theatre may well have been similar to an unknown theatre designed in 1799 (fig.19). A passing reference in 1817 to 'a grand display of beauty and fashion ... within the Box circle, 'suggests a similarity to this design.[3:5] Here too there were upper boxes on either side at the gallery level. It will be noted that a portion of the stage is actually within the auditorium, flanked by private boxes, and approached by Doors of Entry for the actors, with a window or balcony above each door for use by the actors. The whole of this area, usually with a lower ceiling than that to the main auditorium, being

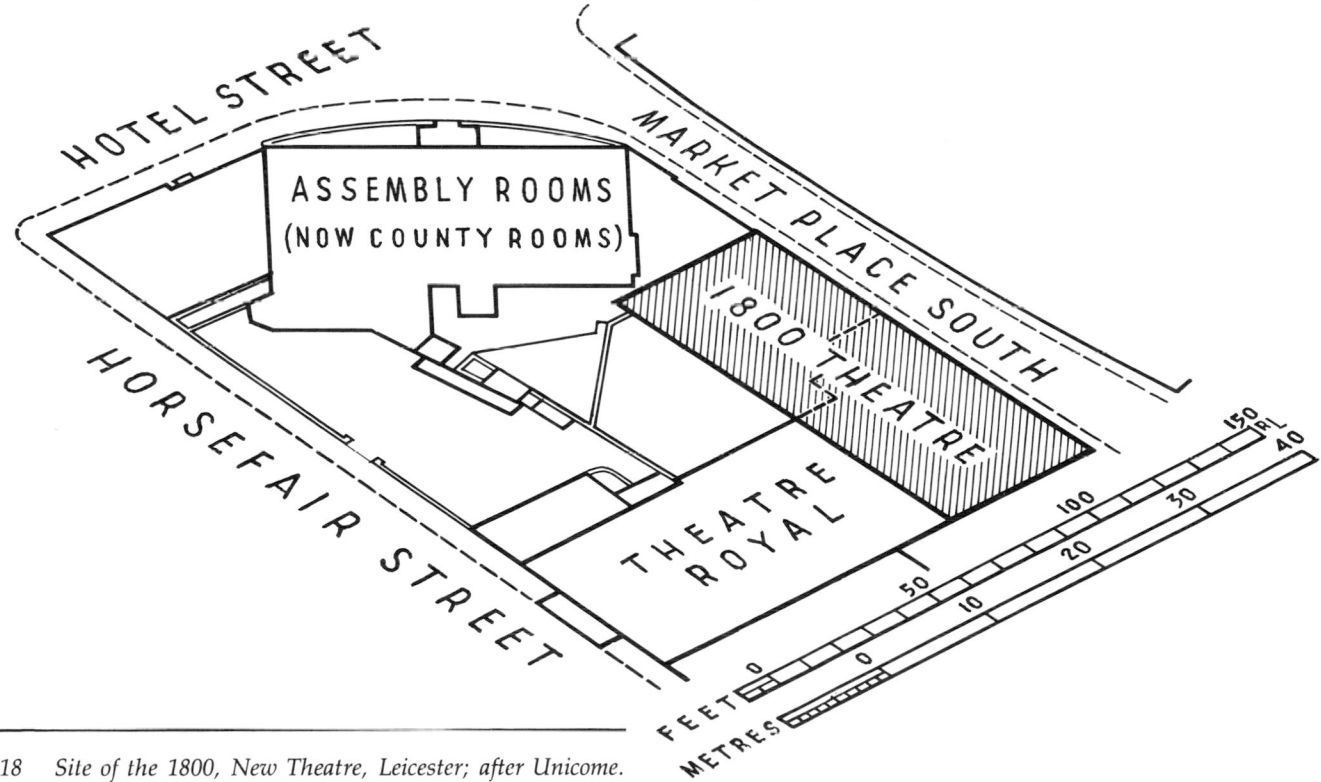

18   *Site of the 1800, New Theatre, Leicester; after Unicome. Details of the theatre not known.*

known as 'the proscenium' (fig.20).

The doors reflect those seen earlier in the medieval halls or the Swan Theatre, but now moved to the side walls to make way for the scenery, which, since the time of Inigo Jones, had become an accepted element of any production. In its simplest form the scenery consisted of side wings (when a scene was to be changed these slid on and off stage in sets of top (figs.62-3) and bottom grooves), with matching lengths of canvas (borders) spanning the stage, which could be raised or lowered to match the changing wings. There were also cloths and special pieces, such as the bridge which fell into the River with the Spaniards on it, in the play *Pizarro*.[3:6] The stage itself had a number of openings in the form of cuts (fig.57:6) for sinking pieces, sliders for bridges, grave and corner traps, and a slot through which the footlights could be raised (pp.46-8).

In January 1802, the Leicester theatre was heated by 'stoves being constantly kept in various parts of the

Theatre'. In 1824 we read that it was 'brilliantly lit with wax', and that

> 'various improvements have been made in every department. A Lobby has been formed at the Box Entrance, some additional lustres have been furnished, together with a quantity of New Scenery and the Old repainted; the former stage lights, so much complained of, have been removed.'

The interior of the theatre was several times repainted: in 1826 when 'A NEW GOLD CURTAIN' was added, and in 1831 when the Theatre was refitted, and 'the house itself is fresh lined and painted.' In 1833 we are told that 'The oil, which, from its smell and smoke, has for so many years been a cause of great complaint ... is *entirely removed* from the interior of the Theatre,' which is now 'BRILLIANTLY ILLUMINATED ... WITH GAS'.[3:7]

On March 17th 1800, the doors of the New Theatre opened at half-past five and the band was in the

19   *Unknown Theatre of 1799. Based on drawings in the Winston Collection at the Theatre Museum, V & A.*

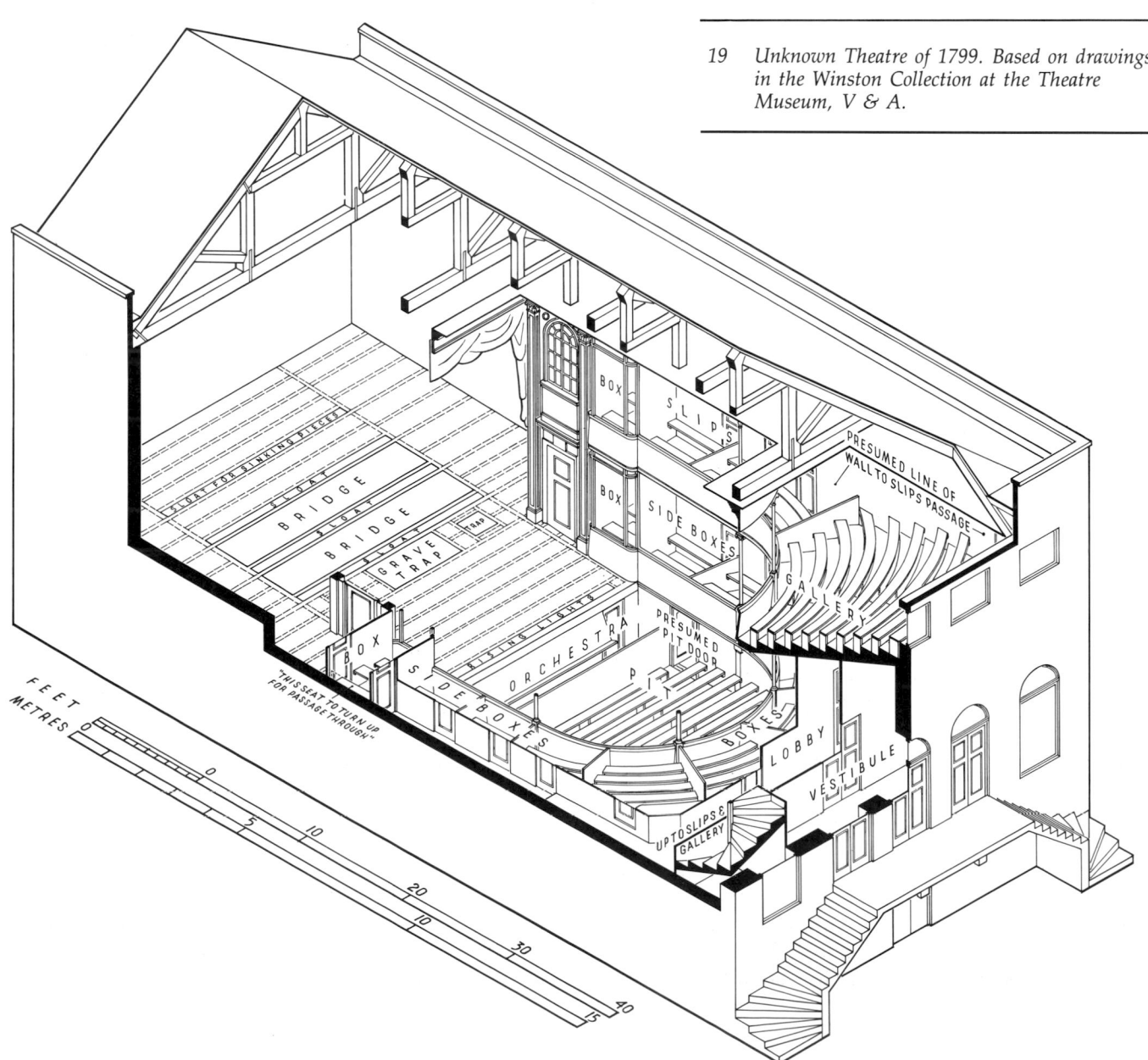

Orchestra at 6 o'clock, the curtain being drawn up at precisely half-past six. The first evening's takings amounted to £21 17s 4d, (after deducting the cost of printing and lights) and were donated by the manager to the Subscription for the Poor.[3:8] This season was very short, closing on March 24th to re-open during the Fair Week in May. From September 1801, until November 1815, the Theatre was under the management of Mr M'Cready, an Irish actor, who had played for ten years at Covent Garden, before becoming a provincial manager. In addition to Leicester he ran companies at Birmingham, Sheffield, Newcastle and Manchester.

From his experiences in London, M'Cready was to introduce many new ideas to the Leicester public. He brought scenery which had been painted in the capital. His production of *Lodoiska,* an adaptation of a French melodrama by John Philip Kemble, had 'The Scenery, Machinery and Decorations invented and executed in London by RUNSIMAN and Assistants. For *Perouse* the grotto scene, composed of shellwork and gold and silver ore, was painted by Mr Whitmore of London, who had invented and executed the original scenery.' Mr Whitmore was to paint many more scenes for the New Theatre. M'Cready also obtained 'at great expence' the manuscripts of plays which had been newly introduced in the metropolis, and which he then staged here.[3:9]

During his management he was also responsible for bringing artistes of note to play with his company. In 1804 he introduced Mr Stephen Kemble, the younger brother of John Philip, who in three nights played in *King Henry IV, The Rivals* and *The Merry Wives of Windsor.* While in November of that year (fig.21) the Young Roscius played *Richard III* and *Hamlet*;[3:10] Master Betty, as he became known, was William Henry West, a child prodigy who took London by storm in 1804-5 playing all the great Shakespearean tragic parts at Covent Garden and Drury Lane. It was on a journey down to London that he stopped to play in Leicester for two nights.

Mr M'Cready's son, William Charles M'Cready, was at Rugby School, and at his father's request he and his cousin were allowed to travel by chaise, reaching Leicester in time to see *Richard III.* They sat in a stage box; behind them were John Philip Kemble and H. Harris, the son of the Patentee of Covent Garden. The play was enthusiastically received by a crowded house, and Master Betty was persuaded to remain for one further performance on Saturday morning, November 24th. For these performances the price of the boxes and pit were raised to 6s and the gallery to 2s 6d. Anticipating crowds arriving at the Theatre, the town authorities set up a one-way system by requesting the drivers of Carriages 'to come up by the Hotel [the County Rooms], and set down and take up with their Horses Heads towards

20   *Vincent Crummles' Portsmouth Theatre. A theatre of similar size and form to the Leicester New Theatre of 1800. (Phiz)*

the Market Place.' Master Betty appeared here again in 1805 (fig.22) and 1806.[3:11]

George Frederick Cooke had started his professional life in 1773 with Mr Whitley's company at Lincoln. He was to become an eminent actor playing at both Drury Lane and Covent Garden. In 1808, M'Cready engaged him to play, among other parts, Shylock in *The Merchant of Venice,* and Archie MacSarcasm in the farce *Love a la Mode.* The *Journal* commented

'The novelty which Mr M'Cready offers to the Town of Leicester, merits every praise and support. *The greatest actor of the present day* he announces for three nights without any advance of admission. All those who wish to see superior *genius* and *merit* will flock to the Theatre, and with delight acknowledge their gratitude for such entertainment.'

Cooke returned the following year to play Sir Pertinax MacSycophant in the *Man of the World.* This was possibly his most famous characterisation.[3:12]

During the 1809 season, Mrs Jordan, the comedienne, was engaged '...to display her superior talents on the Boards of our Theatre'. She became a great favourite with the audiences. They 'had a high treat in the transcendant comic talent of Mrs Jordan', when the 'house each evening was crowded with much of the consequence and fashion of the neighbourhood.' A further innovation which M'Cready made was the juvenile performance. 'To accommodate the Junior Branches of Families that may wish to retire early from the Theatre.' On such occasions the farces and pantomimes were played before the main piece for the delight of the young people (fig.23).[3:13]

Madame Catalini, the opera singer, with her accompanist, Mrs Bianchi, gratified elegant and fashionable audiences in 1810. At her last performance she concluded with 'God Save the King'. The whole house stood up and joined in the chorus 'delighted beyond measure with the loyal tribute of respect'. In the same season William Charles M'Cready joined the company. He had intended taking up the law, but owing to his father's financial position had, of necessity to start earning his living. He first went to the Birmingham company, where he made his debut as Romeo; his father having been a hard task master while he was studying the part. He followed this with Lothair in the play *Adelgitha,* and Norval in *Douglas;* the playbills advertised the parts as being played by Mr William Macready. He repeated these parts at Leicester to great applause. The last night of the season was his father's benefit, 'which proved a bumper. The proprietors of the Theatre also very liberally complimented Mr M'Cready with a present of ONE HUNDRED GUINEAS, as a token of respect.'[3:14]

In the short 1813 season William M'Cready (as he was still billed in Leicester) announced that he would

21   Theatre, Leicester. Playbill of 1804. (Courtesy of the Trustees of the Theatre Museum, V & A)

play Shakespeare's *Richard II*, which had never been acted here before. The other items on the programme were ...'Sylvester Daggerwood and other entertainments as will be expressed in the Bills of the Day.'[3:15] It was the custom for a Bill to be produced every day that the players were performing, giving full details of the performance. Probably when the weekly advertisement was inserted in the newspaper the exact content of a programme was not known,

but by checking the weekly advertisement with comments in the paper, it can be seen that even the main piece was sometimes changed.

The M'Cready company continued to provide entertainments that were well received. In October 1814, Mrs Jordan returned and the houses were crowded for her performances. Whilst on October

THEATRE, LEICESTER.

By Authority.

Mr. M'CREADY has the Honor of making known to the Ladies and Gentlemen of Leicester and its Vicinity, that he has prevailed on

MASTER BETTY,

THE CELEBRATED

Young Roscius,

To perform at this Theatre ONE Night, in his way to London; which will be

On MONDAY NEXT, DECEMBER 9, 1805,

When will be presented the Tragedy of

BARBAROSSA, King of Algiers.

The Part of Achmet, by The YOUNG ROSCIUS.
(Being his first appearance in that Character on this Stage.)
Barbarossa, Mr. FAWCETT.
Othman, Mr. JONES.——Sadi, Mr. LANCASTER.
Aladin, Mr. HELME.
Irene, Miss NORTON.——Female Slave, Mrs. LANCASTER
And Zaphira, Mrs. STANLEY.

End of the Play.

DANCING,

BY Mr. PITT AND MISS S. NORTON.

To which will be added, the Farce of

The Spoil'd Child.

Little Pickle, Miss NORTON.
Old Pickle, Mr. LANCASTER.——John, Mr. HELME.
And Tag, Mr. M'CREADY.
Maria, Miss S. NORTON.——And Miss Pickle, Mrs. STANLEY

Doors opened at Half past Five o'Clock, and to begin at Half past Six.

BOXES AND PIT, 6s....GALLERY, 2s 6d.

☞ Places in the Boxes and Pitt to be had of Mr. Johnson, at the Fruit-Shop.
To prevent Confusion, Ladies and Gentlemen are requested to send for Tickets when they order Places.
✱✦✱ Gallery Tickets to be had at Ireland & Son's Printing-Office, East-Gates.

Printed by Ireland & Son.

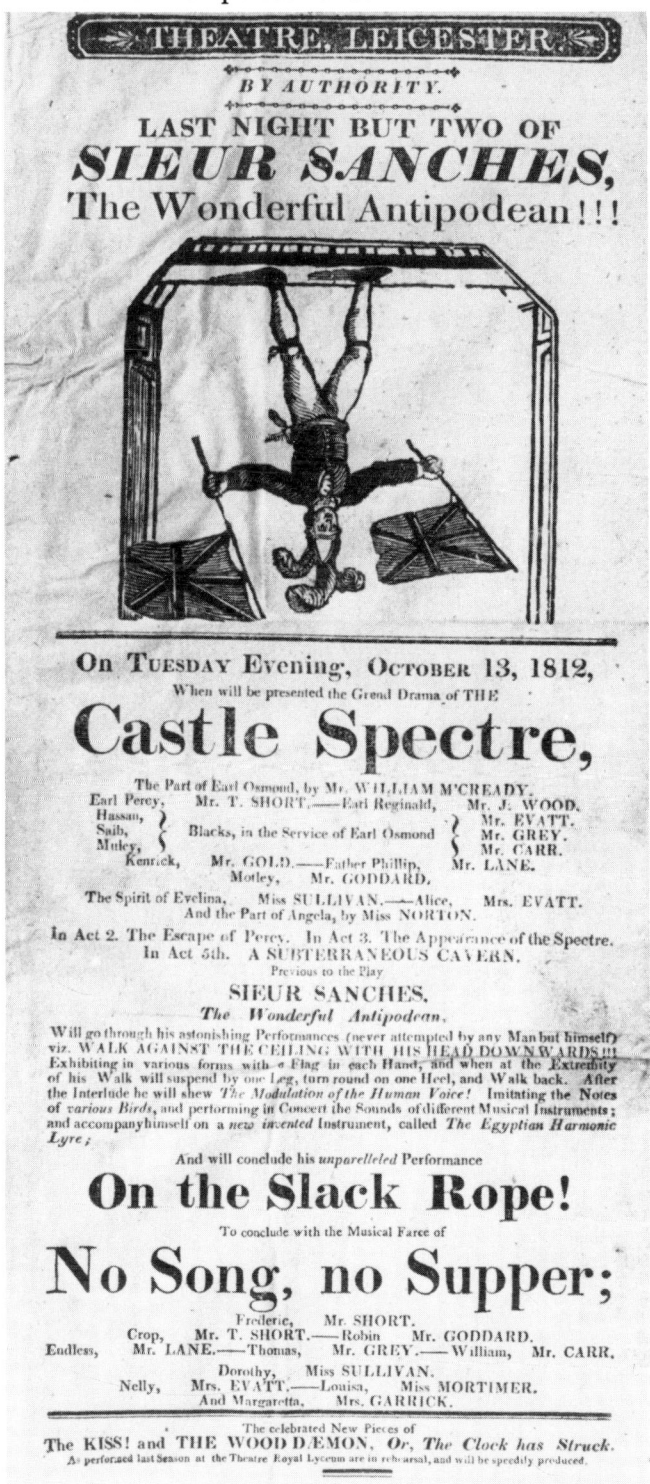

22 *Theatre, Leicester. Playbill of 1805. (R O)*

23 *Theatre, Leicester. Playbill of 1812. (S.H. Veasey)*

THEATRE, LEICESTER.

On MONDAY Evening, OCTOBER 6th, 1834.

Will be performed the admired Drama of THE

FOUNDLING
Of the Forest.

Count de Valmont, Mr. ANDERSON.   Baron Longueville, Mr. WATSON.
Chevalier Florian, Mr. YOUNGE.   L'Eclair, Mr. BODDIE.   Gaspard, Mr. SKERRETT.
Bertrand, Mr. DERBYSHIRE.   Sanguine, Mr. MANDEVILLE.   Lenoir, Mr. BIDDLES.
Pierre, Mr. GENESA.   Albert, Mr. KELLY.
Geraldine, Miss L. MELVILLE.   Rosabelle, Mrs. BELVILLE PENLEY.   Monica, Mrs. ANGEL.
The unknown Female,................Miss SIDNEY.

A Comic Song by Mr. BODDIE.
The celebrated Dance from "La Sylphide," by Miss PARSLOE.

To conclude with (not acted here for many years,) the Melo-Drama of THE

MILLER
And his Men.

Grindoff (alias Wolf) the Miller, ... Mr. ANDERSON.
Count Friburg, Mr. WATSON.   Karl, (his man), Mr. BODDIE.   Kelmar, Mr. WILTON.
Lothair,....Mr. YOUNGE.   Riber,....Mr. DERBYSHIRE.   Golotz, ... Mr. SKERRETT.
Zingra, Mr. MANDEVILLE.   Petro, Mr. BIDDLES.   Jacques, Mr. SPARROW.
Claudine,......Miss L. MELVILLE.   Laurette,......Mrs. ANGEL.   Ravina,......Miss SIDNEY.

PROGRAMME.

Distant View of the MILL IN MOTION.
Kelmar's Cottage, on the banks of a River—The Miller and his Men cross the River in their Boat loaded with grain, and sacks of flour.

THE BORDERS OF A FOREST,
And secret pass, which leads to the cavern where the Banditti meet.

THE CAVERN of the BANDITTI.
Deep recess under ground, with winding stairs, by which the Banditti ascend into the cavern by avenues from the mill.

THE POWDER MAGAZINE.

Lothair, disguised as a robber, in order to discover the retreat of the banditti, enrols himself in their band, and is conducted blindfold into the cavern by Riber and Golotz.—Wolf having fail'd in his addresses to Claudine, as Grindoff the miller carries her off by force into the cavern, where he orders Ravina to treat her with that respect due to his new bride; Ravina fired with jealousy attempts to poison Claudine, but is prevented by Lothair.—Grindoff condemns Ravina to the severest punishment, in the lowest dungeons of the cavern, and leaves Lothair to guard her while the banditti depart; during their absence Lothair, aided by Ravina and Claudine, form a stratagem for their liberty and the destruction of the Banditti, by a coil and train of powder communicating to the magazine, which is conveyed by Ravina under the caverns of the Mill.   The last scene represents,

A NEARER VIEW OF THE MILL,

with a draw-bridge in front across the river, by which means Wolf secures himself from his pursuers.   Ravina is seen ascending the rocks opposite the mill placing the train.   Wolf disdaining to yield himself up, orders Lothair (still disguised as a robber,) to bring forth his bride Claudine, and unless he is suffered, with his band, to pass in safety, to destroy Claudine; at this moment Lothair throws off his disguise, and rescues Claudine from the power of Wolf, restoring her to the arms of her afflicted father.   Ravina at the same time

FIRES THE TRAIN.

THE EXPLOSION TAKES PLACE!!
WOLF and THE BANDITTI are DESTROYED, and are seen falling amidst the FLAMES and RUINS of THE MILL.

AUBER'S GRAND OPERA OF

GUSTAVUS THE THIRD, OR THE MASKED BALL,
WILL SPEEDILY BE PRODUCED.

BOXES 3s.   PIT 2s.   GALLERY 1s.
Second Price at Half-past 8 o'Clock.

Tickets to be had at COCKSHAW'S Library, High-Street; at CHAMBERLAIN'S Printing Office East Gates; and at Mrs. ELLA'S Market-Place, where places for the Boxes may be taken.
Nights of performing Next Week, MONDAY, WEDNESDAY, FRIDAY, and SATURDAY.

COCKSHAW, PRINTER, LEICESTER.

24   *Theatre, Leicester. Playbill of 1834. (R L C)*

31st the audience enjoyed *The Miller and his Men*.[3:16] This became a great favourite with its exciting scenic effects (figs.24-5). 1815 was to be the final M'Cready season. William ran the company for the last month as well as performing. When he left Leicester he was instructed to take home his two sisters 'who had been several years at Miss Linwood's school.'[3:17]

25   *A 1d Plain, 2d Coloured Toy Theatre scene for The Miller and His Men.* (R L C)

It is obvious that on occasions the behaviour of the patrons in the cheaper parts of the house had not been all that it might be, for a notice of 1816 states that

'there is a material and important improvement ... The Gods (as they were terminated) who were heretofore in the habit of RUNNING RIOT, and insulting most respectable characters with *their noise* and *nonsense* and have received a powerful check, by the introduction of some vigilant police officers among them — who have instructions to turn out anyone making a disturbance.'[3:18]

So for a while the occupants of the boxes were able to enjoy the performances in peace.

The court case of 1823 mentioned earlier concerned a fracas between 'three visitants of the Gallery' and 'a dozen of the Box frequenters'. The former had 'quitted the gallery where there had been great disturbance and confusion to get something to drink'. On their return they found the gallery full, and so paid extra to enter the slips. Here they met the constable and another, who pushed them down the stairs, where they became involved with 'the dandies'. Evidence was given that one of the three had been sitting 'in an indecent manner with one leg over the gallery front', holding a jug of ale in his hand. He ingeniously claimed that he was doing this 'to make room for others behind him'.

The description of the whole affair is most confusing, but it is obvious that the theatre was in an uproar. One witness describing how 'he saw scores of apples thrown at the parties in the boxes, from whence many were thrown into the gallery in return.' Another claimed to 'having sent out for a gallon' of apples for that purpose. Unfortunately the report does not tell us if the play was proceeding during the commotion, with the actors, perhaps, dodging the apples which now strewed the stage.

When a 'MASQUERADE' was introduced after the main piece in 1816, the stage was thrown open to members of the public, who, by buying a ticket for 6s and dressing up as a character or wearing a domino and mask, could process and dance with the company to the accompaniment of the band of the Leicestershire Regiment. The entertainment con-

27   *Bosworth Field. Scene design by William Capon. (L C I C): Photo, courtesy of Sybil Rosenfeld*

Theatre, Leicester.

BY PERMISSION.

This Evening, Thursday, October 17, 1816,

Will be presented Shakespear's Historical Tradegy of

King Richard III

OR,

The Battle of Bosworth Field.

King Henry the Sixth,   Mr. BENWELL.
Prince of Wales,   Mrs. TURNER.——Duke of York,   Miss L. BRUNTON.
Richard (Duke of Gloster,)   Mr. ELRINGTON.
Duke of Buckingham,   Mr. HORTON.——Richmond,   Mr. BRUNTON.
Lord Stanley,   Mr. TURNER.——Sir William Brandon,   Mr. PAULIN.
Duke of Norfolk,   Mr. GEORGE.——The Lord Mayor of London,   Mr. ANDREWS.
Catesby,   Mr. CRISP.——Ratcliffe,   Mr. CARTER.
Lieutenant of the Tower,   Mr MORDAUNT.——Blunt,   Mr. JONAS.
Tyrell,   Mr. SINGLETON.——Oxford,   Mr. WILLIAMS.
Queen,   Miss BLANCHARD.——Lady Anne,   Mrs. BRUNTON.
Duchess of York,   Mrs. CARTER.

A FAVOURITE SONG, BY MR. BENWELL.

To which will be added the Farce of

Age To-Morrow.

Baron Piffleberg,   Mr. TURNER.——Frederick,   Mr. BRUNTON.
Hans Molkus,   Mr. JONAS.——Hair Dresser,   Mr. CARTER.
Maria,   Mrs. BRUNTON.——Lady Brumback,   Mrs. TURNER.
Sophia,   Mrs. CARTER.

BOXES, 3s.—PIT, 2s.—GALLERY, 1s.

Places for the boxes to be Taken at Johnson's Fruit Shop, upper-end of the Market-Place
☞ Box, Pit, and Gallery Tickets to be had at Chamberlain's Printing-Office.
Doors to be opened at Six, and the performance to begin precisely at Seven o'Clock.
No Person can be admitted on any account behind the Scenes.

CHAMBERLAIN, PRINTER.

---

26   *Theatre, Leicester. Playbill of 1816. (L C I C)*

28   *A 1d Plain, ?d Coloured sheet of characters.* (R L C)

cluded with the ascent of a 'SPLENDID BALLOON', and a firework display.[3:19]

Mr R.W. Elliston was manager in the years 1817-19. The season opened on the first night of the Races, and patrons were promised the most popular new pieces. Elliston was as good as his word and provided a company that had a 'larger portion of Dramatic Talent than ... ever before witnessed.' He was also responsible for introducing Grimaldi, the famous clown, who performed for two nights and received £70 (fig. 29). He gave a selection of his favourite pantomimes and sang one of his most popular songs — *Typpitiwitchet*. The performance ended with a farce and a scene from *Valentine and Orson*. Grimaldi appeared as Orson, a part he had first played at Covent Garden in 1806. Orson, as an infant, had supposedly been suckled by a bear, and the advertisement promised that the bear would be seen on stage. The house was full each night, and many people were unable to get in.[3:20]

On the last night of the season in 1818, the company joined with the amateurs to present *Richard III* and *High Life below Stairs*. The Infirmary benefited by £50 4s 10d. The following year the amateurs, under the patronage of the Duke of Rutland, gave a performance in aid of the Funds of the Framework Knitters, as trade in the town had been poor.[3:21] Further performances for this cause were given in 1821 and 1822.

William Macready, who had been playing leading parts at the Theatre Royal, Covent Garden, returned

29   *Grimaldi's Last Performance.* (Boz)

THEATRE, LEICESTER.

FIRST NIGHT

Of the celebrated Tragedian

Mr. MACREADY

Who will have the honor of appearing this Evening in

The Character of Hamlet.

This present Evening, FRIDAY, SEPTEMBER 26, 1834,

Will be performed Shakspeare's Tragedy of

HAMLET
Prince of Denmark.

Claudius, (King of Denmark), Mr. YOUNGE.

The Part of Hamlet by Mr. Macready.

Polonius, Mr. BODDIE.   Laertes, Mr. DERBYSHIRE.   Horatio, Mr. WATSON.
Osrick, Mr. GEORGE.   Rosencrantz, Mr. MANDEVILLE.   Guildenstern, Mr. BIDDLES.
Marcellus, ...Mr. NICHOLS.   Bernardo, ...Mr. GENESA.   Player King, ...Mr WILTON.
First Grave-digger, Mr. SKERRETT.   Second Grave-digger, Mr. KELLY.
Ghost of Hamlet's Father, ... Mr. ANDERSON.
Gertrude, (Queen of Denmark), ...Miss SIDNEY.   Player Queen, ...Miss MELVILLE.
Ophelia,........................Mrs. BELVILLE PENLEY.

The Milanese Hornpipe by Miss PARSLOE.

To conclude with a laughable Farce, entitled THE

HAPPIEST
Day of my Life.

Mr. Gillman, ...Mr. BODDIE.   Mr. Dudley, ...Mr. WILTON,   Frederick Vincent, ...Mr. WATSON.
Charles, ..Mr. DERBYSHIRE,   Mr. Jones, ..Mr. MANDEVILLE.   Faddle, ..Mr. BIDDLES.
John, Mr. SKERRETT.   Thomas, Mr. KELLY.
Mrs. Dudley, Miss SIDNEY.   Sophia, Mrs. B. PENLEY,   Mary, Miss L. MELVILLE.   Mrs. Grimsley, Mrs. ANGEL.
Mrs. Taylor, Miss MELVILLE.   Miss Stokes, Miss PARSLOE.

☞ *The Public is respectfully informed that the expence incurred in the engagement of Mr. MACREADY, will prevent the possibility of* HALF-PRICE *being taken during his stay.*

On MONDAY, SEPTEMBER 29th, A TRAGEDY, in which

MR. MACREADY

WILL MAKE HIS SECOND AND LAST APPEARANCE.

On TUESDAY, September 30th, the Opera of GUY MANNERING, the part of

Henry Bertram by Mr. BRAHAM,

Who is engaged positively for TWO NIGHTS ONLY.

Auber's grand Opera of **Gustavus the Third, or the Masked Ball**, will speedily be produced.

BOXES 3s.   PIT 2s.   GALLERY 1s.

Nights of performing Next Week, MONDAY, TUESDAY, and THURSDAY.

COCKSHAW, PRINTER, LEICESTER.

30   *Theatre, Leicester. Playbill of 1834. (L C I C)*

PROGRAMME OF THE PRINCIPAL SCENERY AND INCIDENTS.
ACT I.—SCENE 1. THE EXTERIOR OF THE GEORGE INN.
ACT II.—Scene 1. APARTMENT IN THE INN—Scene 2. EXTERIOR OF FARMER NELSON'S COTTAGE.
3. FRONT SECTION OF THE GEORGE INN. DIVIDED INTO FOUR
APARTMENTS, ACCORDING TO THE FOLLOWING PLAN.

31   *Illustration from a playbill for* Jonathan Bradford *at the Theatre Royal, Edinburgh, showing the four scenes. The Bar and the Little Back Room can be seen through the lower windows. (British Library)*

on three occasions; the last being in 1834 when the house was crowded to excess (fig.30). In June 1828, John Liston, a favourite comedian of George IV, presented eight of his plays on four evenings. His characters included Billy Lackday in *Sweethearts and Wives*; Tony Lumpkin in *She Stoops to Conquer*; Delf in *Family Jars*; Neddy Bray in *XYZ* and Paul Pry. Although prices were not raised, there was no half-price, and several rows of the pit were converted into boxes. In September Madame Vestris appeared for four nights, in which her parts included Don Carlos in *The Duenna*, and Lady Teazle in *The School for Scandal* on her benefit night. Each evening she sang 'several of her most popular songs.' She returned for 'one night only' in October 1830. In November 1829, Edmund Kean, who had earlier appeared for four nights in January 1824, played 'in 2 of his most popular characters,' Shylock and Richard III, under the management of Mr Raymond. When the *Manager in Distress* was presented 'by desire of the Members of the St George's Cricket Club', the 'Countryman in the gallery' was played by Mr Gill, where he sang *The Bumpkin's Life or Fashion in its Glory:* an early example of audience integration.[3:22]

Interspersed between the dramatic seasons were concerts and lectures, although the acoustics were criticised when the theatre was used for music, and it was suggested that there was a need for a separate concert room.[3:23] In January-February 1830, the people of Leicester were given the treat of viewing an exhibition of the celebrated waxworks presented by Madame Tussaud. The theatre was fitted up as a splendid saloon some 70 feet in length. As the weather was very severe, the theatre was kept warm 'with the aid of lighted candles and stoves'.[3:24]

In September 1833, Messrs Penley and Anderson produced *Jonathan Bradford, or Murder at the Roadside Inn*, with elaborate scenery (fig.31). We are told 'an effort will be made in one particular scene (never yet attempted on any provincial stage) so to harmonize FOUR ACTIONS as to produce ONE STRIKING EFFECT! Showing at once THE BAR OF THE INN! THE LITTLE BACK PARLOUR! THE TWO BEDDED ROOM! and THE APARTMENT IN WHICH MR HAYES IS MURDERED!' The review of the play remarked that 'The Exhibition of "four actions" at the same time was strikingly effective, and very creditable to the artists by whom it was executed.'

The following year Mr Charles Mathews presented one of his *At Home* performances (volume 4 of his *Comic Annual*) in which, with quick changes and ventriloquism, he gave imitations of queer people he encountered in a developing plot. Like the *Jonathan Bradford* production, Mathews used two-level settings with practical upper floors, doors and windows, which were at variance with the more normal wing and border scenes. It was at this time that gas was installed in the theatre, but in spite of such ambitious settings and the alterations to the lighting, the managers suffered a heavy loss on the season.[3:25]

In February 1835, *The Celebrated Infant Kean* and the Royal Juvenile Company were advertised with the leading parts being played by juveniles, thus following the tradition of the Children of the Chapel (p.5). They were supported by adults. In announcing a short season by Messrs Penley and Anderson, the *Journal* mentioned that 'it is in contemplation, after the present season to pull down the theatre and build another in its place on an extended scale.' The theatre

32   *Sparrow Hill Theatre, Loughborough, in 1949. (Photo: R L)*

finally closed with a performance by the Leicester Amateurs for the benefit of a Mr Hall on November 23rd.[3:26]

To return to the County. In August 1805, a company was performing at Lutterworth, possibly at the Denbigh Arms where we know that later performances took place. The prices were given as Boxes at 3s, Pit at 2s and Gallery at 1s. One of the pieces played was *Blue Beard* which had 'new Sceneries, Dresses and Decorations, particularly the Blue Chamber with Changes of Pictures in Transparency.' *Blue Beard* also appeared on stage riding on 'An ELEPHANT as large as life.'[3:27]

In Loughborough Mr Beynon's Company had been playing in 1788 at The Theatre. Mr Stretton, however, was performing in the Assembly Room in the George Inn in 1794, while, in 1801, the Cheltenham Company of Comedians ran a short season of plays at the Town Hall, which was 'rendered warm and commodious'.[3:28] But in 1822 a purpose-built theatre was erected in Sparrow Hill by a Company of local Shareholders at a cost of £700.[3:29] The theatre was opened on Monday, June 2nd 1823 (figs.32-5). It was

described as having an interior of 'extreme elegance', 'The proscenium has a lofty and imposing appearance and instead of the usual heavy green curtain, a drop, of light drapery, corresponding with a very handsome ceiling, painted to represent variegated marble and intersected octagonally with fanciful wreaths, greatly added to the general effect and gave a pleasing finish to the whole.'

The manager was the Mr Bennett of the Theatre Royal, Worcester, who had previously included Ashby and Loughborough in his circuit. He informed the public that he had engaged 'a respectable company of approved talent' and 'hopes by diligent attent[ion] to the comfort and convenience of his patrons to be favoured with their kind support.' The season was to last for six weeks with performances on Mondays, Wednesdays and Fridays. The first performance commenced with the singing of the National Anthem by the whole company. The pieces presented were *Speed the Plough* and the Melo-Drame of *The Warlock of the Glen*, which were much appreciated by the crowded and elegant audience.[3:30] The papers do not contain any advertisements for the

33   Conjectural reconstruction of the Sparrow Hill Theatre, Loughborough, 1823

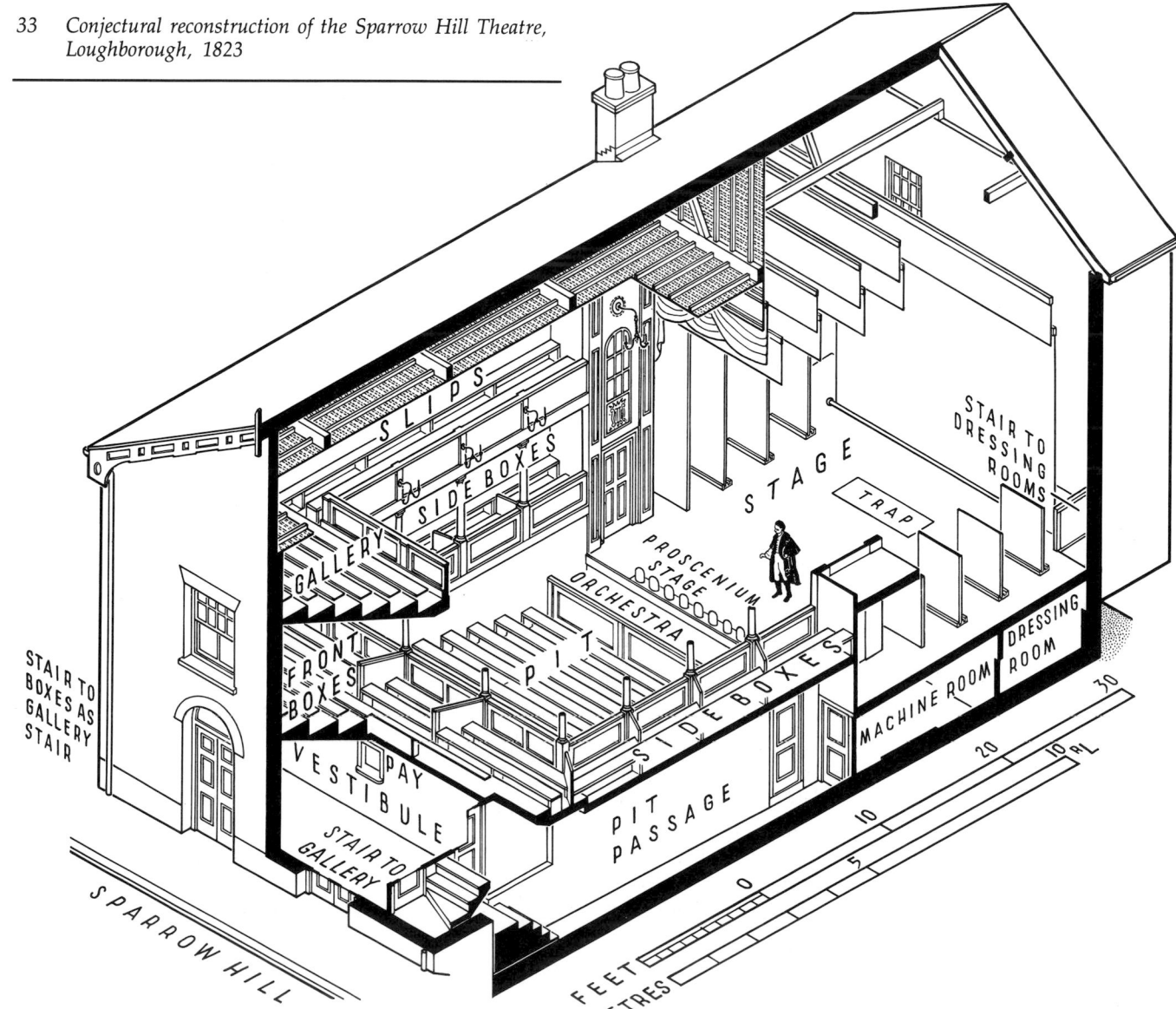

34   *Sparrow Hill Theatre. Markings indicating the position of the Pit floor on the reverse side of the wall to the Pit Passage shown in the reconstruction. (Photo: R L)*

following weeks, these were probably announced by Bills of the Day.

In 1836 a performance was given on January 25th by Master B. Grossmith, the celebrated Juvenile Actor (fig.36). In 1839, Mr Watson of the Leicester Theatre opened for a short season after the theatre had 'been closed for several years'. A company that was unable to play at Leicester performed for a week in 1840, and in the same year Mr Batty presented his exhibition of wild animals, after showing them at the Leicester Theatre. Mrs and Master Owen played at the theatre for a week in 1841, but when a company appeared in 1842 their performance was so poor 'that there never was any attendance. They left the town.'[3:31]

A Mr Carter was manager for a month in January-February 1843, when 'the little place of amusement was crowded out by an audience eager to witness the popular piece of *Oliver Twist*', and the greatest satisfaction was given by the performers. The *Leicester Journal* commented when they left the town to go to Derby, 'They appear to have met with pretty good encouragement, principally from their having lowered their charges to three-pence the gallery and other places in proportion.' For the winter season of the same year the theatre was occupied by Messrs C. and T. Hildyard, whose performances were received with great applause. They were followed by Mr White's company.[3:32]

By February 1845, Mr Ryan, the then manager, had greatly improved the interior and the theatre was now 'Brilliantly Illuminated with Gas'. However, during a performance of the farce *The Galvanic Ring*, the lights suddenly disappeared and the place was left in darkness. The stage manager, Mr Donnelly, who was on stage at the time attempted to reassure the audience, but failed. The general buzz indicating

35   *Sparrow Hill Theatre. The blocked up Pit Passage, from the stage end, with Pit wall on right (Photo: R L)*

that the audience were rushing for the doors. Mr Ryan returned the following year, when prices are given as Boxes 1s 6d, Pit 6d, Gallery 3d with 2nd price to Boxes only, at 9 o'clock 1s.[3:33]

Mr Gill, the lessee of the Leicester Theatre, took over the management of the Sparrow Hill house in 1848. His season started on February 3rd with a

'more talented company than has appeared on the stage here for many years past. The Theatre has been thoroughly cleaned and newly decorated, and presents such an appearance as few persons in the town have witnessed there before. Ladies may now pass an evening in it in comfort'.

Nevertheless the *Journal* had later to note that 'The lessee has not yet received that degree of support which his efforts deserve, but we hope he will yet be rewarded for his spirited determination to make the Theatre respectable. In January 1852, Mr Holloway, the 'well-known travelling comedian', achieved 'tolerably good houses' with his company.[3:34]

On May 9th, 1848 the building was put up for auction, and was purchased by T. Cradock, Esq., for £288, but the sale fell through. After this the theatre appears to have been used only very occasionally, and in 1855, after undergoing extensive internal

36   *Loughborough. Playbill of 1836. (L.Simpson)*

37   *Bath Street Theatre, Ashby. Exterior in 1949 with the entrance doorway to the theatre in centre (Photo: R L)*

38   *Bath Street Theatre. Interior in 1949. (Photo: R L)*

alterations and repairs, it was opened as a Free Church. In 1856 it underwent a further 'transform-ation, being now let as a Lecture Hall and Music Salon, for which, after the internal alterations that have been made, it is admirably adapted.'[3:35] It is probable that it was now that the theatre suffered the fate of so many similar theatres throughout the country, when the boxes were removed and the pit floored over level with the stage to make a 'useful hall'. In 1949 when the building was surveyed, only the understage walls remained, together with some marks on the walls indicating the original positions of the floors to the pit, boxes and gallery (fig.34), sufficient at least for the preparation of the con-jectural restoration of the theatre (fig.33).

On February 9th 1857 the first meeting of the Manchester Unity of Oddfellows took place in the building, which they had purchased the previous year. Occasional use was made of the hall for music or lectures by such bodies as the Temperance Society or the Nottingham Band of Hope. Our last record of the Oddfellows Hall, prior to its later use as an auctioneer's mart, concerns a prophetic lecture by a Mr Jerrad, entitled '"Burning up of the Earth in 1867"' ... several paid their money and took their seats, and although they waited a long time for the "Prophet", he was not to be found, and a pretty hubbub followed. The lights were put out, and the audience demanded their money back, which after some demure was returned.'[3:36]

After Loughborough, Mr Bennett had turned his attention to Ashby, where he opened the New Theatre in Bath Street on June 2nd 1828. This theatre was at first floor level, approached by a passageway through a terrace on the street frontage, where there were double doors with, originally, a bust of Shakes-peare over (figs.37-40). The interior was 'neatly fitted up with Boxes, Gallery and Pit. ... The House will hold about £50.'[3:37]

The advertisement for the first performances announced to the 'Nobility, Gentry and Inhabitants of Ashby' an engagement for three nights of the 'celebrated and fascinating Actress MISS FOOTE.' Boxes were 3s, Pit 2s, and Gallery 1s and there was to be 'No Half-price to any part of the House' (fig.41).[3:38] In his book, *Nine Years of an Actor's Life*, Robert Dyer wrote of his experiences in Mr Bennett's company. Although the house was thin on the first night, 'the tide of public favour set in full upon us, which continued to the last night of the season', and he compared 'the excellent taste' of Ashby with Mr Bennett's other theatre, where they had 'to suffer the purgatory of a Loughborough audience'.

William Macready played a short season in 1830, and in 1835 'the well-conducted place of rational entertainment' was once again opened for a limited season by Mr Bennett.[3:39] In 1837, however, a per-formance of *Richard III* received scathing criticism in the *Journal*.

'Could our immortal bard have witnessed its representation, he most certainly would have dropped a tear to the March of Intellect, and scolded dame Fortune for allowing him to witness such a mangled hodge-podge as that represented. ... The hero of the piece was Mr Laws, ... and had he died sooner he would not have been missed. ... Miss Pernley ... with a better company would have performed her character respectably, but with the present tadpole set she was lost. The orchestra was well supplied with cat-gut scrapers.'[3:40]

In 1840 Mr Batty displayed his animals, but for the next few years there was little dramatic activity, although in 1854 Mr H. Lacey of the Theatres Royal, Worcester and Coventry, staged a six week season with some success. In 1860 a Mr W.P. Dewes of the Hastings Rifle Company staged an amateur pro-

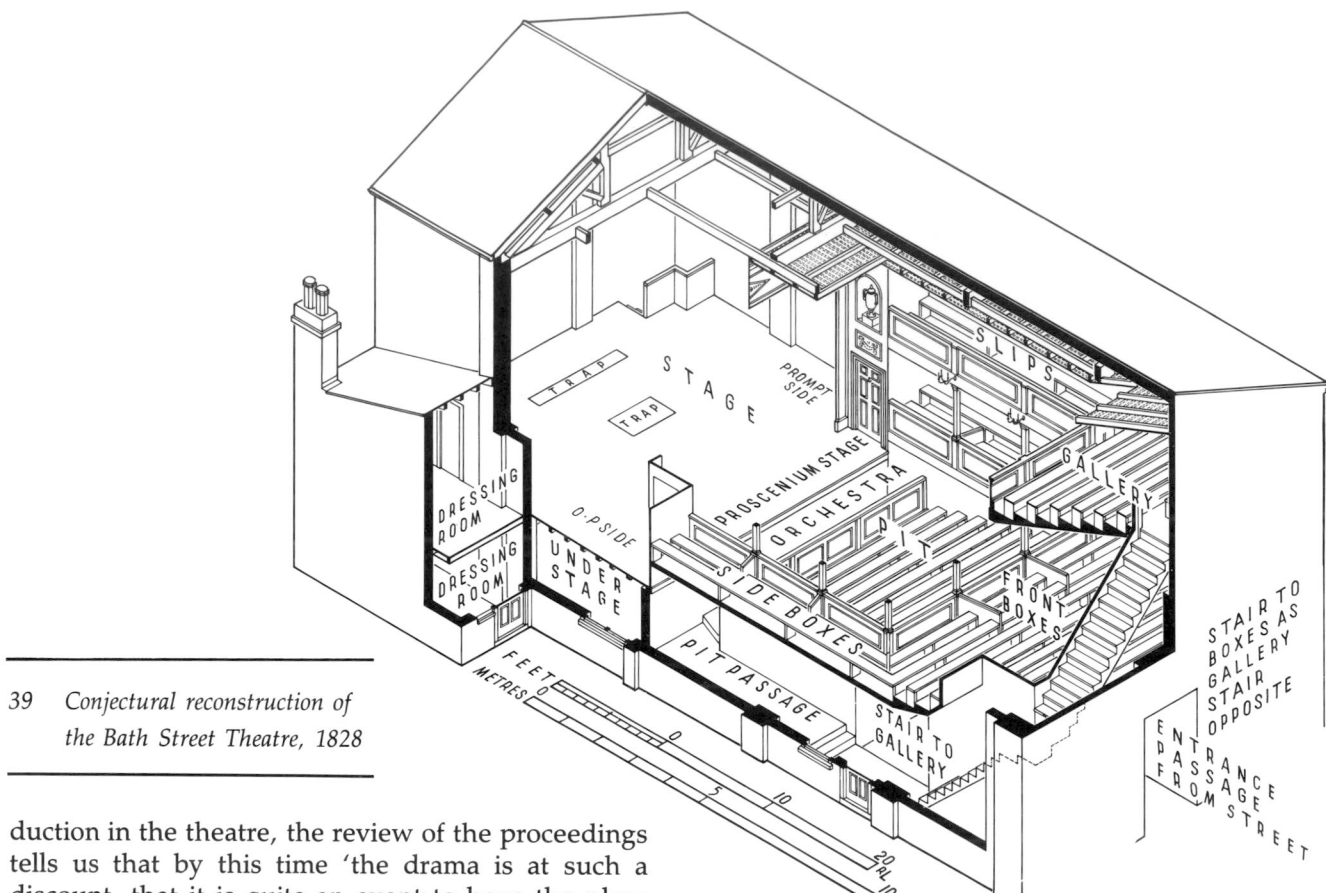

*39   Conjectural reconstruction of
        the Bath Street Theatre, 1828*

duction in the theatre, the review of the proceedings tells us that by this time 'the drama is at such a discount, that it is quite an event to have the place open. ... The theatre, a compact building, although much in decay, is not capable of holding more than 250 persons', and it adds that the production 'was hardly suitable for so small a stage.'[3:41]

In June 1862, the 'Theatre Royal' presented *Othello*, when the Boxes were at 2s, Pit 1s, and Gallery 6d, but by 1867 it had suffered a similar fate to the Sparrow Hill Theatre, with the removal of its internal furnishings, and the pit and stage floored over.[3:42] In 1890 it had 'fallen into the hands of an enterprising tradesman, and the decorator and carpenter have transformed the delapidated structure used alternately as a furniture store room, a chapel, and eventually as an auction room, into a fine Hall'. The Floral Hall opened with a concert on April 21st (fig.42) and was available for hire for 'meetings and addresses.'[3:43] A survey carried out in the same year as that at Loughborough made it possible to prepare the conjectural reconstruction (fig.39). The building was demolished in September 1967.

It would seem that both of Bennett's theatres differed from the 1800 Leicester theatre in that the pit and enclosing boxes were rectangular, following the pattern still to be seen in the 1788 theatre at Richmond, Yorkshire (figs.43-4). Like this theatre it is reasonable to assume that both had a proscenium stage within the auditorium, flanked by Doors of Entry.

40   Bath Street Theatre. Rear view in 1949. (Photo: R L)

Theatre, Ashby-de-la-Zouch.

FOR THE BENEFIT OF

Miss FOOTE,

And the Last Night of her Engagement.

On WEDNESDAY Evening, JUNE 4th. 1828.

Will be performed Mrs. Centlivre's Comedy of THE

WONDER

A Woman keeps a Secret!!

Don Felix,	Mr. DYER.	Frederick,	Mr. ROBERTS.
Don Lopez,	Mr. WIGHTMAN	Lissardo,	Mr. CASSUP
Don Pedro,	Mr. LOVEDAY.	Gibby,	Mr. HALL.
Colonel Britton,	Mr. HAZELTON.	Vasquez,	Mr. WATSON.

Donna Violante, by Miss FOOTE.

	Donna Isabella,	Miss SIDNEY.	
Inis,	Mrs. WATSON.	Flora,	Mrs. DYER.

In the Course of the Evening Miss FOOTE will sing the following Songs :—

THE MERRY SWISS MAID,

A Characteristic "Dancing Song,"

AND "THE LITTLE HIGHLAND LAD,"

The whole to conclude with the Musical Farce of

THE

HIGHLAND REEL.

Moggy M'Gilpin, ... by Miss FOOTE.

Charlie . . . . Mr. BENNETT.

M'Gilpin,	Mr. LOVEDAY.	Serjeant Jack,	Mr. DYER.
Shelty,	Mr. CASSUP.	Laird of Raasey,	Mr. WIGHTMAN.
Croudy,	Mr. HAZELTON.	Sandy,	Mr. WATSON.
Captain Dash,	Mr. HALL.	Benin,	Miss SPRAY.
	Jenney,	Miss SIDNEY.	

THE PIECE WILL CONCLUDE WITH

A Scotch Reel by Miss FOOTE and the other Characters.

*** Doors to be opened at Half-past Six, and the Curtain to rise precisely at Seven o'Clock.

BOXES 3s.—PIT 2s.—GALLERY 1s.

Tickets, and Places for the Boxes may be had at the Box-Office of the Theatre, at Beadsmoore's Printing-Office, Kilwardby-St. and of Mr. BENNETT, (Manager) Bath-Street.

41   *Bath Street Theatre, Playbill for 1828. (R O)*

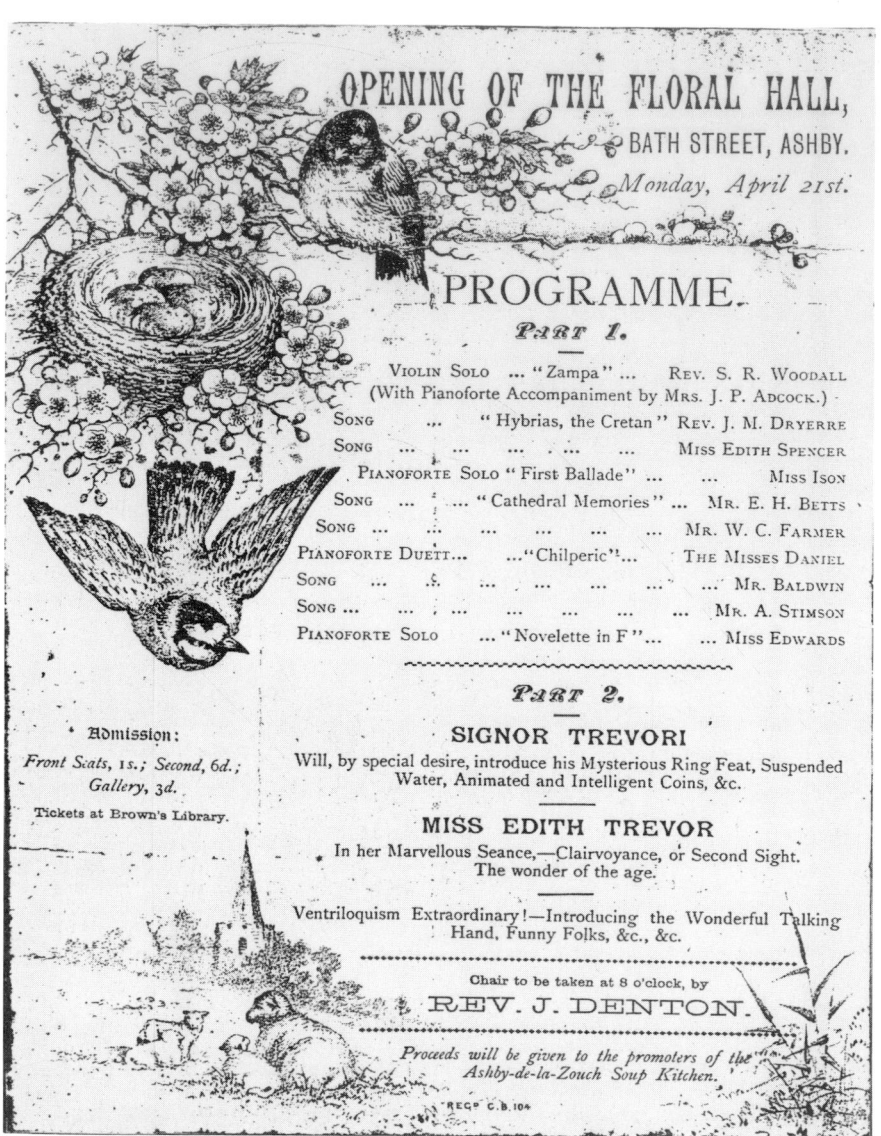

42   *Floral Hall, Ashby. Programme for 1890. (Mrs Gilbert)*

43   *The Georgian Theatre, Richmond, Yorks. 1788. A theatre similar in size and layout to the Loughborough and Ashby theatres. (Photo: R L)*

44   *The Georgian Theatre, Richmond. (Photo: R L)*

Amateurs & Private Theatricals

We have already seen the players performing in the halls of manor houses, and, at Ashby, in the home of the nobility, where members of the household took part. Such theatrical performances, often with professional actors giving assistance, were to continue into the 18th and 19th centuries. As a setting for such activities a room in a stately home might be fitted up as a theatre; or a converted barn could be used. Leicestershire had few great houses, but there were mansions and hunting lodges to which the aristocracy and gentlemen's families came for a few weeks in the year, and where theatrical entertainment was enjoyed.

Joseph Cradock of Gumley Hall staged performances in a room at his house. As an author he had gained some experience of the professional theatre, when his tragedy *Zobeide*, had been performed at Covent Garden. It was repeated in the Coal Hill Theatre by Messrs Whitley and Herbert's Company of Comedians on December 18th 1772. There is no evidence concerning the appearance of the Theatre at Gumley; but it must have been of a reasonable size and well fitted up, as Lady Craven borrowed scenes from Cradock for her theatricals at Combe Abbey in Warwickshire.[4:1]

On September 9th and 10th 1773, the tragedy of *Mahomet* with an entertainment of *The Lyar* were played at Gumley. The newspaper commented that Cradock's 'distinguished tastes and abilities in dramatic performances cannot be sufficiently admired'. In the same year, Joseph and his wife went into Northamptonshire on November 29th-30th to assist their neighbour Mr Hanbury with his theatricals at Kelmarsh Hall. The play was *Venice Preserved*, also taking part was Mr D. Garrick, a nephew of the famous actor. A review reads 'the Entertainments of each evening were conducted with singular elegance and propriety and gave universal satisfaction.' The 'famous actor' did not himself play at the Leicester theatre, but an impromptu performance of Falstaff given with Cradock and some friends in the Three Cranes Inn for their own amusement, was shared with some townsmen who overheard them from an adjoining room.[4:2]

It was at Edward Hartopp's residence, Little Dalby Hall near Melton Mowbray, that many performances were given for the pleasure of the participants and the neighbourhood (fig.45). Although there were breaks, the family continued the tradition from 1777

until 1878. In 1777 an epilogue was spoken which was found among Cradock's papers.[4:3] Evidence of performances at Little Dalby comes from the Hartopp papers, when George Bunney was employed in preparing scenery. From his bills we learn that he made scenes and sewed rollers on to them, he also made bags to store the cloths. He prepared a frontispiece and a floor covering for the stage, and made coverings for the seats. The theatre, which was set up in the hall, must also have had a green front curtain, as Bunney spent a day working on it between November 1798 and October 1799.

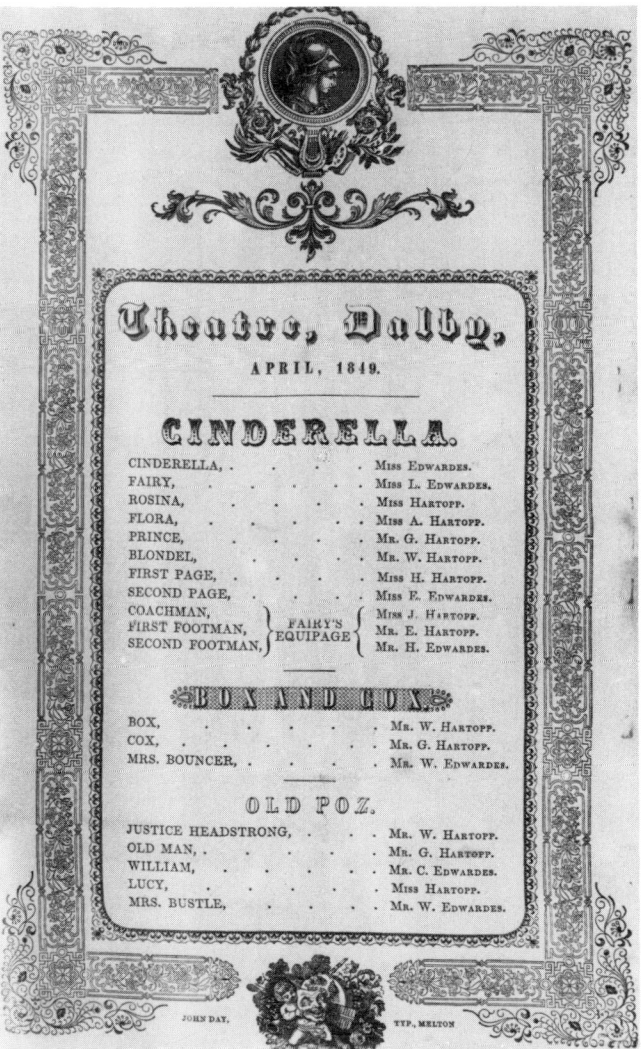

45   *Hartopp Theatre, Dalby. 1849. (N H M)*

In 1798 Richard Johnson, a builder, worked on the theatre. The bill for his services and those of a man totalled £23 6s 8d. Apart from the number of days worked, the only details given are for painting the dressing room, and taking down the music room, dressing rooms, scenes, stage and clearing away. The performances took place in August, and the plays presented were *Othello*, followed by *High Life Below Stairs*, *The Trials of Temper* with the *Commissary*, *Romeo and Juliet* and *High Life* repeated. The cast had the assistance of professional players from the Stamford Theatre and from Melton Mowbray. The Band of the Melton Mowbray Infantry Corps provided the music. Mr Bilsborrow, a friend of the family, not only acted but wrote *The Trials of Temper* and also painted the scenes. The audience was composed of guests from the nobility and gentry, but certain nights were set aside for tenants and tradespeople. Similar performances were given for six nights in August 1799.

In 1800 the building of a proper theatre, adjoining the hall, was commenced. It had a gallery and place for the orchestra, whilst the stage contained a trap which had iron work to wind it up. There was also mechanism for changing the scenes, and raising and lowering the lights.[4:4] It opened in July 1801.

'A new and beautiful Theatre has been built by Mr Hartopp, capable of containing, with ease, between three and four hundred people. ... The private amateur performers were the two Mr Hartopps, Mr Bundy and Mr Bilsborrow. They were assisted by the whole of Mr Hamilton's Company and detachments from the Cheltenham, Stamford and Drury Lane theatres. ...After each night's performance, cold collations were provided for the company in all the principal rooms of the house, and followed by gay and sprightly dances.'[4:5]

Similar theatricals were staged during the summer until 1804, with the addition of a Christmas entertainment in 1803. Further evidence of performances comes from playbills dating from 1833 to 1878, which were in the possession of a member of the family.[4:6] By 1847 the theatre had been demolished and when theatricals were presented in that year, they took place in a theatre which had been 'erected in the entrance Hall, the proscenium of which was tastefully decorated with the arms of this ancient family.'[4:7]

The Leicestershire papers do not carry notices of all amateur performances, but through the 1850s and '60s there are sufficient to tell us that private theatricals were an important part of the activities of families when they were in the Shires. Lord Wilton's Hunting seat, Egerton Lodge, Melton Mowbray, was the setting for theatricals in 1850

'The genteel company began to assemble at 9 o'clock and were ushered into the corridors, which

had been neatly and appropriately fitted up as a private theatre, in which the more juvenile branches of this graceful family were to display their histrionic powers ... At precisely a quarter past nine, the prompter's bell was rung and the curtain drew up, and revealed a scene of surpassing loveliness.'[4:8]

The Duke of Rutland presented theatricals in the ballroom at Belvoir Castle in 1851. The pieces played were *A Day After the Wedding*, *The Village Lawyer*, an Epilogue and a farce. The curtain did not come down until 2 o'clock in the morning. The performance of 1854 (fig.46) had ... 'a very beautiful drop scene ... representing Belvoir Castle with the woods and also the Vale of Belvoir in the distance.'[4:9]

Colonel and Mrs Markham gave entertainments at their hunting residence, 'The House', Melton Mowbray, in 1877. The audience was by invitation and consisted of leading members of the Hunt and local tradespeople. 'The handsome drawing room was specially seated for their accommodation and the Library, entered by large sliding doors, served as a stage.'[4:10]

Whilst the nobility and gentry staged performances in their own homes, there were also amateur theatricals which took place, either in a Theatre, or in an available hall. Mr Bernard de Lisle and the Musical and Dramatic Society, presented plays in St Winifred's School, Shepshed. In 1887 the inhabitants of the village and surrounding areas were given 'an opportunity of witnessing one of those fine dramatic performances which are so seldom to be witnessed in country places'. The piece was the *Eumenides* of Aeschylus, with performers from the University of Cambridge. The orchestra was composed of local musicians. The costumes were designed by Miss Lucy Haynes and Miss Lawrence Alma-Tadema. A special feature was the scenery, painted by Mons. Wante, Academie Royale de Peinture, Antwerp. The room was crowded for every performance.[4:11]

The Earl of Denbigh was patron of an amateur performance on January 21st 1863, in the Town Hall, Lutterworth. At Hinckley, two amateur concerts were given in the Corn Exchange in 1859 to promote the Penny Bank, and for the benefit of the poor.[4:12] It was Mr Trivett, landlord of the George Hotel, Hinckley, who in 1874 built St George's Hall adjoining his inn. This was used by the Hinckley Amateur Dramatic Society for a performance in aid of the Free Library Fund. The house was full and £21 was taken. The hall was still in use for dramatic purposes in 1893 and 1894.[4:13]

As early as 1767 Mr Springthorpe, Master of the White Hart in Ashby, had performed with Mr Miller's Company at the Coal Hill Theatre in Leicester, playing the part of Young Hob in *Hob in the Well*, to the loud applause of the audience. The company, however, possibly unused to the piece, were 'shamefully imperfect' with their lines.[4:14]

After the closing of the Sparrow Hill Theatre in Loughborough, theatrical presentations took place in the new Town Hall. When the Amateur Dramatic Society played in January 1867, 'the room was well filled ... nearly the whole available space being appropriated for reserved seats.' At the fifth annual concert of the Loughborough Institute held in the Victoria Room in the Town Hall 'the characters were sustained principally by local amateurs and the performance throughout would have been no discredit to professionals. On the first evening the front seats were filled by the elite of the neighbourhood'. By 1892 there were two amateur societies in the Town. 'The Dramatic Society depend upon popular prices and Bank Holidays, their friends in amateurism look

to the wearers of evening dress, to ''carriages at 10.30'', and to fashionable nights.'[4:15]

Amateur performances were held at Melton Mowbray Corn Exchange in 1860 (fig.47). The actors included E.B. and Captain Hartopp. The room had been fitted up as

'a capital theatre, ... capable of holding some 400-500 persons, was splendidly decorated for the occasion, a very neat and compact stage, with all suitable scenery and appliances, having been erected at the far end, surmounted by various flags, and the Melton arms, together with a beautiful drop scene of the town of Melton, with a view of Egerton Lodge, painted by a local artist. A temporary gallery was added at the opposite end of the room decorated with the Wilton arms. ... The whole of the decorations, stage accessories,

46 *Belvoir Castle. Programme. (R O)*

&c., were the work of the Melton amateurs and tradesmen.'[4:16]

Later extra accommodation was added to the gallery, and artists from London, under the direction of Mr Hawes Craven, the well-known scenic artist,

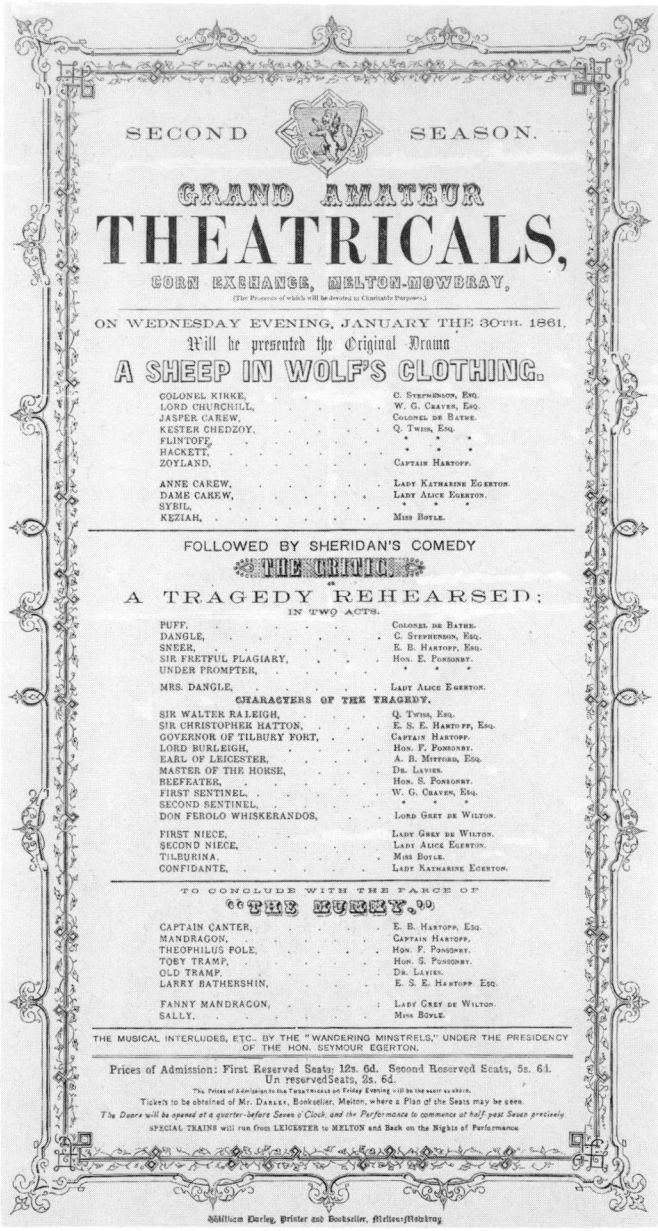

47   *Corn Exchange, Melton Mowbray. Playbill for 1861. (G. King)*

were painting the scenery. Special trains were run from London to Melton for visitors to the plays. When the Society of Gentlemen Amateurs, known as the Windsor Strollers performed on January 29th and 30th 1867, Earl Wilton 'kindly placed at their disposal the scenery and other stage accessories, which were prepared at immense cost, for the previous entertainment held here.'[4:17]

In Leicester, the Leicester Dramatic Society was 'instituted on January 22nd 1851, for the Relief of Indigent and Infirm Actors and any other persons or Charitable Institution'. It gave many performances at the Theatre Royal for such causes. A benefit was held for Mr Tadman, an actor who, during a performance was, 'accidentally wounded by the explosion of a paper shell. His clothes were set on fire and a hole two inches deep burnt in his back, near the spine. He was immediately removed to the Infirmary.'[4:18]

In the 1890s the Westbury Amateur Dramatic Society performed for the inmates of the Workhouse, and at the Recreation Room at the Gas Works, where the Gas Department Society also performed . Other entertainments were staged at the Co-operative Hall. The Leicester Amateur Music and Dramatic Club performed at the Royal Opera House. Their presentations were mainly Gilbert and Sullivan operas, which were great favourites with their audiences.[4:19]

Pupils of the local schools performed for the enjoyment of their parents and friends, including the young gentlemen of Mr Piggot's School, Collegiate, Stoneygate, Loughborough Grammar School and Appleby Grammar School, Ashby. Horace Twilley, a local man who was much concerned with amateur societies in Leicester, wrote in *Drama* in 1932 of the Belmont House Society, a group formed in 1856 by the past pupils of Belmont House School. 'A high standard of excellence was achieved'. In the early days the performances were at the Great Meeting in Bond Street, as, 'there was no other stage so good in the city.' Their last production was in 1933 in the Lancaster Hall. Twilley also commented on the religious and old morality plays produced by the Wycliffe Players under the Rev. Seaward Beddow at Wycliffe Church, now the County School of Music. The villages were not left out, in most there were Penny Readings, and dramatic entertainments and pantomimes in the school or village halls, often with the addition of a meat tea or supper.[4:20]

The Theatre Royal; The Building

On March 17th 1836,[5:1] demolition of the 1800 theatre began, and the site was prepared in readiness for its successor.

'in its place will be erected one which will not only prove an ornament to the town, but be far more convenient for the play-going public. The entrance will be in Horsefair-street, ... and will outvie in appearance most of the public buildings. The stage we understand will be 41ft long, and 24ft 6in wide, part of which will be movable, and constructed after the manner of the London Theatres. The house-part will contain two tiers of boxes, a pit, and a gallery, and will be very spacious.'

'Builders and Others' were informed that they could 'see the Plans and Specifications at the office of Mr WILLIAM PARSONS, Saint Martin's, Leicester, from Monday, the 21st day of March'.[5:2]

The New Theatre, as it was called until January, 1837, when it was (on one occasion) referred to as the Theatre Royal,[5:3] opened on September 12th 1836. The *Leicester Journal* tells us that it reflected 'great credit upon the Architect, Mr W. Parsons [the County Architect], and the Builders, Messrs W. & C. Herbert.' The Horsefair Street frontage (fig.48) in the 'Grecian Ionic School', was built of brick faced with stucco; even the fluted Ionic columns being of stucco on a core of special-made bricks. The rear elevation to the Market Place (fig.49) with its rusticated stucco base and six pilasters, was crowned by a pediment forming the gable end to the roof, which was, at this time, continuous over both stage and auditorium (fig.52).

The auditorium was in the form of a horseshoe, with a pit seating some 450 persons on benches, 'every second one having a rail at the back'. Above was the Dress Circle, divided into Centre and Side boxes, and above these were Upper Boxes on a level with the Gallery. The boxes held 'about 350 persons ... and the gallery, from 450 to 500.' The internal decorations were by Mr Crace, 'Ornamental Designer of the Theatre Royal Drury Lane and the Royal Olympic and St James's Theatres'.[5:4](A reference to Samuel Beazley as the designer of the theatre [5:5] perhaps suggests that Beazley — who had designed the St James' Theatre — may have given Crace some help or advice.) The decorations were

'of a chaste arabesque character on a light ground in the style of the well known Baths of Titus relieved with light gilt ornaments. The ceiling is divided into eight compartments, forming open pannels through which a rich specimen of clouding is seen. The centre flower is a gilt ornament of a light elegant appearance. The cove is divided into pannels, in the centre of which are cameo paintings of heads of celebrated dramatic authors. The front of the upper tier of boxes is decorated with festoons of flowers, with light honeysuckle ornaments. The dress circle is formed into pannels, in which are painted arabesque scrolic ornaments, in & the centre of which are various kinds of birds of elegant plumage on a dark ground ... From the centre of the ceiling a magnificent chandalier, executed by Mr Morland Broderip, is suspended, and when lighted [by gas] presents a most brilliant and imposing spectacle.'

The scenic department, including the act-drop and curtain, was under the control of Mr Finley of the

48   Theatre Royal, Leicester. Horsefair Street frontage, May 1947. (Photo: R L)

Theatres Royal, Drury Lane and Covent Garden, and Mr Alfred Finley of the Theatres Royal, Birmingham and Liverpool. The stage and machinery were by Mr Evans of the London Theatres; and the lighting 'of the most novel description', was executed by Mr Handley, of Berwick-Street, Soho.[5:6]

This is, in effect, all we are told regarding the interior of the theatre, and one must put together such small fragments of information as come to light piece-meal. In 1855, for example, we note 'Private Stage Boxes, 3s' which in 1859 'seated 4 persons', and for which, in 1869 '12 cane seated chairs were obtained'.[5:7] In the same year complaints were heard regarding 'the three end boxes close to the stage on each side of the building, sit on a back seat and one can see nothing of the performance, and those in the front row have to bend in a very uncomfortable fashion to obtain a glimpse of what is going on.' In 1873 we read that 'The old stage boxes have been entirely removed, and a concave wall placed instead of the abutting obstruction which has in the past been effectual in hiding the stage from those who had the misfortune to sit near it.'[5:8]

The depth of the stage alone was given above as

49   *Theatre Royal, Leicester, Market Street facade, with fly tower erected in 1888. Compare with fig.52 (Photo: R L)*

41ft, but we are now told that 'The length of the stage including the proscenium is 48 feet, & its breadth at the proscenium 25 feet.' As noted earlier (p.15) 'the proscenium' was that part of the stage which projected forward into the auditorium, flanked originally by stage doors, but later by stage boxes in a similar manner to those at Drury Lane in 1823 and Covent Garden in 1824.[5:9] It would therefore seem there was such a 'proscenium' unit here (fig.50), which would have projected 7ft into the auditorium, flanked by stage boxes.

Separated from the proscenium stage by a railed space for the orchestra, it is more than likely that the Pit was contained within the lines of the Dress Circle. In 1840 a correspondent to the *Chronicle* complained that smoking was being allowed in the theatre, citing two individuals who 'were so employed in the side slips of the pit on Saturday night'. Although these could simply have been open spaces on either side of the pit benches, there were in Holland's 1794 Drury Lane, 'eight dull and inconvenient slips, ... on each side of the pit,' which were also described as boxes.[5:10] There may well have been three such boxes on either side containing the Leicester pit, which could then have opened out beyond them to the full width and depth of the auditorium.

In 1850 there was a 'SPLENDID EXHIBITION OF ARTS', for which the theatre was transformed into an Assembly Room, when the pit was boarded over, and in 1854 it was again 'boarded over, and made level with the stage to form one large saloon', for a series of Promenade Concerts. 'The upper portion of the stage was closed in with white glazed calico falling in graceful folds (fig.51), giving a light and pleasing effect. An orchestra was erected in the centre of the stage, decorated with banners and an illuminated arch of gas jets.'[5:11]

It would have been easier to 'board over' the pit, if it were enclosed by 'slips boxes', and this factor has been taken into account in preparing the reconstruction (fig.50). In 1871 seat prices included the 'Pit and Promenade, 1s', the latter was also mentioned in 1877, when Mr Clinton Hall 'removed the Pit Stalls and added that amount of accommodation to the Pit, and ... formed a promenade at the back of the Pit.'[5:12] Before the theatre was opened 'constant fires' were 'kept in every part of the Theatre', and later we learn that new 'Iron Fender Guards' were 'needed for the Fires in the Pit'.[5:13] Fireplaces on either side of the pit, and in the Box Passages above, came to light during the demolition of the theatre (fig.59).

In addition to the upper (private) boxes in the proscenium area, there were 'upper boxes' which appear to have been open, although approached by doors at the rear. In 1850 these were divided from the gallery by a partition, which was considerably raised in 1857, when curtains were placed at the front of the boxes. By 1862 the lessee was asked to replace the boards that had been taken away from the Upper Boxes, and not to 'use the upper tier of boxes at a lower charge for each person than is made to parties frequenting the pit.'[5:14]

At an inquest held on the 20th January, 1868,[5:15] on a youth who died as the result of an accident in the theatre; we are told that he went 'through a side door into the side slip, which is generally thrown open to the occupants of the gallery, when that portion of the building is overcrowded. ... Whilst he was in the upper boxes, a door which had for many years stood in the lobby of the upper boxes' fell on him. In the unknown theatre (fig.19) there are side slips in the form of boxes. At Leicester the 'upper boxes' had to be priced at not less than pit prices, while the side slips could be open to the gallery, so it is possible that here there were open boxes in front, with a raised slips behind. Without a plan or a view of the interior, any attempted reconstruction remains highly conjectural. Unfortunately no illustration prior to the mid-1900s has come to light, and the only early plans which date from the 1888 reconstruction are full of inconsistencies, and raise as many problems as they solve.

There is little information on the stage machinery, which would have been similar to that described earlier (p.16). In October 1850, the 'sinkings and flyings' were put to use in a performance of *Macbeth* in which Mr James Anderson appeared.

> 'deserving of notice was ... the witch scene at the end of the 3rd Act. It was so arranged that the clouds appeared to descend over the moon to the stage, and arise again with the witch Hecate amongst them, while the other witches disappeared through the floor of the stage. It was so successfully done that it drew forth a hearty round of applause from the house.'[5:16]

The Corsican Brothers was performed several times, and for this a special trap had to be prepared to permit the 'apparition of M. Louis' to appear 'making a lateral ascent across the stage. The *tableau* is very striking; and the manner of introducing the Ghost is such, as to claim for this piece, a superiority over all others in which ghosts are introduced by mechanism.' Following this the Proprietors noted that the joists under the stage to right and left of the centre had been displaced, and the large trap (used for raising Pianofortes, etc) had been cut through the

50   *Theatre Royal, Leicester;*
      Conjectural reconstruction
      of the original interior

51   *Theatre Royal, Drury Lane. The stage decorated for a promenade concert, with similar drapes to those described at the Theatre Royal, Leicester. (Courtesy of the Trustees of the Theatre Museum, V & A)*

middle and a beam placed under it. They complained that these alterations had not only made the centre trap useless, but had also impaired the stability of the stage.[5:17]

By 1863 they noted that the stage required new flooring, and the scenes new frames. Two years later they requested that guards be placed over the foot and side lights, and knives and a small Fire Engine be kept in the Flies: the knives being used for cutting down any scenery which might catch fire. In 1869, it was noted that a new carpet was needed for the stage, and a new Green Baize to cover the Stage Carpet. At the same time it was decided that a new Green cloth Drop curtain was required, and that a Brass Rod should be fixed in front of the Gaslights on the stage as a protection to the Dancers.[5:18]

52   *Theatre Royal, Leicester; photographed from the spire of St. Margaret's. Showing the original roof continuous over both auditorium and stage. (R L C)*

53   *Theatre Royal, Leicester; with fly tower of 1888. (R L C)*

With gas lighting and general wear theatres were in constant need of renovation and redecoration. Such work was carried out five times between 1847 and 1860, not always meeting with the approval of the patrons. In 1854, the decoration in the boxes was described as 'being a very dull bedroom paper'. In 1860 the renovation of the ceiling was put in hand.[5:19]

An even more thorough restoration was carried out in 1865,

'The ceiling is of pale green and gold, the circle surmounted by tablets of light brown and gold. The front of the boxes and gallery represents a highly finished colonnade of oak with gold edging, and interwoven with wreaths and garlands of bright flowers; the base consisting of slabs of two marbles, green and pink. The proscenium, by Mr Channing, is light and in extremely good taste, the prevailing colours being a delicate pink marble upon a base of rich dark red, and florid shields and basso relievos in white contrasting with the rich and well painted crimson drapery of the sides and top.'[5:20]

The side boxes had been decorated with a handsome green patterned wallpaper, and the seats covered with green American cloth. Gas lights and globes were attached to each pillar and mirrors hung on the walls. The centre boxes were now completely separated from those at the sides, and their walls, partitions and doors were decorated in a pink paper with a white lace pattern over. Both these and the private (proscenium) boxes were surrounded with gold fringed crimson velvet curtains. The chairs were covered with American cloth in crimson. Chandeliers were suspended over both the private and the centre boxes. In 1869 the theatre was again 'entirely cleaned and re-decorated; the flooring of the stage has been

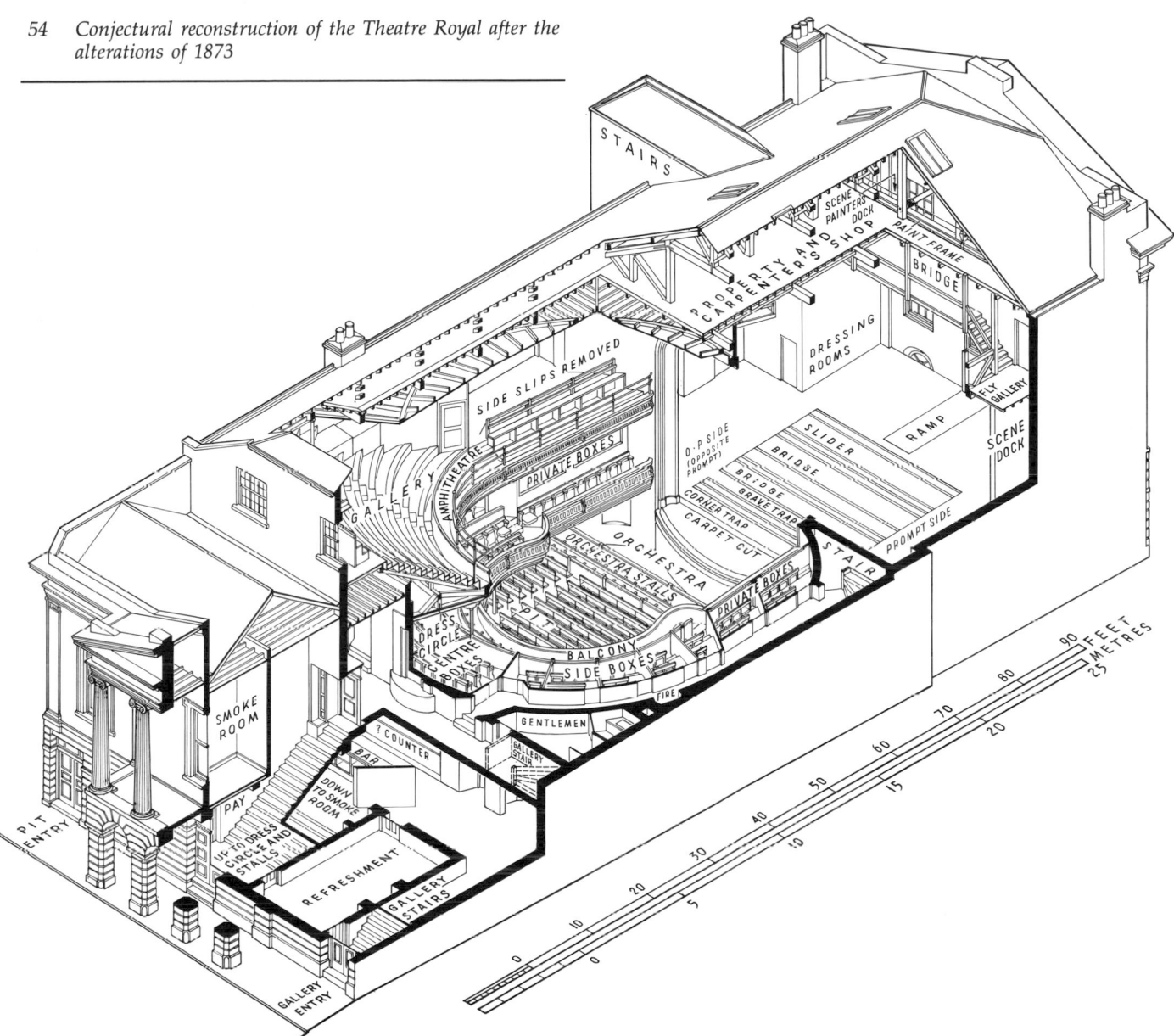

54   *Conjectural reconstruction of the Theatre Royal after the alterations of 1873*

restored, and new scenery and drop curtain provided.' In 1872 'a cloak and Retiring Room' was fitted up in the Box Corridor 'for the convenience of visitors to the Boxes.'[5:21]

In 1873, a more thorough re-modelling of the interior took place (fig.54). The new lessee, Mr Elliot Galer, who, in his younger days had practised as an architect, made proposals which the owners accepted, and the work was put in hand in March.[5:22] We noted earlier that the stage boxes were now removed, and it would seem that with them went the whole proscenium unit, as Galer was able to create a new ceiling to the auditorium which was

> 'brought six feet nearer the stage than previously, and instead of being flat, as hitherto, is now dome-like and pannelled — showing figures of Griffins finished in arabesque, and in the several panels

medallions of Shakespere, Byron, Dante, Goldsmith, Mozart, Mendelssohn, Beethoven and Rossini. ... the work of Mr Earle, of London, one of the best scenic figure painters of the day. ...The centre sunlight is a gorgeous piece of mechanism, giving forth the lights of 190 gas jets in nineteen clusters.'[5:23]

Galer took the opportunity to bring the theatre more into line with the London theatres by making the front of the stage curved.

> 'The proscenium has been thrown back three feet [presumably the distance to the front of the curve] in order to obtain additional seating accommodation for about 500 persons. Above are the royal arms, in white and gold [see frontispiece]. The drop-scene, a representation of Bradgate Ruins, painted by Mr Herbert and assistants, ... is a

delightful and splendidly-coloured picture, ... In front of the stage is the orchestra, and between it and the pit the orchestra stalls, which are seated in bright-coloured maroon rep; as are the balcony and boxes. ... doubtless the lovers of luxurious accommodation will here find an enviable position. The front of the dress circle and gallery above is constructed in sunk wood, ornamentally picked out in warm grey, salmon, and gold;'

'The front of the boxes has been projected about three feet, to form a balcony' (fig.55) 'on the plan adopted in the "Gaiety" and other metropolitan theatres', 'consisting of two rows of armed seats, which may be lifted up at pleasure, to allow of the free movement of the visitors. At the back of the balcony are other seats of the same character and material as those of the orchestral stalls. The boxes are entered by two doors, instead of one as before; thus at once contributing to the convenience and safety of the playgoers. The orchestral stalls are approached by passages at the back of the boxes, and by stairs at the ends of them; near which are the private and stage boxes.'[5:24]

'In the pit the means of ingress and egress have been much improved, two doors having been provided in place of the old one, ...One of the double rows of columns which were an obstruction to the view has been removed, and by an improved principle the remaining row has been made to serve the purposes of both. A new floor has been laid, and two gangways down the house have been substituted for the old fashioned ones at the sides. New and comfortable seats with separations between every sitting have been provided.'[5:25]

The owners later requested that these iron bar 'separations' be removed. Sight lines from the gallery were 'improved by the carrying forward of the domed roof six feet, and the additional space gained' has permitted 'the formation of amphitheatre stalls in front, and the addition of two rows of seats behind' (fig.56).[5:26]

We are further told that the removal of the stage boxes would improve sight lines from 'the ends of the pit' which 'were formerly dark and useless corners — in future they will be properly seated and afford a good prospect of the stage. ... Private boxes (fig.54) will be provided behind the ordinary boxes, near the stage, to suit the convenience of the class of visitors who require them.' and 'The side-slips, formerly existing above the end-boxes, will be removed, and the gallery carried quite round on both sides.'[5:27]

The introduction of the gallery amphitheatre 'in the same style as the boxes' was commended when it was explained that

'This will have a double object in meeting the requirements of those whose tastes incline to this high altitude, and preventing the discomfort which used to arise to the people in the pit from the practice indulged in the "gods" of throwing down edibles.'[5:28]

There had been numerous complaints regarding the gods. In 1841, when Charles Dillon was playing Lear, their conduct was

'most disgraceful during the whole evening: not only were the most disgusting oaths bandied about, but several fights took place, and the police were two or three times obliged to be called in. Coats and hats were flung into the pit: the dregs of beer-bottles were emptied on the heads of those below — and worse things than that even.'

In 1869 it had proved necessary to line the front of the Gallery with sheet iron to protect it from the rough usage of the "Gods". In 1870 'the gallery boys' were still hurling 'apples at the heads of the players.'[5:29]

In 1873, the front of the building had been repainted and five elegant lamps had been placed in the spaces between the Ionic pillars. A new office and other rooms had been provided on the ground floor, to be used as a box-office. The stairs had been considerable widened, and a spacious hall now led to the dress circle. A bust of Shakespeare was placed in a niche opposite the stair. On the right-hand side there

55   *Theatre Royal; the auditorium. (Crown copyright)*

was a spacious refreshment saloon, with elaborate paper, and a richly ornamented counter. Adjoining this, with a separate entrance, was a large and comfortable saloon.[5:30]

On the stage the old green curtain had been replaced by a red one, and the new stage, which was set back, had been laid out with all modern appliances. The footlights were sunk so as not to interfere with the view of the stage.

'All the stage machinery has been renewed and fitted up on the principle of the best Metropolitan stages. New dressing rooms have been added, and ... The lights are fitted up on the most modern system.'[5:31]

The following year the orchestra stalls were raised, and the footlights lowered still further to improve sight lines. But a more radical renovation was undertaken in 1881, when the interior was

'in the French style of internal decoration for theatres, ... the principal staircase ... being decorated in the Pompeian style. All the seats for the dress circle have been made expressly, and a ... new feature in that portion of the building is the provision of easy chairs.'

The proscenium was formed from carton pierre (a form of papier mache imitating stone) which was said to be in keeping with the rest of the decorations. The seats in the pit were now stuffed and upholstered. On either side of the stage was a niche containing a handsome statue in white. The green baize curtain was a facsimilie of a Parisian blind, and was described as being the first of its kind introduced into an English theatre.[5:32]

'Round the whole of the boxes will be hung elaborate curtains of crimson velvet, trimmed with gold, ... The private boxes have been rendered much more comfortable, more commodious, and better to see from. Hitherto there have been a row of seats in front of them, but this has been removed, and the private boxes have been brought to the front of the tier, 'with' their sides so sloped away that ... one may accept a seat anywhere in the dress circle, with the certainty that, as could not be said in old times, an adequate view of the stage will not be obstructed.'

The lessee, Mr R.W. Key, had asked permission of the Theatre Directors 'to alter the front of the stage to make it square — to put four new Private Boxes, recover and alter some of the seating of the Balcony and decorate the place generally.'[5:33] It had previously been assumed that Key was cutting back the stage to line with the proscenium wall, but this was not the case. Surprisingly we are told,

'The stage itself has been lowered and brought out more into the house, which has the desirable effect of allowing everyone in all parts of the house to see perfectly well. This is a decided improvement, and

56   Theatre Royal: the gallery. (Crown copyright)

one which has been long felt necessary.' 'the front which was circular, has been made straight, and a new place made for the members of the orchestra.' It would seem that the stage front had been restored to what we earlier assumed to be its original position. According to one report the new stage was one foot lower than the old, and the *Era* tells us that a 'new proscenium has taken the place of the old flat sides.'[5:34]

Prior to these alterations the Directors had noted that the Stage needed 'to be thoroughly repaired, put in a new Bridge, have new levers, and put the whole in working order.' It was also necessary to 'Repair the back Bridge'. If the stage were lowered by a foot, it would seem that all the machinery would have had to be adapted or replaced, and this may well have been the case. In future the stage was 'to be lighted with Tollerton's patent lighting apparatus,' and new scenery will now take the place of that which has done good service.'[5:35]

We learn something of the stock scenery in use in the theatre from an inventory of 1883, which includes '4 French Chamber Scenes,' which consisted of

'1 Oak Chamber, 18 feet high by 24 feet wide, the Framework attached is 9 feet by 24 feet.
2 Oak side pieces right and left, making 4 pieces in all, 18 feet high by 6 feet wide each.
1 light Chamber ... 2 Light side pieces right and left... 1 Front Chamber, Baronial Hall' of similar dimensions, and '1 Front Flat, 18 feet high by 26 feet wide, the Framework attached is 12 feet by 26 feet.'

In addition it was thought 'desirable to purchase from Mr R.W. Key for the sum of Ten Pounds a complete Wood scene, now in the Theatre, as it could not be properly worked without one.' Consisting of

'3 Borders, 6 feet high by 31 feet wide, and
1 Border, 11 feet high by 32 feet wide.

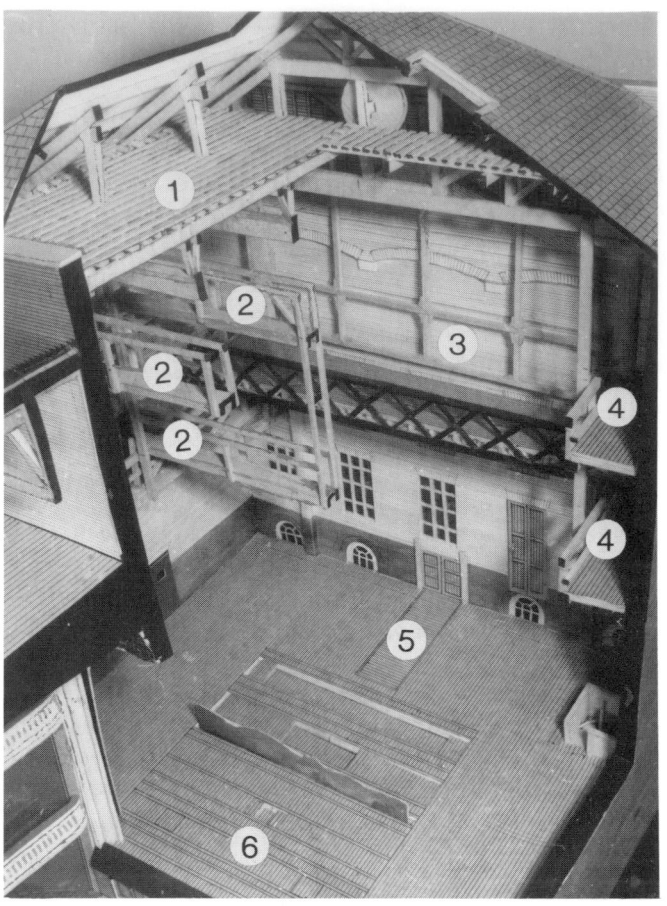

6 Wings, 18 feet high by 6 feet wide.

1 Cut Cloth 18 feet high by 26 feet wide.

1 Back Cloth, 12 feet high by 15 feet 6 inches wide.

1 Set tree, 9 feet high by 8 feet at the base and 2 feet wide with Border to match 10 feet to 14 feet high by 30 feet wide.'[5:36]

As early as 1866 an oxy-hydrogen lime light was being used 'in the tableau finale' of a production of *Faust*, and in 1886 there was an accident when the lime light exploded, injuring one woman and blowing out two windows. We are told that after the woman had been removed to the Infirmary the performance continued.[5:37]

The Magistrates, with the new duties in mind due

57   *Model of the Theatre Royal; showing the stage and fly tower. 1: the Gridiron. 2: Catwalks. 3: Paint frame. 4: Fly floors. 5: Ramp to street. 6: Stage cuts. (photo: R L)*

58   *Model of the Theatre Royal; cut open to show interior. with fly tower of 1888. (Photo: R L)*

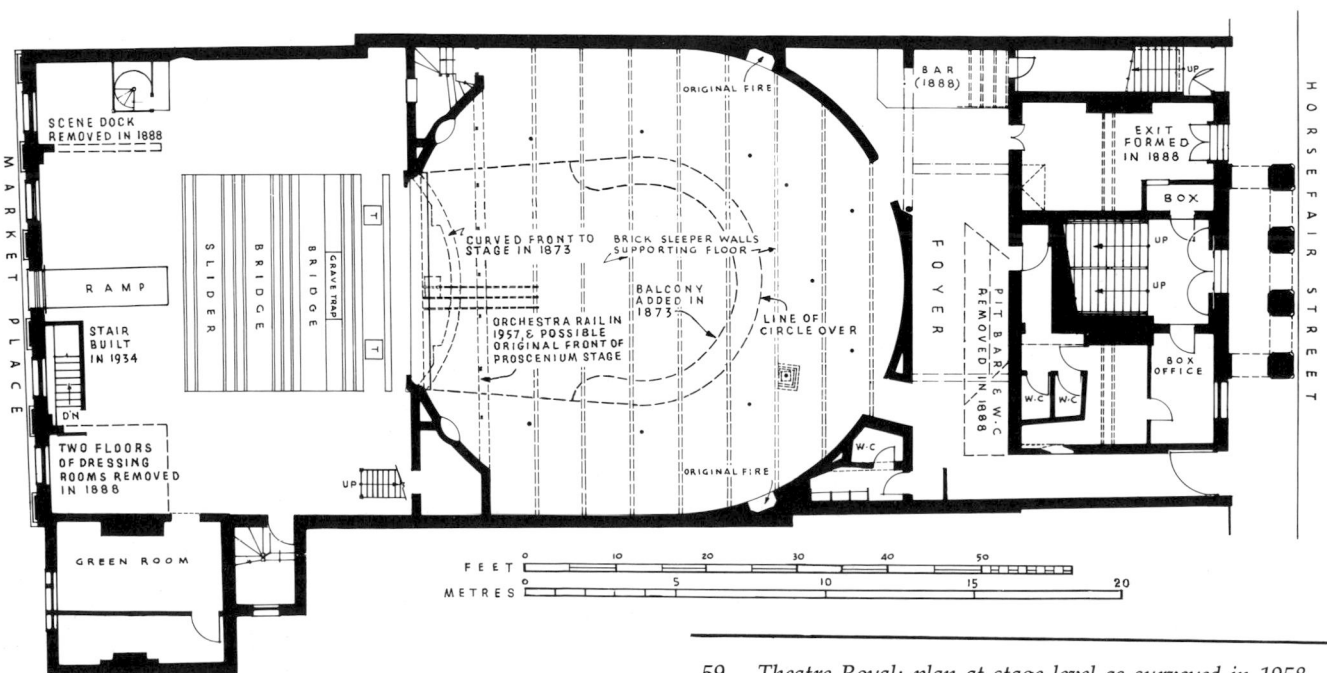

59   *Theatre Royal; plan at stage level as surveyed in 1958, including various alterations noted in the text.*

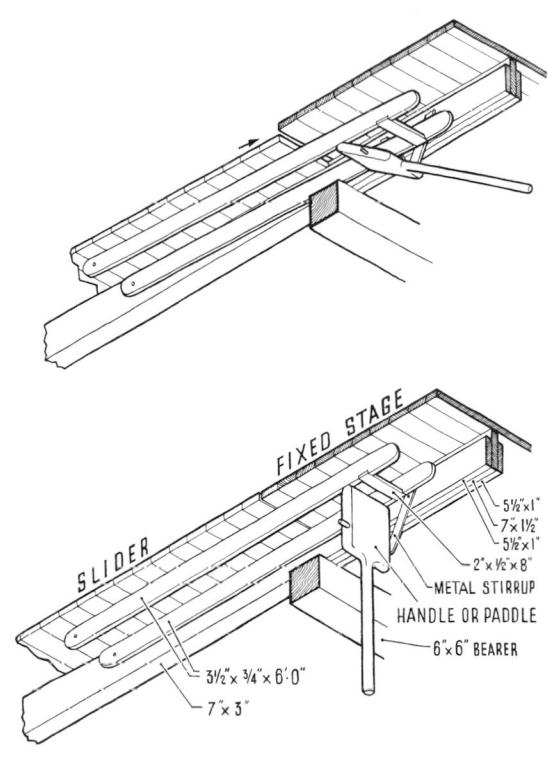

to be imposed on them by the Local Government Act, 1888, 'inspected the whole of the theatres and places of amusement in the town, and found that in a great many of them structural alterations were desirable, and in some cases absolutely necessary.'[5:38] At the Theatre Royal they required that the entrances to the pit and gallery should be widened and improved, the winding stair to the latter being thought very dangerous. 'Iron doors should be provided on each floor to the staircases next the stage.' They were particularly concerned that 'The scenery and property room in the roof over the auditorium is exceedingly dangerous and should be abolished, and the opening in the proscenium wall 24 ft in width should be built up, and the wall carried through the roof.' They also required that 'A drop curtain of asbestos or some other uninflammable material should be provided.'[5:39]

This was done — being later referred to as the Iron Curtain. Originally it was hung on hemp lines, and so it not surprisingly gave trouble; and in 1892 these were replaced by wire. Further hydrants were required, 'there being none in the auditorium. ... The Borough Surveyor recommends the carrying up of pipes on to and above the flies with perforators therein at that level so that by simply turning the water on, the fire and all inflammable material could be played upon by heavy showers of water.'[5:40]

It was to deal with these requirements that Mr I. Barradale prepared the drawings mentioned earlier,

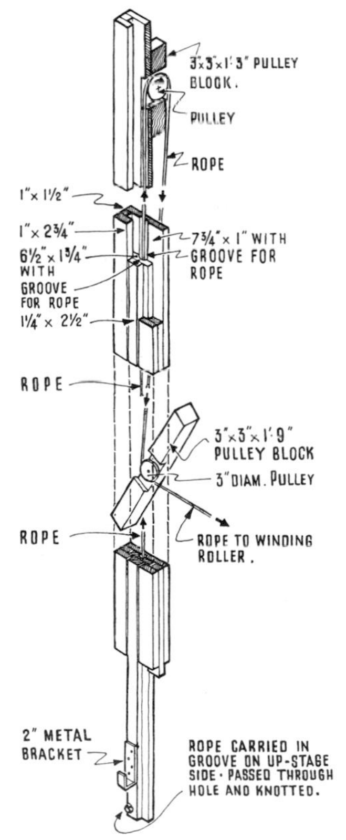

60   Detail of stage sliders: (above) in raised position; (below) dropped ready to be drawn off under fixed side stage

61   Detail of sloat (left) and sloat cuts (right). 1: sloats. 2: sliders. 3: slider for bridge. 4: fixed side stage. 5: handle or paddle. 6: stabilizing metal bar.

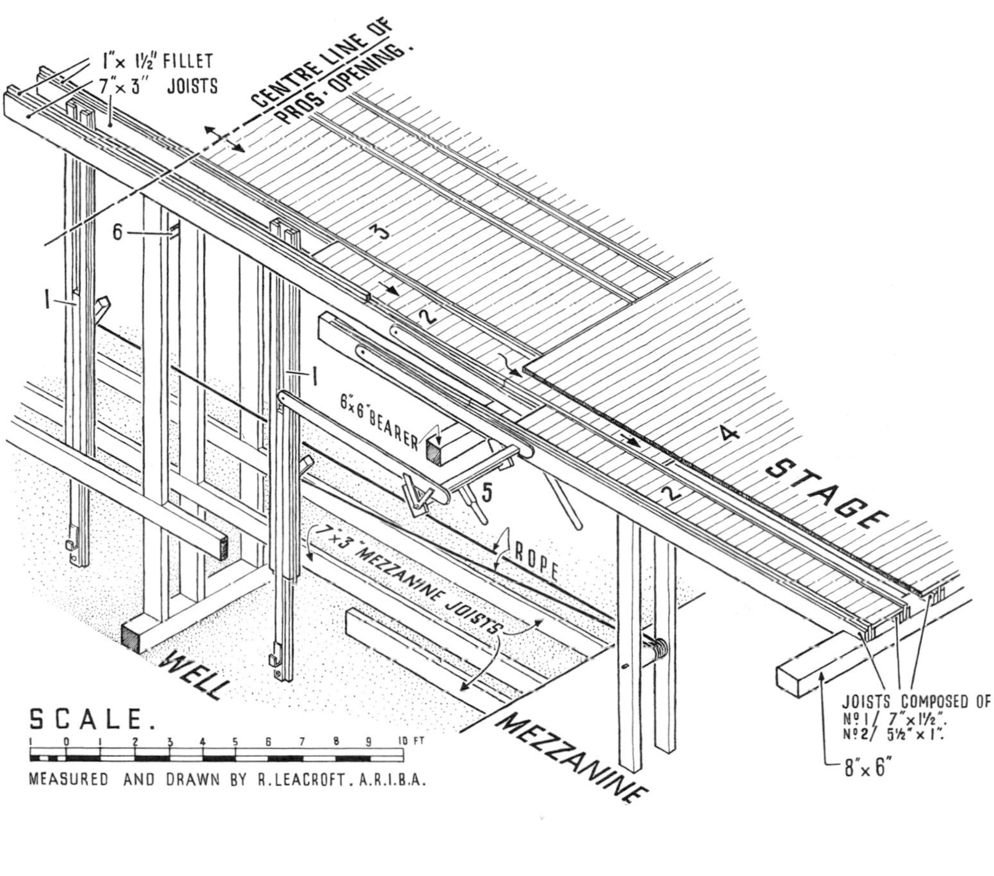

SCALE.

MEASURED AND DRAWN BY R. LEACROFT. A.R.I.B.A.

(p.39) and the opportunity was taken to bring the stage into line with current practice by forming a fly-tower (fig.53). The Directors' Annual Report for 1889 announced that

'The roof and walls have been raised an additional 16' in height, which enables the scenes to "hang" without being rolled up or folded, which not only prevents damage to the scenes by creasing, but also allows twice the number of scenes to be used.'

The roof trusses were raised to provide the extra height, which permitted the insertion of a second fly gallery on either side. Both levels of gallery being connected across the stage by catwalks (figs.57-8). The whole of this work being carried out during the month of July under the charge of Mr Albert Hubbard.[5:41]

Dressing rooms and an old scene dock were removed from the stage to give a clear floor space of 40 feet by 50 feet. The stage entrance was enlarged, and by the introduction of a hinged portion of stage which let down to form a ramp from street level, it was made possible for the whole of the scenery to 'be placed direct from the street on to the Stage.' Previously the scene door had been at stage (first floor) level. 'The old Carpenter's Shop and Property Room

in the Basement have been transformed into four first-class Dressing Rooms, properly fitted with dressing table, lavatories, &c. erected for supers.' An extra exit from the Pit was formed in a refreshment room (fig.59,B), and a new stone stair, with straight flights and square landings, was built 18 in wider than the old winding gallery stair.

Drawings based on a 1947 survey of the stage area (fig.65) show these alterations, together with the remains of the stage machinery which was presumably installed in 1881, although some elements — as for example the upper grooves (figs.62-3) — may be from an earlier date. The stage front is shown on Barradale's drawings as lining with the proscenium wall. Directly upstage of the footlights (the stage sloped up in the then normal manner) was a narrow cut, with a hinged lid, known as the "carpet cut" into which the front edge of the stage carpet was trapped. Next to this were two square "corner traps", through

62　*Upper grooves in position on prompt side (stage left) fly floor, with the proscenium opening bottom right. (Photo: R. Hunt)*

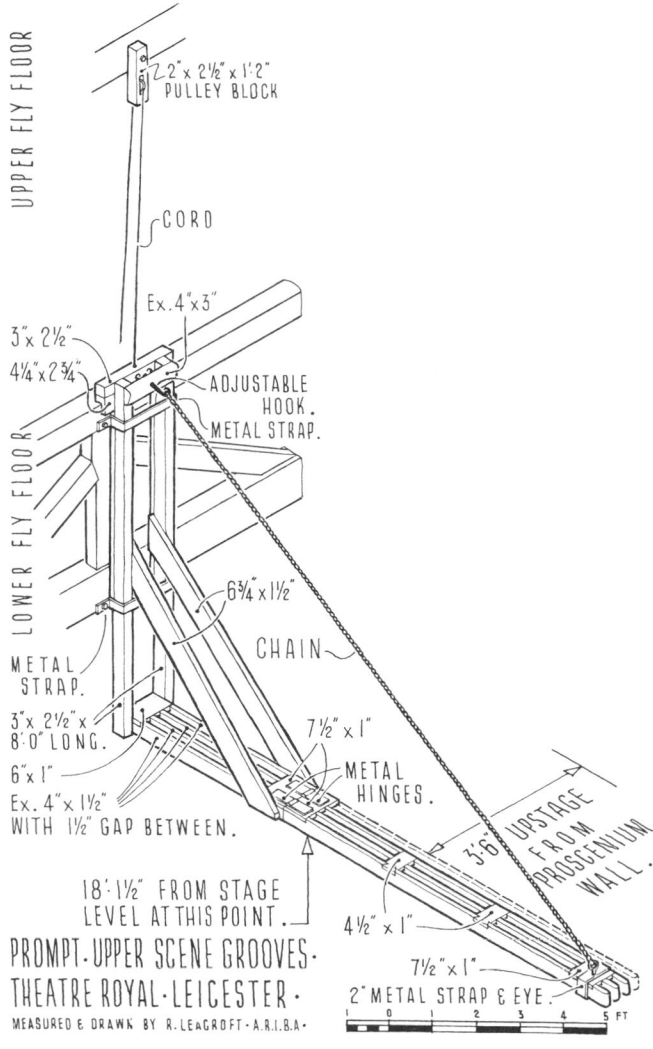

63　*Upper Groove, with hinged section lowered for use with sliding shutters (see fig.64)*

64   *Backstage view of a Wing and Border setting, with sloat cut and bridge in use, and stage hands leading on a pair of shutters*

which a single figure could rise or sink to or from the basement (fig.59,T). Beyond were two further cuts, each about one foot wide. These are known as "sloat cuts", and each was equipped with two T-shaped posts — "sloats or slotes" — rising and falling in a similarly shaped channel. Each sloat had a metal bracket near its foot into which a piece of scenery, known as a ground row, could be placed, to be raised by ropes and winches to stage level (fig.61).

Next up-stage was a central, wider, trap known as a "grave trap" (fig.59) for use in such plays as *Hamlet*, and adjoining this was a larger cut (these varied from 2ft 6in to 3ft wide) equipped with a "bridge", which, like the grave trap, could be raised and lowered between four corner posts; two in the case of the corner traps. The bridges, traps and their

loads could be made to rise and fall with comparative ease by the use of counterweights.

When these cuts were to be used it was necessary to remove the related portion of stage. This was made up of two movable pieces, each half the width of the proscenium opening, known as "sliders". These ran on rails, or battens, fastened to the stage joists between each cut, which sloped down so that the sliders might be drawn off beneath the fixed portions at either side of the stage. Normally these sliders would be held level with the stage by means of "paddles" (fig.60). When these were moved, the slider dropped on to the sloping rail and was drawn off by ropes and winches to leave an open space through which the performers or scenery could be raised or lowered (fig.64). To keep the stage stable

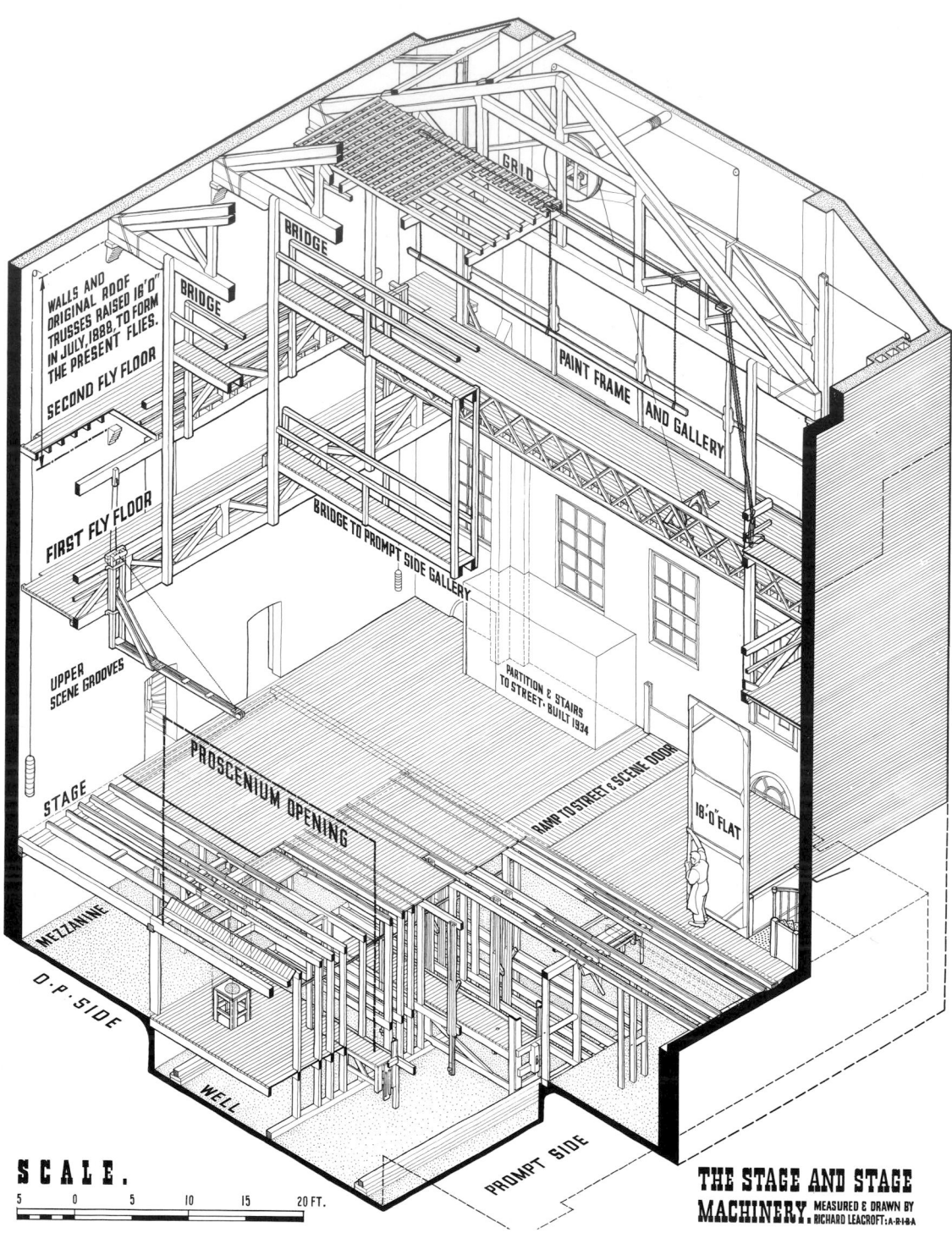

*65   Measured drawing of Theatre Royal stage and fly tower,
      as surveyed in 1947*

metal bars were fixed to the central posts supporting the joists, which could be unhooked when a particular space was to be used.

Our drawing of the stage area (fig.65) shows the Paint Frame and Gallery as it was in 1947 (fig.66). Barradale's 1888 plan and a later plan of 1891 (for a new Gallery Bar) both show a much wider Scene Painter's Dock (approximately 13ft), with a Painter's Room at one end, and in the latter case, a Wardrobe at the other. Both plans show an 'old bridge removed' adjoining the dock. On plan the painter's dock and room are shown to be level with one of the fly floors, but the section shows them part way between, and some 9ft 6in wide, which relates more closely, but not correctly, with the arrangement as surveyed. The 1891 plan also shows what may be interpreted as a paint-frame on the down-stage side of the dock. It seems possible that these plans record the earlier Painter's Dock and Frame, for which a windlass was purchased in 1883.[5:42]

A timber 'gridiron' now formed a ceiling to the stage, on which were carried the pulleys needed for raising and lowering the scenes. Sets of pulley blocks were fixed at approximately 1ft 6in intervals parallel with the stage front. Each set consisting of a single pulley placed centrally above the stage, with a further single pulley some 12ft to either side. Above the rail on the prompt side fly gallery was a headblock, containing three pulleys. Lines led over the single pulleys down to stage level, and at their opposite end they passed over the headblock to be tied off to a cleat on the upper fly rail. The stage ends were tied to the top batten of a cloth, which could be hauled up into the flies by fly-men working on the top gallery. When raised to the correct height, the lines were tied off to the cleat, and the surplus rope coiled neatly (!) on the lower fly floor (figs.67-8).

In spite of all these alterations it was not long before the building was once again being criticised. In 1897 the lessee, Mr Revill, was calling attention

66   Theatre Royal: author at work on scenery attached to paint frame. (Photo: R. Hunt)

67   Stage of the Theatre Royal: in foreground; the lower of the two up-stage catwalks or bridges, and beyond the girder supporting the paint gallery. On right; upper and lower prompt side fly galleries. (Photo: R. Hunt)

68   *Stage of the Theatre Royal: left; proscenium opening and upper grooves attached to the lower O.P. (stage right) fly gallery. Lower up-stage catwalk or bridge across centre of picture, with underside of paint gallery at upper right. (Photo: R. Hunt)*

'to the most unsatisfactory accommodation which the theatre affords to the public — owing to the extremely bad lines of sight the side Boxes are but poorly patronised while the amphitheatre and gallery scarcely holds 350 people who can see the stage, it is owing to the small holding capacity of the Theatre together with the poor accommodation that prevents the better class Companies from booking with me at Leicester. ... We can neither hold the people nor the money when it can be taken.'

'In order to prevent opposition springing up in the Town it is really time that the interior of the building be reconstructed. I think that for an outlay of a few hundred pounds the Theatre could be made to compete with the Opera House [which opened in 1877]. If the directors fall in with this proposal I would suggest asking Mr Matcham the Theatrical Architect to submit a scheme for approval.'

This was done, but 'the alterations suggested by Mr Matcham ... were upon too extensive a scale', and they were turned down.[5:43]

In 1905 estimates were obtained 'for fixing an electric light installation on the stage', from Gent and Hurley; T.H. Wathes and Co and S. Noakes. Sanction was given in 1908 to remove 'the partition to the first private box on either side of the Theatre, the stage box on each side to be left intact.' In 1912 the gangways on either side of the pit were widened, and in the following year permission was given to remove 'the two private boxes one on each side of the theatre.' In 1917 the problem of heating the theatre was considered, and the use of gas radiators was turned down in favour of 'an efficient hot water heating apparatus.' In the following year the pit was 'reseated with upholstered leather tip-up seats.'[5:44]

The Theatre Royal; Plays & Players

The opening performance at the New Theatre started with an address spoken by Miss Booth; the whole company then joined in singing the National Anthem. *The School for Scandal* was the first piece presented by Mr Monro, who had leased the theatre for three years. This was followed by selections from Ballets and popular dances, terminating with a Farce. A completely new programme was staged each night until Friday — the company was now playing for five nights of the week. The players had been chosen from the London theatres and the leading provincial houses.

However, only a fortnight later we read that though the company did well in comedy, in the tragedy of *Macbeth* the performers were

'more guilty than innocent of the crime of murder … As a whole the piece went off lamely, for not only were parts improperly filled, but cues were not caught, passages were perverted, and the scenery became infected with the blundering mania.'[6:1]

Matters were put right in the following week when enthusiastic applause greeted the performances of Mr Warde, the tragedian and a member of M'Cready's old company, when he appeared for three nights.

Mr Monro continued the custom of introducing star performers to play with his 'stock' company, and on October 10th, Mr Charles Kean, son of Edmund, made his appearance as Hamlet, to be followed by Macbeth, Lear and Richard III. Because of the expenses involved in presenting such a week's entertainment, the free list was suspended except for the Press.[6:2] It was expected that Mr Kean would be well received, but the newspaper reports were adverse.

'His Hamlet … was a sorry realization of Shakespeare's philosophical Prince of Denmark. … The puling, whining, ranting Hamlet of Mr Kean, was not the Hamlet of the play: we had the words of Shakespear (in part), and the *name of Kean* — but nothing more. Genius here has not been hereditary: what of merit Mr K. displayed, was apparently the result of study, and not of natural talent; and the study, without the talent, has been to little purpose.' His 'representation of' Macbeth 'was even inferior to the previous performance of "Hamlet".'

the other parts were well sustained.[6:3]

For this first season which ran from September to December, the presentations consisted, as we have seen, of plays by Shakespeare, and the type of comedy and farce such as had been played in the earlier theatres. The performance of *The Jewess* was an opportunity for a

'glittering show, … but at its close, it is "an unsubstantial pageant faded" leaving behind little more than a confused recollection of flags, armour and ermine … to those who love splendour and spectacle, the piece must prove acceptable.'

The newspaper report, however, continued to say that theatrical managers had been complaining that the public were taking less interest in the drama, but if this were so the policy …

'should be, not to concoct trumpery exhibitions, but to conjoin with good plays such matter as is daily becoming more popular with the people — short lectures for instance on science, moral and physical with such striking experiments as are best adapted for a large house.'[6:4]

On Monday, January 2nd 1837, there was a 'GRAND MASQUERADE' for which the Interior was 'most brilliantly illuminated, representing Vauxhall on a Gala Night! … A communication will be made between the Boxes and the Stage, which will form a perfect promenade! Refreshments in the Saloon, and in the Apartments behind the Scenes.' During the 1837 season the audiences were given the opportunity of seeing *Black Anna's Bower or The Maniac of the Dane Hills*, which, based on a local legend, had been written by Mr Higgie, a popular member of the company. He chose this for his benefit. Mr Pridham, the box book-keeper, was also given a benefit, and performances were patronised by the MPs for Leicester and the Mayor.[6:5]

In May 1838, the theatre was let for a short dramatic season to Mrs Christian. Her tenure did not prove successful, as in June six members of her company advertised that they were to play for a farewell performance. The Proprietors having given them free use of the theatre, they hoped that their influential friends would support them, as they had been unprofitably employed for three weeks. They had lost their expenses from London, and presumably they had not been paid at all! A situation with which actors were only too familiar.[6:6]

In September 1838, Mr Monro announced his farewell season. The plays which he had produced had been (after the first season) of a very mediocre calibre; and the company were often lacking in competence.

On October 18th 1838, the performance was 'By Desire and Patronised by the Proprietors of the Theatre, and the subscribers to the Card and Billiard Rooms', (which were situated at the front of the building). The paper comments that attendance continued to be scanty.

'In a town like Leicester the boxes should not be deserted every evening, and we do not think it too much to expect from the principal inhabitants of the town, at least an occasional patronage of an amusement which affords such satisfaction to many of their humbler fellow-tradesmen, but which from the small support it meets with seems likely to be altogether abandoned.'[6:7]

The last performance of the season was Monro's benefit, he 'took the opportunity of alluding to reports of a want of liberality on the part of the proprietors ... and intimated his intention to form an establishment of his own.' Which he did in 1840 when he opened the New Amphitheatre in Humberstone Gate.[6:8]

The early months of 1840 saw the presentation of a tamed animal show, together with rope dancing; anti-Corn Law and Reform meetings and a course of lectures. A short drama season, from September to November, under the management of Mr Battie, included a performance of *Hamlet* by a gentleman of Leicester, and a night of opera, and Signor Joel il Diavolo made his 'TERRIFIC FLIGHT From the Back of the Gallery to the Back of the Stage.' In November Mr Battie and some shareholders attended the Exchange when the rating assessment of the Theatre was considered.

'The overseers contended that the rate should be on an assessment of £200 ... as though the Theatre was professionally, occupied only three months of the year, yet the resources derivable from lectures and other casual exhibitions were considerable. The shareholders were willing to admit £110 rental and £18 for the Billiard Room...'
£140 assessment was agreed.[6:9]

The 1841 season saw Mr W.S. Wallett (fig.105) as Acting Manager and Mr Charles Dillon, well known in London, as Stage Manager and also playing leading parts. The *Leicester Chronicle* did not carry any advertisements for the 1842 season and there were few in the *Journal*; probably indicating that business was poor, as there is mention elsewhere that there was considerable distress in the town due to unemployment. Perhaps the building of a larger theatre had been over ambitious for the times. On October 14th the *Journal* informed its readers that the proprietors were intending to sell the building to pay off their outstanding liabilities as they were 'not likely to be discharged by returns in the shape of rent, within any reasonable period, judging by past experience.' A new company of shareholders finally agreed terms

for the purchase at a meeting held on the 30th March 1847.[6:10]

In 1843 the performances were restricted to three times a week and the season lasted only from September 18th to October 20th. The following week the proprietors advertised for 'a married man without incumbrance, to reside at the Theatre, and take charge of the property.'[6:11] This would seem to indicate that the theatre was now closed.

The 1844 season, again very short, saw a varied programme of plays and opera. The theatre was acknowledged to be well conducted, and the press were able to say

'It affords us great pleasure to be able to recommend all who would wish to avert the closing of another avenue of desirable relaxation ... for the toil-worn artizan and the labourer, no less than the scholar and the gentleman ... a means of mental relaxation and intellectual pleasure ... to tender the manager their support.'[6:12]

Mr Macready appeared once more in October 1845, in *Hamlet*, but although he gave a masterly portrayal, the house was practically empty. Even when Mr Saville engaged Miss Helen Faucit to play Pauline in *The Lady of Lyons*, a part she had introduced to London audiences, and Rosalind in *As You Like It*, 'which was, indeed, a piece of the finest acting of the highest class,' the audience was 'sadly small considering the occasion.'[6:13]

Mr Charles Gill was the lessee from 1847 to 1853. At the opening of the season the Duke of Rutland patronised the performance. Gill provided the audience with a series of old English comedies for which

'the house was remarkably well attended ... the dresses and scenery and indeed all the appointments of the present company, are very superior, and a most efficient band has likewise been engaged.'

The plays continued to please and the management paid particular attention to the scenic effects. In *Ben the Boatswain* there were representations of

'the coast of Sussex, the Mediterranean sea with picturesque views amid the Sicilian mountains, the hold of the pirate and the cabin of the king's ship. The grand tableaux of the ship on fire was well managed.'[6:14]

However, a later report comments once again on the poor attendance in the boxes.

Mr Gill revived the Juvenile performances, and staged a benefit for the Widows and Orphans Society of the Leicester District Manchester Unity of Odd Fellows. Further patronage came from the Freemasons, Leicester Town Cricket Club, the Literary and Philosophical Society, and the Mayor and leading townsmen. The season concluded with four nights of opera in which Mr Travers of La Scala, Covent Garden and Drury Lane appeared.[6:15]

THEATRE, LEICESTER.

Celebrated Historical Play,

GREAT VARIETY OF ENTERTAINMENTS.----THE PANTOMIME FOR THE
LAST TIME. To conclude with a
Grand Masquerade Scene, Positively for this Night Only.

On MONDAY, October 14th., 1839,

will be presented, the Grand Historical Play, written by Sheridan Knowles, Esq., entitled,

VIRGINIUS;
Or, The Liberation of Rome.

Virginius,	MR. ANDERTON.	Icilius,	MR. DYOTT.
Appius Claudius,	MR. PENN.	Caius Claudius,	MR. WOODLEY.
Dentatus,	MR. HUDSPETH.	Numitorius,	MR. YOUNG.
Marcus,	MR. J. THORNHILL.	Lucius,	MR. FRENCH.
Servius,	MR. HEMING.	Centurions, Romans, &c. &c. &c.	
Cneius,	MR. T. HEMING.	Soldiers, &c.	
	Virginia,	MRS. DYOTT.	
Servia,	MRS. J. THORNHILL.	Female Slave,	MRS CONNER.

A COMIC SONG BY MR. HUDSPETH.

The whole to conclude with for the last time, the much applauded Pantomime, called

GAMMER GURTON;
OR, THE MAGIC NEEDLE.

IN WHICH WILL APPEAR

TWO HARLEQUINS.   TWO CLOWNS.
TWO PANTALOONS.   TWO COLUMBINES.

Colin, (afterwards Harlequin White Sword) Mr R. HEMING............Clod, (afterwards Clown) Mr. W. HEMING.
Gaffar Grunt, Mr. E HEMING...................Snip, (afterwards Harlequin Black Sword) Mr. FRENCH.
Gammer Gurton, Mr. HEMING.................Trace, (afterwards Pantaloon) Mr. J. THORNHILL.
Blossom Bluebell, Miss CONNER.....................afterwards Columbine with Harlequin White Sword, by Madame SEARLE.
Fairy of the Needle, Miss BRONSDORPH ....afterwards Columbine, with Harlequin Black Sword, MRS. DYOTT.

GRAND MASQUERADE SCENE.

Amongst other Incidents and Entertainments, will be introduced the following.

A PASS SEUL, BY MISS CAMPBELL.

The Celebrated Ode of Alexander's Feast will be recited by
MR. ANDERTON.

A GRAND PAS DE DEUX, BY MADAME SEARLE & MISS CAMPBELL.
Chinese Contortions, by Brothers Heming.

Comic Song by Mr. HUDSPETH.-Comic Song by Mr. YOUNG.

Several Characters from Shakspeare's Plays, will occasionly appear besides Groups, Dominos, &c.

Acrobatic Exhibitions by Brs. Heming

A SAILOR'S HORNPIPE, BY MR. FRENCH, in conclusion,
A MAYPOLE DANCE BY THE CHARACTERS.

On Tuesday, the Favourite Play, THE FOUNDLING OF THE FOREST, and the DUMB SAVOYARD, for the Last Time.
Doors to open at half past six, and the Performance to commence at seven o'clock.—BOXES, 2s. 6d.—PIT, 1s.—GALLERY. 6d.
Half-price to the Boxes only, at 9 o'Clock, 1s. 6d.
Places for the Boxes, with Tickets, to be had at the Theatre, from 11 till five o'Clock each day: Tickets also may be had at Mr. Fowler's
Printing Office, St. Martin's.

69   *Theatre Royal: Playbill for 1839. (R L C)*

In the Spring of 1848, Mr William Macarthy provided dramatic entertainment, he promised the appearance of, amongst others, Mr and Mrs Charles Kean and Macready, but they never materialised and the company played for only a fortnight. Macready, under Mr Gill's management did take a farewell of Leicester audiences on September 27th 1849, when he played Richelieu. There was not even standing room for the many who waited to get in.[6:16]

During the Autumn the papers speak of cholera raging in the country, and this was to affect theatre attendances. Nevertheless Gill continued to provide a varied programme of entertainments, and when the actors were not upon the stage in February and March 1850, Mr Thiodan's Exhibition of Arts was to be seen. It consisted of Tableaux, Fireworks and 'an AUTOMATON' on the slack wire. There were such crowds that numbers were nightly turned away.' We do not remember anything being so popular in Leicester before, and glad we are, for it is so most deservedly.'[6:17]

Mr Ira Aldridge played during January 1851. An American negro, he became known as the African Roscius and was an eminent Tragedian in this country, in Europe and America. The Leicester programme included Othello, The Slave, Revenge and Father and Son. At his last performance a skating ballet was introduced on 'the Patent Metallic Ice.' The reports commented 'The African Roscius has been attracting large audiences this week. Pit and Gallery crowded to excess, and attendance in the boxes was much larger.'[6:18]

Holiday fare after Christmas and in early 1852 included three Masquerades, and the prices for dramatic presentations were reduced to Boxes 1s 6d, and Private Boxes 10s 6d. Mr Henry Betty of Covent Garden, son of the English Roscius (p.17), was engaged for four nights and the African Roscius made a return visit. 'The manager continues to play at half price ... Better attendance than of late.' But when the season closed Gill told the house that 'it has not by any means been a profitable one, the Exhibition [at the Crystal Palace] and the bad trade, have had a great effect upon it.'[6:19]

The season which commenced in September 1852, was notable for two presentations. The Corsican Brothers, a play of revenge (p.39), which was much acclaimed, and for the first time in Leicester, Uncle Tom's Cabin. The theatre was closed the night before the first performance to allow for the getting up of the scenery. The play was repeated three times in the following week. Both these plays were chosen by Mr Gill for his benefit on the last night of the season. In February Mr Popham gave two panoramic lectures on 'The Heavens', and over Christmas George Payne presented his two and a half hour moving Panorama of the Australian and Californian Gold Fields. [6:20]

On September 16th 1853, the following advertisement was inserted in the Leicester Journal,
'LEICESTER THEATRE — ON SALE — Two shares of £25 each. The Dividend paid last year was £76. Two shares give a vote for the Southern Division of the County; also free admission to any part of the Theatre at every performance during the Season except Benefits.'
This indicates the advantages a shareholder had. The ownership of two shares giving property rights and so the right to vote in Parliamentary elections.

Mr Gill had once more been granted the lease of the Theatre for twenty weeks for a rent of £200; the proprietors had resolved that it should not be let for a theatrical season before he took up his tenancy, but only for odd nights for the Amateurs. The company was new and talented and 'well patronised on the race evenings.'[6:21]

In October Sardanapalus, or The Fall of Nineveh was presented. The scenery was based on Sir Austen Layard's archaeological excavations in Mesopotamia, and there was great interest in his finds. The play was given every night for a week, with a change of afterpiece (fig.71). Mr E. Stirling took his benefit on November 4th when the play was The Spirit of the Loom! A Leicester Poor Man's Story (fig.70). This was a play which could be localised to fit any area. It had been performed in Norwich in 1848 with East Anglian locations.[6:22]

After Christmas, prices were reduced for a performance of Uncle Tom's Cabin and The Corsican Brothers. 'The six Front Boxes 2s, Side Boxes 1s, Pit 6d and Gallery 3d.' These prices remained for the rest of the season, which was to be Gill's last. In his farewell speech 'he assured his audience that though it would not require a wagon and 4 horses to draw away the profits of the season', he had not suffered any loss but had a small balance in his favour. He also alluded to a rumour that this season was the last, 'it being contemplated to turn the building into a Corn Exchange or Chapel'. It if should be so 'converted he hoped ... to preach 1st sermon.'[6:23]

The spring of 1854 saw a short season under the management of Mr Eaglesfield, but houses continued to be thin. When he introduced Mr Barry Sullivan, who was popular with provincial audiences, the Chronicle reported that he 'left on Wednesday after two mutilations of Shakespeare and a couple of nights' unseemly brawling on the stage with the other performers.' The manager did his best to restore order after Sullivan's departure.[6:24]

Mr J. Spencer Harris took on the lease from June 21st for seven years, at a rental of £225 per year. But houses were poor and on April 2nd, 1855, Mr Berridge, secretary to the proprietors, applied to Mr Harris for the payment of rent. Harris promised to pay all within a fortnight, but nothing was forth-

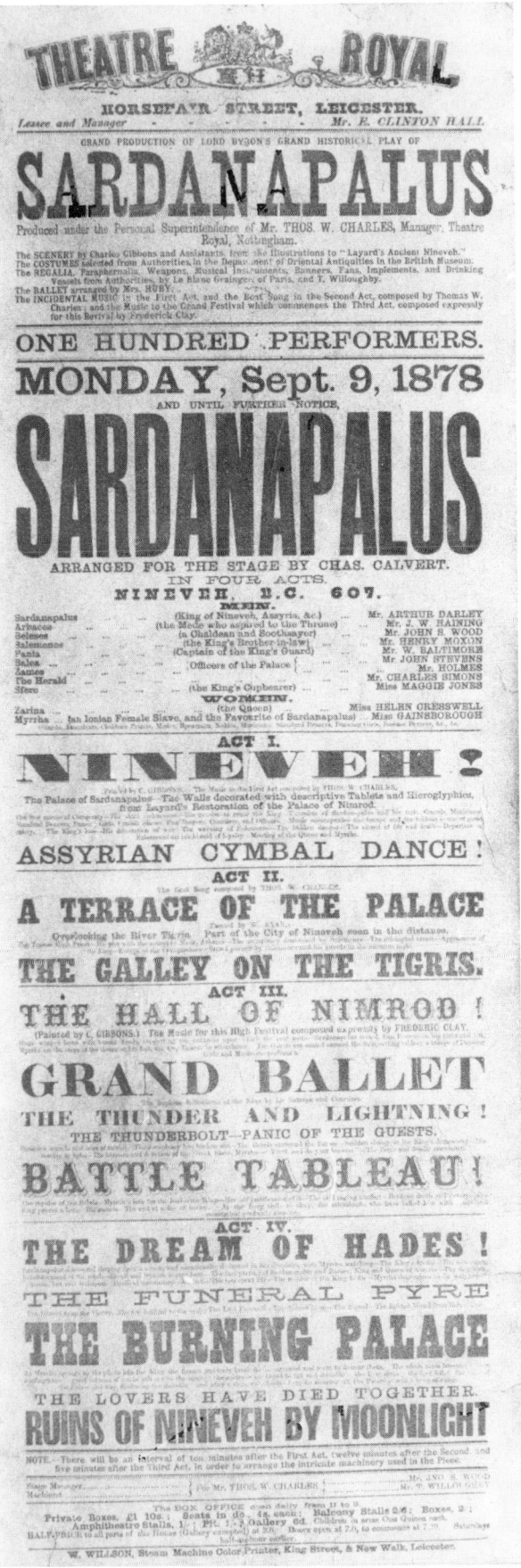

70   *Theatre Royal: Playbill for 1853. (P. Davies)*

71   *Theatre Royal: Playbill for 1878. (R L C)*

coming. As he had let the theatre for a short season to Mr Elliot Galer, the proprietors wrote to Galer requesting that he pay the rent to them rather than to Harris. He agreed, subject to being indemnified against loss or expenses 'by reason of non-payment of the same to Mr Harris.' As a further measure timber and goods in the theatre were seized under duress and sold, and his lease was cancelled.[6:25]

The season started as usual in September under the management of Mr Blanchard. Throughout the time that he was lessee, the main attraction was opera. 1856 saw Elliot Galer again at the house with the London Grand Opera Company. Houses were well attended, except for the boxes. 'This was no doubt owing to the absence from town of many of our leading families who have not yet returned from the country and the sea-side.'[6:26]

Mr William Sydney, lessee for the dramatic season, presented the usual varied entertainments with his stock company. But at its close he had to admit to the audience that he had been a loser. The theatre was closed over the Christmas period. In the new year Mr George Owen took on the lease. In March he presented the Opera Company under the direction of Miss Rebecca Isaacs and Elliot Galer; the engagement lasted for six nights and there was a full band and chorus. The African Roscius returned for a farewell week, 'which may well be considered an event in the history of the Leicester stage'. His impersonation of Othello was 'a matchless performance ... To Mr George Owen, the admirers of legitimate drama owe much (fig.72). His taste and judgement ... prove his sincere attachment to the drama.'[6:27]

There were various lettings during the Spring and Summer before the dramatic season opened under Mr Clifford. On December 15th he wrote to the Proprietors saying 'I am sorry to say that I cannot possibly pay anything before Xmas. The business has been so frightfully bad that I have lost everything and am completely drained'. In a further undated letter written after Christmas, Clifford wrote

'The Pantomime on which I depended ... has been a miserable failure ... during the first week the receipts came down to £4 13 0 and during the second £3 1 6 ... wearied as I am with disappointed hope and constant struggle. Beset on every hand with debt and difficulty — with my wife in a position that will necessitate her retirement from professional duty and an anticipated increase in my family. — I would fain throw myself upon your consideration and hope to be released from an engagement which has already proved one of the most unfortunate of my life.'[6:28]

It was the return of George Owen from March to May 1858, which was to see crowded houses, attractive bills of fare with well staged productions, including the Opera Company with Elliot Galer and Fanny

Reeves; who was to become Mrs Galer. When Owen announced that he had arranged to open the theatre for the following season, the applause was deafening. He 'intimated that the present season had not been a very lucrative one, but he was satisfied.' Every member of the company took a call, and 'for Mr J.H. Windley (a young and promising fellow-townsman) ... the cheering was of a most vehement description; and for upwards of twenty minutes continued unabated.'[6:29]

The new season opened on September 20th and Owen provided much to please the audiences, particularly his presentations of Shakespeare in which both he and Charles Dillon were loudly cheered. He re-engaged the English Opera Company, and in November leased the theatre to Mr Henry Powell, whose company gave great satisfaction with such melodramas as *The Corsican Brothers*, *The Warlock of the Glen* and *The White Slave*. Powell returned as manager for a Spring season which ran until the beginning of July, when Owen took over for a month. So the theatre had been occupied by the drama through the summer for the first time.[6:30]

In the Autumn of 1859 Mr Townsend, late MP for Greenwich, became the lessee (fig.73). Apart from the Race and Yeomanry Weeks he had met with little encouragement, particularly from people who should have taken box seats. Even the pit and gallery were poorly attended because trade was now flourishing and the normal occupants of these parts were having to 'work very late hours.' In a speech from the stage Townsend said he had 'heard much of the "Decline of the Drama", and of theatres not paying. I believe it to be attributable almost entirely to the continued "Blood and Murder Pieces".' His ambition was to produce entertainment more worthy of the countenance and support of a refined, enlightened and discriminating public (loud applause).' Townsend left the theatre in March 1860. Having suffered considerable losses, he was unable to pay his rent.[6:31]

Mr Powell now returned, as lessee for three years. In addition to the usual types of drama, he introduced Emidy's *Circus Troupe and Stud of Trained Horses* from Astley's Amphitheatre. He was responsible for presenting the melodramatic spectacle of *Mazeppa*, a story of a young man, who as the result of a love affair was tied naked to the back of a horse and carried off into the country of the Cossacks. There was a splendid stud of horses in *Timour the Tartar* on November 12th, when horses were also introduced into the procession for *Lady Godiva*.[6:32] There was considerable interest by the public in equestrian and animal acts at this time (p.81).

The Christmas Pantomime of *Valentine and Orson* was well received. After the conclusion of the fairy

72 *Theatre Royal: Silk playbill for 1858 (D. Duxbury)*

story, which we today would look on as the panto-mime, we are told 'Then the Pantomime proper commences, and Clown, Pantaloon, Harlequin and Columbine take the places of the heroes of the burlesque. Now the genuine fun begins.' When the drama season finished it was followed by the Grand English Opera Company under Madame Ruders-dorff, while in March Mr Galer and his opera company returned once more. Mr Powell's Spring season, for which he engaged leading players from America and London, was not successful, as the prices had been doubled, and not even the gathering of the Yeomanry for their exercises led to the full houses which might have been expected from past experience.[6:33]

In September, 1861, the management of the company was directed by Mr Charles Harrison, Mr Powell being engaged at one of his other theatres. When *The Colleen Bawn* by Dion Boucicault (author of *London Assurance* and *The Corsican Brothers*) was staged, it was well received. The *Journal*, however, pointed to a difficulty that provincial managers now faced: the coming of the railway and of cheap fares to London, enabled people to see drama in London theatres, so these were now in direct competition with the provincial houses. Mr Harrison's Panto-mime of *Jack the Giant Killer, or Harlequin King Arthur on His Royal Progresse to Leycestre, and ye Knychts of ye Rounde Table* was performed nightly for three weeks to large, delighted audiences.[6:34]

Although the season of 1862 opened in August, there were few advertisements or comments in the papers, and the same applies to 1863 when the only mention was of a number of performances by the Leicester Amateur Dramatic Society. We do know, however, that by January 29th 1864, Mr Owen was once again lessee, and 'sparing no pains to make performances worthy of public support.' Although

there were no advertisements in the papers, Owen must have opened his season before Christmas, as he invited the children of the Workhouse to see the Pantomime, free of charge, and each child was given a cake.[6:35]

Among the attractions which Owen staged in the Autumn was a season of opera; when Madame Tonnelier took her benefit, the performance was patronised by the Gentlemen of the Quorn Hunt. The Adelphi Drama of *Leah* was given on two occasions, with Mrs Owen in the title role. The play was in high favour with the frequenters of the Theatre. Mr Owen's Pantomime was, as usual, very attractive.[6:36]

A disagreement between Owen and a member of the company ended in the County Court. On April 19th 1865, he sued an actor for refusing to play, which resulted in the piece being changed and many patrons asking for the return of their money, or not even entering the theatre; so Owen suffered a poor night's takings. The case was decided in his favour.[6:37]

J.L. Toole, the comedian, appeared in September 1867, when the house was 'crammed in all parts'. He performed in *The Steeplechase*, in which he introduced his catch phrase "It does make me so wild", — which was no doubt heard on the lips of every errand boy the next day — and *Ici on Parle Francais*. These two farces were to remain in Toole's programme for nearly thirty years. An advertisement for the panto-mime *Red Riding Hood*, tells us that the theatre was to be 'perfumed by Rimmel's Patent Vapourizer.'[6:38]

John Windley of Leicester (fig.74), earlier noted playing parts at the Royal when a young man, took over the management for a short Easter season in 1868. He had become well known as an actor, and as a manager of provincial theatres. He was responsible for engaging many famous performers to support his company, and introducing spectacular productions.

73   *Season ticket to the Theatre Royal.*

(R O)

He also raised the admission charges. By 1860 the price for the pit was sixpence and threepence for the gallery.

'Matters at last became so bad that in the early part of 1868 orders to admit two persons for the price of one were being issued nightly, thus virtually reducing it to a threepenny pit and three halfpenny gallery. ... On my opening night the occupants of the ''celestial regions'' were so outrageously unruly that I had to lower the curtain three times during the progress of the play. ... In 1870 I decided ... on the important steps of restoring the prices of admission to their original standard.'[6:39]

On August 30-31st 1869, Leicester audiences were given the opportunity of seeing *Our American Cousin*, in which Edward Sothern played Lord Dundreary. For this part he displayed a fine set of whiskers down either side of his face, these were very popular with the gentlemen of the period and soon became known as ''Dundrearies''. As so many people wished to see him, holders of tickets for the Orchestral Stalls and Pit Stalls had to be admitted at the Stage Door entrance in the Market Place. Henry Irving also appeared for one night in *The Uncle*, with the principal players of the Birmingham Company; J.L. Toole was heading the bill with a repetition of his favourite farces. In September of the same year Samuel Phelps, the tragedian, performed for three nights.[6:40]

Windley was responsible for presenting *Under the Gaslight*, a play which was

'Received nightly with acclamations of applause. ''Hats, caps and tongues'' applauded to the skies. ... Scene after scene is witnessed with almost breathless anxiety, ... until at length ... the Down Express Train dashes along at lightening speed, and the curtain falls to the greatest applause ever heard within the walls of a Theatre.'[6:41]

The mechanical effects were by Mr Green, the limelight by Mr Jackson and Mr William Laffar painted the beautiful scenery.

In 1871 the audience was treated to *Across the Continent*, a sketch of life in New York, and on the Pacific Railroad. The scenery was again by Mr Laffar, the resident artist. The review stated

'the word ''sensation'' as applied to the present play is indicative of stage ''sets'', scenery and terrific situations ... the endeavour to work the audience to a high pitch of excitement has been perfectly successful.'[6:42]

Opera had continued to be presented between the dramatic seasons, and various theatrical companies took the theatre for very short periods. Each Christmas Windley presented his Pantomime with his own company. It was in 1871 that he announced that he would be bringing 'all the best companies he can get during the winter season, continually chang-

74   *John Windley. (W, Feb.19, 1897)*

ing them instead of pursuing the old course of keeping one class of performers through the winter months.'[6:43]

The movement of theatrical companies about the country was facilitated by the ever growing railway network. It was now much easier for a complete company, with properties and scenery to move from town to town. As yet the weekly touring company had not arrived, but the end of the stock company was in sight. As we have seen people could travel to London to visit the theatres, and on December 29th 1871, the *Journal* carried advertisements for special trains to the Pantomime in Nottingham, and on January 5th 1872, for a train to Leicester from Derby, and all intermediate stations, for a visit to the Panto, with a return journey at a suitable time.

Conditions outside the management's control have always affected attendances, and in April 1872, in spite of performances of Shakespeare and legitimate drama, houses were not good. This was blamed on the number of strikes which were then taking place in the town. As we noted earlier dramatists used their plays to comment on the social climate, and in November *True as Steel*, a play about a strike at a

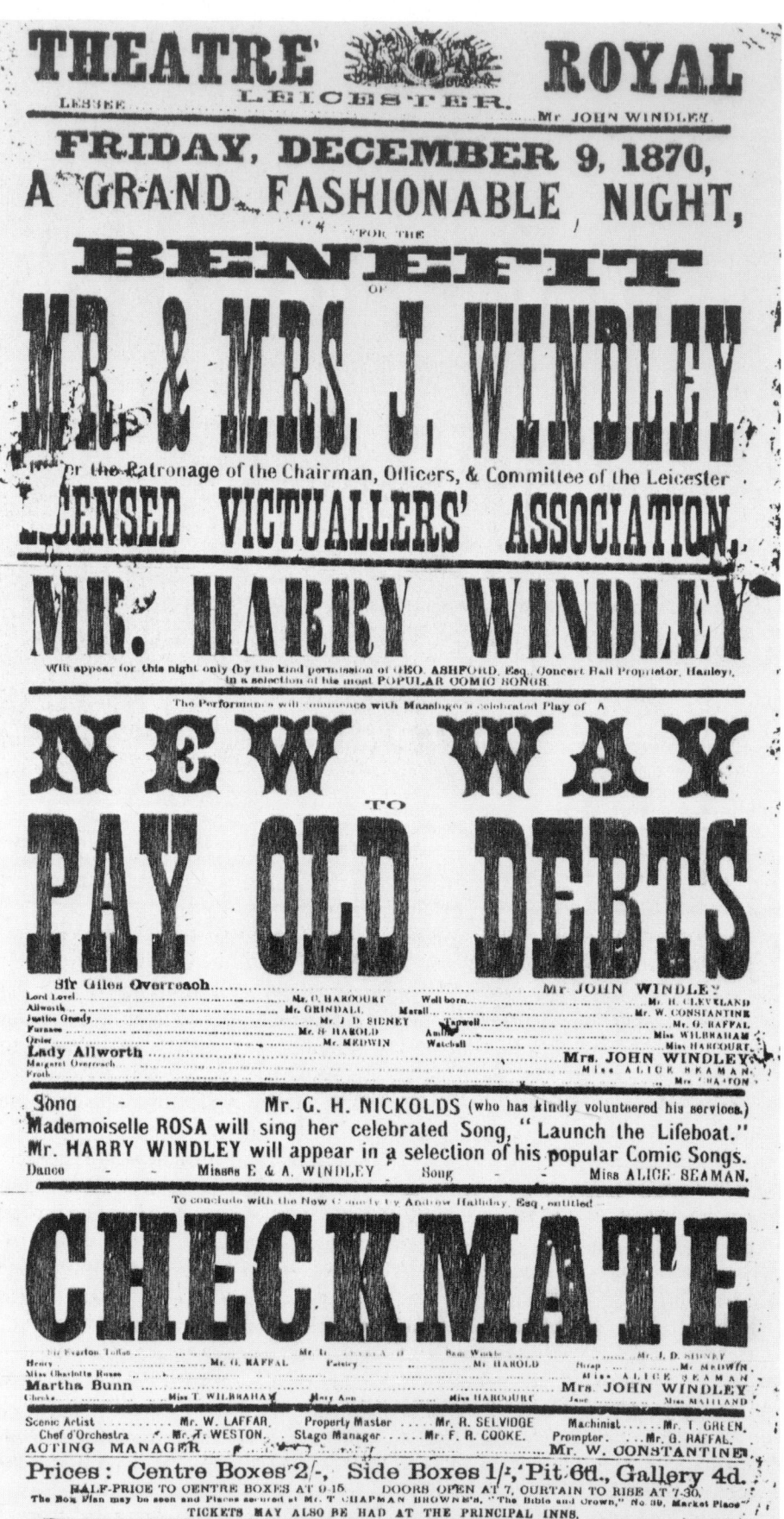

75   *Theatre Royal, Leicester. Playbill for 1870. (R O)*

northern iron works, was presented.[6:44]

Mr Windley continued as lessee until February 1873, when he retired from theatrical management and, settling in Leicester, took up journalism. But he was not forgotten by his friends on the boards, and in 1897 he was given a most successful benefit at the Theatre Royal.[6:45]

After his major alterations to the building (p.41), Mr Galer (fig.76) opened his season at the Royal on September 15th 1873, in a cheerful, gay theatre. The Acting Manager was Mr Chas. Reynolds. Prices varied from 6d to £2 2s 0d, and the doors opened at 6.30 for the performance to commence at 7 o'clock. Carriages were to be ordered for 10.35. The first production was *Twixt Axe and Crown* with Mr and Mrs Rousby in the leading parts. It was seen by a brilliant audience, and bouquets were thrown on to the stage at the conclusion. Performances took place every evening of the week to houses crowded in all parts. The following week Mrs Rousby played Joan of Arc, and was received with acclamations. The week ended with performances of *Hamlet* and *Romeo and Juliet*.[6:46]

Mr Galer's policy was to bring established companies to his house, and from the opening until November, five such companies played, including Mr Eldred and his Opera Bouffe Company; Miss Heath and Wilson Barrett's Company and Mr Charles Wyndham's Company, the last two both playing *The Happy Land* by W.S. Gilbert, which was very popular at the time.[6:47]

When Mr Galer introduced his regular drama season on November 16th, he lowered the price of the orchestral stalls from five to four shillings, and issued family tickets to admit four people for 14s. On November 28th he announced that the doors would open at 6.45pm, to commence at 7.15pm. The programme included such classics as *School for Scandal* and *The Rivals*. *The Honeymoon*, a verse drama which played to good houses, and the old favourite *Richelieu*. Preparations were also being made for the Christmas Pantomime — *Harlequin Graceful and the Fair One with the Golden Locks*. Mrs Galer made her first appearance of the season in this, and there were skating and ballet troupes and the Royal Clown — Charles Lewis. The management provided Juvenile Nights and Morning Performances, which took place at 2pm. Special trains were laid on from Nottingham and Derby and the show ran until February 21st, 1874.[6:48]

The resident drama company continued until March, to be followed by visiting drama companies and Madame Tonnelier and the Grand English Opera Company. Miss Heath and Wilson Barrett were booked to appear on July 13th when *East Lynne* was on the programme. The *Journal* agreeing that the performers played well, expressed concern that the public had been given too much of the struggles of

76   *Elliot Galer. (W, Feb.2, 1894)*

fallen women, and their efforts to rise up again, or their miserable despair

> 'we doubt the moral effect of the too frequent repetition of these pictures, before the susceptible young people who visit our theatre, who from having their sympathies so much and so often awakened on behalf of the sinner, may begin to think less of the value of their virtue, which after all is the basis of a happy family life, if not of the more important life of the nation.'[6:49]

When Mr Galer applied to the magistrates for his yearly licence for the performance of stage plays, the Mayor said that the Bench had much pleasure in granting it because the theatre had been well conducted. The Winter season was successful. *The New Magdalene* by Wilkie Collins was received with frequent applause and 'the rapt attention that gratifies every sensitive artist.' Mr Galer put *The Beggar's Opera* back on the stage, playing Macheath himself. He also staged *Macbeth* with an efficient chorus and all the original music. A letter writer to the *Journal* pointed to the reasons as to why the Drama should be supported; he wrote

> 'a perfect tragedy is one of the noblest productions of human nature, so it is capable of giving the

mind one of the most delightful and most improving entertainments.'

However, when *Macbeth* was being played to enthusiastic and crowded houses, some noisy occupants of the gallery, who had been offered their money back at the end of Act 1, had persisted in staying and making a nuisance of themselves.[6:50]

The pantomime season for 1874-5 was occupied with *Robinson Crusoe,* written by Mr Galer and with music by Mr Bartle. Clown was played by Mr Harry Croueste, and items were given by The Royal Christy Minstrels. Although it drew good houses until February 18th, with special trains bringing visitors from Northampton and the Harborough side of the County, and a benefit for the Infirmary, the *Journal* felt that parts of the slapstick were crude and violent, and once again set a bad example. It suggested that 'the public do not care to see the clown and pantaloon put on night gear and go to bed together, catch fleas, frizzle people with red-hot iron and throw them out of the window for snoring and squash babies and pitch them into the street for crying.' It also thought that it was wrong for the suggestion to be made in the course of the pantomime that 'the

working-class' should do 'less work and more pay for it, which are simply unsuitable in a world where men in general must live by their labour.'[6:51]

Among the companies playing in the Spring of 1875 was Mr Craven Robertson's 'Caste' Company (fig.77). This play, first produced in London in 1867, had established Tom Robertson as a serious dramatist. He used drama to describe life and social conditions as they were, moving away from the theatricality of contemporary plays. The settings were conceived as real rooms in which the characters could actually have lived, and they spoke the language of ordinary people. Robertson's plays were domestic dramas dealing, as Lillo's *George Barnwell* had done, with the middle and lower classes. Written as comedies, they became known as ''cup and saucer drama'', and laid the foundations for the British drama of the future. The company also played Robertson's *School* and *Ours.* The usual season of opera followed, during which Mr Galer took his benefit, 'the boxes and orchestral stalls being filled with the beauty and fashion of the neighbourhood.'[6:52]

77   *New Leicester Theatre company setting for* Caste, *Dec. 1946. (Photo: R. Hunt)*

The Royal Opera House: Two Theatres in the Town

For some time dissatisfaction had been expressed regarding the state of the drama in Leicester, and suggestions had been made that the cultural level of entertainment could be raised if provision were made for a new theatre, particularly one related to the presentation of opera.[7:1] At the Theatre Royal Galer had raised the quality of production as well as altering the form of the theatre. His efforts led to the formation in 1869 of 'The Leicester Opera House and Music Hall Company (Limited)', with T.T. Paget, the High Sheriff, as Chairman. Its prospectus included the provision of a building suitable for 'operatic, Dramatic and other entertainments of a superior character'. It was also intended that the building could be used for 'Public Dinners and Meetings.'[7:2] At the time some 400 shares out of a proposed 1000 £10 shares had been taken up, but it was not until seven years later that work on the theatre was begun, when the greater part of the funding was supplied by Mr Paget, described at the opening of the theatre as the Proprietor.[7:3]

In August 1876, Chas. J. Phipps, the architect, advertised that 'Builders desirous of TENDERING for the erection of the ROYAL OPERA HOUSE to be built in Silver-Street, Leicester, are requested to send me their names at once ...' Followed in September by a notice that builders tendering could see Drawings and Specifications at the site office after October 3rd. Drawings prepared by Phipps were approved in November, on which the reconstruction (fig.82) was partly based. On October 23rd the site was pegged out, and by early November the foundations had been dug and work was well in hand by the following February.[7:4]

This was described as Phipps' seventeenth opera house, all seventeen having been supervised by Mr Frank Stripling, as Clerk of Works. The main contractor was Mr Kellett. The total cost of the building was given as approximately £35,000, of which some £10,000 or £14,000 was for the site.[7:5]

The front elevation to Silver Street, in red brick with white stone dressings, was in the Queen Anne style (figs.78-9). Arched openings, leading to a large Entrance Vestibule, gave access to the circles and boxes, and adjoining this a separate entrance, next to

78   *Royal Opera House. Silver Street facade. (Read)*

79   *Royal Opera House. Silver Street facade. (N H M)*

an office for advanced bookings, led directly to the Pit, which accommodated some 1000 persons. This had a railed portion beneath the Circle, which could be curtained off, when smaller audiences were expected for intimate occasions.[7:6]

The main area of the Pit was designed so that the front of the floor could be jacked up level with the stage. This permitted the theatre to be readily adapted for balls or promenade concerts. Between the Orchestra and the Pit there were 50 Pit Stalls, approached directly by a corridor from the Entrance Vestibule.

In the main Vestibule there was a spacious and well-lighted staircase; the first landing led to the Balcony Stalls or Dress Circle, seating some 150, while the second led to an Upper or First Circle, seating 250, which could also be curtained off. There were three Private Boxes on either side at Balcony level, with four Boxes at stage level, seating in all 50 persons. There were large retiring rooms for ladies and gentlemen in connection with all parts of the house, and refreshment bars for liquors and non-intoxicants. There was also a fine conservatory off the Balcony corridor, with a choice collection of plants and shrubs, and a charming fernery, with rustic fountain and fish.

The Gallery, approached by a separate stair from Cank Street, was to accommodate some 1000 persons, and Phipps included here a feature introduced by Galer at the Theatre Royal (p.42), namely an Amphitheatre, consisting of a single row of seats for 50, railed off at the front of the Gallery. It has a separate staircase approached from the front of house. In 1952 this area was increased to five rows of seats at the expense of the Gallery, where 'comfortable rubber seating' was installed.[7:7]

When first opened the Gallery was described as being well ventilated, but by 1894 a member of the

81   *Royal Opera House. The auditorium. circa 1953. (N H M)*

audience was complaining that 'The ventilation of the gallery is execrable. The place smells from Monday evening to Saturday night like the sweating room of a Turkish bath.' Why he asked 'in the name of the ''Gods'' ... should we be suffocated because we only pay sixpence.'[7:8]

What were considered at the time to be effective arrangements had, however, been made for the proper ventilation of the building. A huge shaft, five feet in diameter, had been fixed in the roof immediately over the sunlight, down which fresh air could pass as the heated air made its ascent through eight windows or skylights, placed circular fashion around the shaft. These could be closed by shutters painted to form part of the ceiling, or when they were raised, the apertures could be closed with glass panels pivoted on the sides. The gallery was additionally ventilated by square windows, which could be opened at will. These would light the house during the day, when it was used for 'bazaars, flower shows, morning concerts, promenades,' but there are few references to its use for such purposes.

The main auditorium lighting was provided by the sunlight or starlight, containing 175 burners; in addition there were innumerable brackets throughout the house. The decorations were in the Renais-

80   *Royal Opera House. The proscenium, circa 1953. (N H M)*

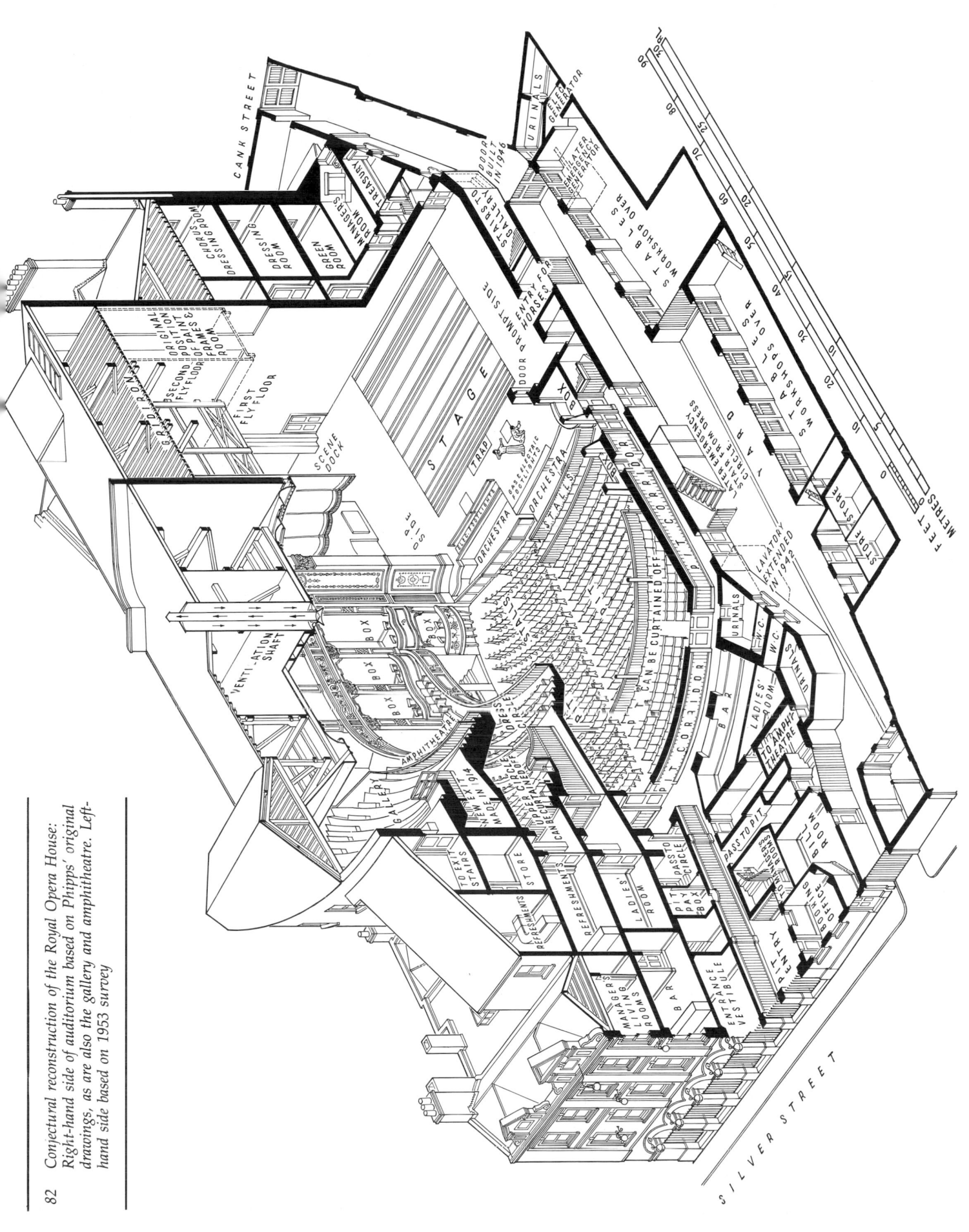

82   *Conjectural reconstruction of the Royal Opera House:*
Right-hand side of auditorium based on Phipps' original
drawings, as are also the gallery and amphitheatre. Left-
hand side based on 1953 survey

CANK STREET

CHORUSROOM DRESSING

DRESSING ROOM

GREEN ROOM

MANAGERS ROOM

TREASURY

ORIGINAL POSITION OF PAINT FRAME ROOM

SECOND FLYFLOOR

FIRST FLYFLOOR

GRIDIRON

SCENE DOCK

STAGE

TRAP

DOOR PROMPT SIDE

DOOR BUILT IN 1946

STAIRS TO GALLERY

ENTR'R FOR HORSES

URINALS

GENERATOR

THEATRE EMERGENCY GENERATOR

STABLES OVER

WORKSHOP OVER

STABLES OVER

WORKSHOPS OVER

STORE STORE

ELEVATOR

O.P. SIDE

VENTILATION SHAFT

BOX

BOX

BOX

BOX

BOX

ORCHESTRA

ORCHESTRA

STALLS

BOX

PIT CAN BE CURTAINED OFF

PIT CORRIDOR

PIT CORRIDOR

BAR

URINALS

W.C.

W.C.

URINALS

LADIES' ROOM

LAVATORY EXTENDED IN 1942

STAGE ENTRANCE FROM DRESS CIRCLE

AMPHITHEATRE

GALLERY

NEW EXIT 1914

NEW STAIRS MADE IN 1914

DRESS CIRCLE OFF UP & CURTAIN

TO EXIT STAIRS

STORE

REFRESHMENTS

REFRESHMENTS CAN BE

LADIES' ROOM

BAR

PASS TO PIT

PIT PASS TO D'CIRCLE

PIT PAY BOX

PASS TO AMPHITHEATRE

TO AMPHITHEATRE

MANAGERS LIVING ROOMS

BAR

ENTRANCE VESTIBULE

BILL ROOM

BOOKING OFFICE

SILVER STREET

FEET

METRES

0 10 20 30 40 50 60 70 80 90 100

sance style, cream and gold being the predominating colours, and blue the chief colour in the private boxes and dress circle. The circle front had blue velvet edging and was decorated with panels in the manner of Wedgewood cameos, 'the figures being represented in gold, crimson and other glowing colours on a cream ground.' The chairs of the circle were the same colour.

There were three exits from the pit, and the same number from the gallery, and 'from the higher priced parts of the house equal accommodation' was provided, 'so that it is believed that the entire building can be emptied in less than five minutes.' Further precautions were two rain-water cisterns at the front and rear of the building, each holding 15,000 gallons of water. In addition there were 'six of Merewether's patent hydrants with hose attached placed in various parts of the building so that in case of fire there would be every facility at hand for at once having it extinguished.

It was earlier noted (p.45) that a prime area of possible danger was the use of the roof space over the auditorium by the carpenter's and property master's workshops. Here these were sited 'in a yard at the side of the theatre, entirely away from the main building,' with stabling for horses 'during the equestrian season' underneath. One reason for raising the pit floor was to make provision for such productions, but the building seems to have been used for this purpose on only one occasion. In 1879, as an 'Attraction for Fair Week ... This handsome house having been transformed into an elegant amphitheatre, was opened on Monday evening as a circus ... An extensive circle has been formed out of the stage, the orchestra and part of the pit,' with 'a gallery for spectators at the back of the stage' including 'an elevated box for the band.'[7:9]

Adjoining the orchestra well, which was 'sunk in front of the pit stalls, so as not in any way to obstruct the view,' was a narrow forestage, approached from either side by stage doors in the curving flanks of the proscenium opening.[7:10] It may be surprising to read once again of 'stage doors', as this traditional feature had fallen out of use prior to the building of the Theatre Royal. The sensational productions and naturalistic scenery popular at this time had led to long waits between scenes while the spectacular scenery was prepared behind the front curtain. At the Theatre Royal in 1879 the 'Elaborate properties and massive staircase used in Acts 1, 2 and 4' of the play Peril had necessitated 'a wait of five minutes' after Act 1 and ten minutes after the second and third Acts. In 1880 a criticism of the performance of Drink at the Opera House was 'the extreme length of the performance, which is occasioned to a great extent to the elaborate nature of the scenery.'[7:11] 'Front scenes' had been included in some productions to

overcome this problem, which resulted in the introduction of a fore-stage with doors, such as we see here.

The stage was some 43 feet deep by 60 feet wide, with a height of 54 feet 6 inches to the gridiron. 'The space below the floor as well as over the stage is replete with all the latest improvements in stage mechanism:' i.e. the usual bridges, sloat cuts and traps. 'The scenery ... is fitted to go up and down wholesale, [p.49] doing away with the old-fashioned style of pulling off at the wings.'[7:12] Tom Robertson's Caste and the productions of Madame Vestris, made use of more realistic scenery (rooms with ceilings or what we would today call box-sets) (fig.83) in place of the earlier side wings: so there was never the need in this theatre for any upper or lower grooves.

In 1895 we hear from Ernest Liston (fig.84), the Clown in the Pantomime, that as an apprentice to Messrs Gimson and Co., the Leicester engineers, he did the tracings 'for the mechanical arrangements under the stage at the Opera House, little thinking at the time that I should use them.' In the Harlequinade there were 'thirty-two appearances and disappearances in eighty-five seconds' made through the traps. He had 'to be very careful when springing through the "star" traps, as I'm rather big for that job, and have to stand on one particular spot beneath the stage. There are ten men with ropes, besides heavy weights to send me up.'[7:13] One of the corner traps was removed, circa 1953, to be installed in the Palace Theatre (fig.85).

There was a large scene dock on the O.P. side of the stage (fig.82), entered from Cank Street, with an adjoining property store. Like the reconstructed Theatre Royal of 1888, there were two fly floors, with a 12 feet wide scenic artist's room spanning the stage at second fly floor level. This had two paint-frames, on which the Journal tells us Mr Malton of London, and Mr C. Frampton, the resident scenic artist, were preparing scenes for the opening of the theatre.[7:14]

Following contemporary ideas the accommodation for stage staff was separated by a brick wall from the stage, to which it was connected by two doors. It included 'spacious and separate rooms for supers, music room, Manager's room, treasury, green-room, "star" rooms, and ladies and gentlemen's dressing rooms,' and a wardrobe.

The theatre was opened on Thursday, September 6th 1877, with a Grand Concert of Vocal and Instrumental music. For this

'the stage was so fitted that the whole gave the appearance of a concert room. The screen behind was painted ... to correspond exactly with the front part of the house; there were no footlights, but instead two large candelabra springing from the stage, each bearing ten lights. This was the design of the lessee, the effect being very pretty, ...

83   *The parts of a Box Setting: a: ceiling. b: top rail. c: line and hook. d: brace. e: plywood corner. f: sandbag on vacant line. g: cloth.*
h: cleat. i: toggle. j: plywood keystone joint. k: canvas flat. l: toggle shoe. m: stile. n: throw line. o: split-pin hinge. p: brace
eye. q: proscenium opening. r: footlights. s: tie-off cleats. t: extension brace. u: door and jamb for fixing in v: opening. w: electric
dip. x: cill iron. y: bottom rail. z: stage screw or weight.

The stage and private boxes were hung with rich curtains of satin Creton, the colours being blue homburg and black and crimson.'[7:15]

After the inaugural concert, at which the acoustics were described as superb, Galer presented more opera and Mr Sims Reeves in a second concert. On October 8th the dramatic season commenced with Mr Buckstone and his Haymarket Company, which was generally favourably reviewed, but some of the dialogue was not as audible as it should have been, either because of the large size of the stage, or because the performers were not used to it. The Christmas presentation, *The Invisible Prince* attracted good audiences.[7:16]

The prices for the theatrical performances were given as Private Boxes, £3 3s £2 2s and £1 1s. Balcony Stalls (numbered and reserved) 4s. First Circle (numbered and reserved) 2s 6d. First Circle (unnumbered) 2s, Pit Stalls 2s 6d, Amphitheatre 1s 6d, Pit 1s, Gallery 6d.[7:17]

During the spring and early summer, 1878, the fare was provided by Mr Galer's Company and visiting tours, including Wilson Barratt's *Proof* Company, and Mr W. Ducks' *Our Boys* Company which returned

many times. After the Summer break, J.L. Toole and Sothern presented plays from their repertoire, including *Uncle Tom's Cabin*, which had remarkably excellent houses. Mr and Mrs Bancroft appeared in *Diplomacy*, with Mr Bancroft playing Orloff, one of his most famous parts. The houses continued to be well filled.[7:18]

The Pantomime of 1878-9 was *Sinbad the Sailor*, and the theatre closed on December 17th to allow for the necessary preparations. Ten members of the Lupino family appeared. Originating in Italy, the Lupinos were acrobats, dancers, pantomimists and actors. It was Lupino Lane who, in 1937, created the character of Bill Snibson in the musical comedy *Me and My Girl*, revived in 1984 at the Leicester Haymarket. Sinbad played to crowded houses, and was followed by Edward Compton and Maud Brennan in *Macbeth*.[7:19]

When Ellen Terry played in *New Men and Old Acres*, the house was filled with a fashionable audience. Miss Terry's 'delicious abandon, ease of manner, unforced gaiety, clear and telling delivery … gave the greatest pleasure.' In the period to Christmas 1879 there were performances of opera, and Leicester was given the opportunity of seeing *Pink Dominoes*, which was considered rather risque, *Ali Baba and the Forty*

84   *P.E. Liston (W, Jan.25, 1895)*

85   *Corner trap. Taken from the Opera House in 1953, and installed in the Palace (Photo: T. Buckeridge)*

Thieves, with a harlequinade by the Lupinos, filled the stage for the holiday period, and drew over 30,000 patrons.[7:20]

The season of 1881 followed the pattern Galer had instituted. He provided the town with good entertainment, which included for the first time Edward Compton's Comedy Company performing plays in repertoire. A high spot was the D'Oyly Carte Opera Company, which was always a great favourite playing Gilbert and Sullivan, in *The Pirates of Penzance*. The staging of *Les Cloches de Corneville* was a novelty, as it was sung and acted entirely by children. Later the old favourite Toole again brought his company to the theatre. In 1883 Galer staged *Mazeppa* with Maud Forrester playing the young man. This lady, of 'somewhat remarkable proportions,' was borne on the 'ghastly ride most efficiently by her horse.'[7:21]

Galer was himself a dramatist, and many of his plays were tried out in Leicester before being transferred to London. Opera continued to be well supported and when the Carl Rosa Company gave *Falka* in 1885, the papers said 'Never ... has there been anything like the enthusiasm ... all the best parts of the theatre were bespoke.'[7:22]

A manager often has to face difficulties, and Galer was no exception. The company booked to appear on January 22nd 1888, was unable to play, so another was booked very hastily. When the performance started both Galer and the audience realised that the type of entertainment was unsuitable. He intervened, closed the performance, and returned all money at the doors. When *Lily* was being played in February, there was great applause at the end of the second act, and Madame Gaylord, taking a call, was hit on the head by the weights of the descending curtain, and nearly fell into the orchestra. In 1862 Charles Harrison, manager of the Theatre Royal, had to cancel a performance of *Othello*, due to the non-arrival of the costumes. The pittites greeted the announcement with stamps and groans, while the gallery resorted to their usual practice of throwing apples.[7:23]

In April 1888, Galer booked F.R. Benson's Shakespearean Company, but in August he gave up his management and Colonel Winstanley took over. Galer continued to live in Leicester until the death of his wife in 1897, when he left his house in Anstey and settled in Surrey.[7:24]

Under Winstanley's lesseeship Lily Langtry appeared as an actress in 1889, when she was described as 'no Venus', and in 1892 Miss Vesta Tilley and her Burlesque Company performed. The resident scenic artist in that year was W.R. Buist (fig.87). He returned to the Opera House during the war years, and in 1926 painted the 'beautiful scenery' for Fred Clement's pantomime, *Sinbad the Sailor*. His youngest son, Robert, helped in the paint room above the

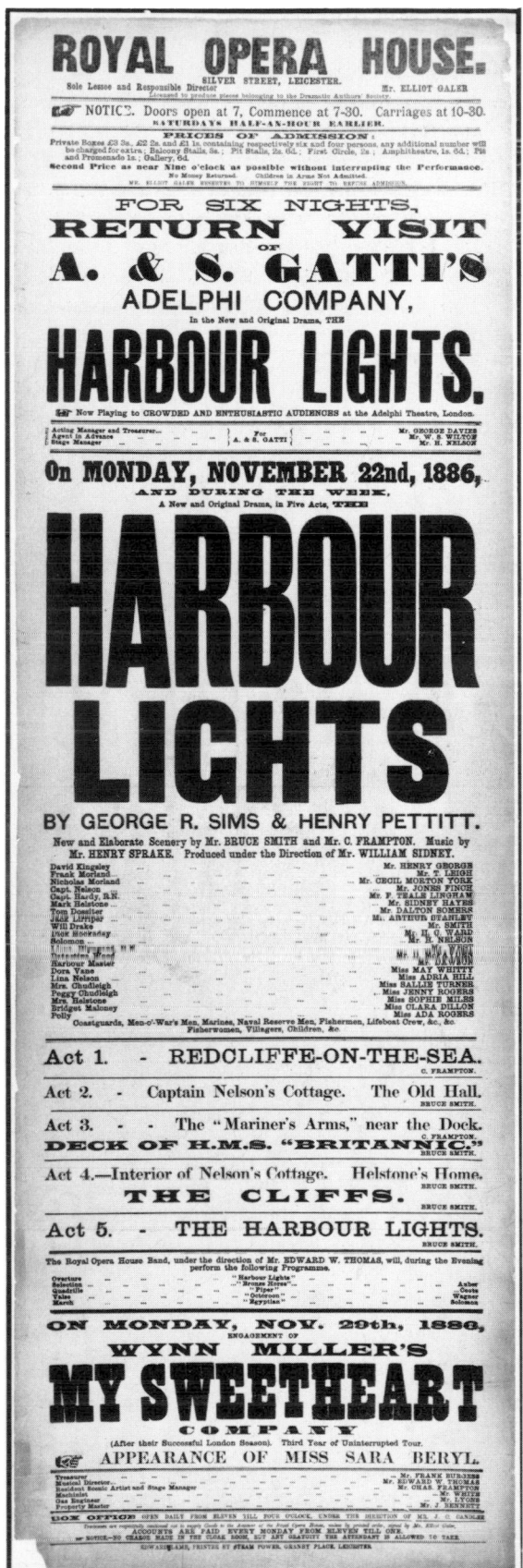

86 *Royal Opera House. Playbill for 1886. (R O)*

stage, and in June 1922, as a founder member of the Little Theatre, played Mr Livens in their production of *The Silver Box* at the Opera House (p.113). 1893 saw the first performance in the town of *The Second Mrs Tanqueray*, and in April 1894 *The Gaiety Girl* performed to very large houses. December saw the first performance of a play by Bernard Shaw, *Arms and the Man*, with a company selected and rehearsed by the author. *The White Heather*, which had been eagerly awaited after its success at Drury Lane, included a realistic representation of a struggle between two men on the sea bed; 'it is difficult to persuade the senses that they are not beholding real water, real fishes and a real sub-aqueous struggle.'[7:25]

Alterations had been carried out at the Opera House in 1888, of which the *Advertiser* said 'The crowded state of the house every night this week

87   *W.R. Buist (far right) working in No.1 room of H.O. Richardson's Scenic Studios, Oldham. (R. Buist)*

88   *Royal Opera House. Pantomime of 1896. (W, Dec.24, 1896)*

renders a detailed description of the decorations unnecessary, for most of our theatre-going readers have no doubt seen them for themselves.' A comment which is not very helpful to us, luckily the *Chronicle* and *Stage* were more informative.

'Mr Elliot Galer, as a last graceful act prior to his withdrawal from the scene, has had the whole building entirely redecorated and upholstered.' 'Soft grey, apple green, dead yellow and gold are the prevailing tints. The panelling is rich with delicate tracery picked out in artistic colours. Maroon curtains are hung to the private boxes and the beautifully designed ceiling is panelled in olive green relieved with salmon and gold.' 'On the proscenium ... is the motto "All the World's a Stage," surmounted by Shakespeare's arms and crest.'[7:26]

In 1896 the 'seats and fittings' were re-covered with green plush, and the boxes were draped with curtains to match. The auditorium was now redecorated in the 'Italian Renaissance style ... The front of the Dress Circle and other woodwork has been skilfully renovated in cream and terra cotta, relieved with gilding. The panels at the sides of the proscenium have been filled with appropriate scenes by Mr Edwin Talbot.' There was a new act drop, 'The Greek Dancing Girl', and 'those who have gazed for so many years on "Sorrento", will find much to charm and relieve the eye in the new design.'

In October the theatre was offered for sale by Mr Wade, of Warner, Sheppard, and Wade, including 'the scenery, properties, stage and other effects ... with dwelling-house, extensive outbuildings, stabling accommodation, &c.' The property was advertised as being 'held on lease by Major Winstanley at a yearly rent of £1,000'. Bidding started at £12,000, but 'the property was ultimately withdrawn at £25,000.'[7:27]

At the end of June 1903 the theatre was 'handed over to the workmen for 5 weeks.' Two rows of chairs were added to the stalls, and, so that the accommodation in the pit should not be curtailed, the apron in front of the proscenium was removed, and the orchestra placed further back. The plan for these alterations is noted, 'The footlights, which are at present composed of Electric & Gas Lights, will in future consist of Electric Lights only.'

The Stalls were

're-seated, upholstered and recarpeted, the prevailing colour being a light blue. The new hangings in the boxes and portiers are of turquoise blue and gold, and the plush cappings of the dress circle and upper circle are in harmony. In the upper circle 224 armed upholstered seats have been added, and the floor space has been richly carpeted in a light blue. The grand circle corridor has been carpeted with a turquoise blue Axminster

89   C.D. Leigh. (L G, Aug.26, 1905)

pile, as also have been the grand circle cloak-room and lounge.' The Upper Circle was also reseated with 'comfortable chairs of a more up-to-date style.'[7:28]

It appears that some electric lighting had earlier been installed on the stage, but now it was introduced throughout the theatre. A spacious office was provided for the travelling actor-managers, and a new Act Drop was painted by Mr C.D. Leigh (fig.89), the resident scenic artist and stage manager. In his younger days he 'was apprenticed to Gilbert of Brighton, and afterwards worked with Greaves'. He first visited Leicester when the late Mr John Windley was lessee of the Theatre Royal.

'In those days travelling companies did not carry scenery with them, but they retained the services of a scenic artist, and sent him on ahead to the theatres they proposed to visit, that he might paint scenes for them. In this capacity Mr Leigh was engaged by Mr L.F. Sefton, who was running "Pygmmalion and Galatia", round the country, and who included Leicester in his tour. Later on, while still with Mr Sefton, Mr Leigh was in Leicester again, this time doing work for "Broken Hearts".'[7:29]

In August 1904, an additional staircase and exit from the dress circle, and an extra exit from the pit, were constructed, and in June 1906, approval was given for a new proscenium wall of 18in brick replacing the original lightly-structured coved wings. Steel stanchions and a girder carried a 14in wall over the proscenium opening, and some three feet above the roof. This work was presumably carried out as part of redecoration done during the summer recess. A new asbestos curtain had been fitted in 1904, which suggests that this replaced an earlier fire curtain which had presumably been in place in 1888, when the authorities appear to have required no more than an asbestos lining to the proscenium.[7:30]

Elliot Galer had given up the management of the Theatre Royal in August 1877, to devote his time to the Opera House, and his position at the Royal was taken by Mr E. Clinton Hall. He continued with a resident company interspersed with touring shows, presenting the type of plays which the patrons of the Royal enjoyed; light comedies, melodramas and spectacular productions such as *Sardanapalus* (fig.71). A highlight of the 1878 season was the appearance of Henry Irving in *Hamlet*, *The Bells* and as Mr Jingle from the *Pickwick Papers*. The house was crowded and he was given a most enthusiastic reception.

In May 1879, Miss Emily Soldene and her Comic Opera Company presented Bizet's *Carmen*, having acquired the sole right of 'representation in English, in the Provinces.' When the D'Oyly Carte Company played *H.M.S. Pinafore* in November the price of the Balcony Stalls was raised to 4s. Houses had generally been good, but early in 1880 Clinton Hall gave up his management, as he had been ill for some time. The theatre was taken over at Easter by Frank Emery. Programmes continued on the same lines, played now by touring companies, and we now learn that 'Bonnets' are 'not allowed in Balcony Stalls.'[7:31]

In 1881 the lease of the Royal was granted to Mr R. Key, an experienced London manager (fig.91). In October he presented *After Dark* for which he engaged Sam Torr, the proprietor of the Green Man in Wharf Street and Geo. Leybourne, the lion comique, to play the music hall scene. They were well applauded and were recalled many times. The Pantomime, *Babes in the Wood*, included a 'Grand Moving Panorama of local views.' It was a great success, drawing crowded houses. On May 8th *The Squire* by Pinero was presented, together with a series of performances by music hall artistes, among whom was Lily Langtry, the Jersey Lily. Despite having provided companies of a high standard and reviews speaking of good houses, Key gave up his lease in February 1883. The theatre was closed except for a few odd weeks until August, when S. and J. Horner took over, programmes being then well suited to the popular parts of the house.[7:32]

In September 1884, the proprietors determined to run the theatre by themselves, and Mr J. Spencer, the clerk, applied for a six month's licence. He booked weekly touring companies, as well as Mr Hamilton's *Panstereorama of Passing Events*, which occupied the house throughout November, to be followed by two performances by the Amateurs. At Christmas Mr and Mrs Romaine Callender presented *Jack the Giant Killer*, which had thirteen scenes including a 'GRAND CLASSICAL TRANSFORMATION' and a Harlequinade. It was a marked success, and when patronised by the Mayor and Mayoress, the boxes were well filled. At an afternoon performance 'The older men and women of the Union, numbering over 100' were invited. While on another occasion 2,500 children from the denominational schools filled the auditorium.[7:33]

The Autumn drama season of 1885 was under the management of Mrs Kennion; Captain Kennion being the business manager. Mrs Kennion was a well known actress and brought her own company to the theatre, in addition to providing a good list of plays for the Winter and the following year. In 1887 she booked Augustus Harris's *A Run of Luck* from Drury Lane. There were thirty players in the well balanced company, several horses, a pack of hounds and professional jockeys and trainers.

'The marvel is that the drama should be so perfectly produced on our limited stage, ... Everyone should see the canter across the stage, which

91   Theatre Royal: Souvenir fan, 1881. (L Me)

AT

Christmas

WILL BE PRODUCED

A GRAND COMIC

CHRISTMAS PANTOMIME,

WRITTEN BY FRANK HALL, ESQ.,

ENTITLED—

LITTLE BO-PEEP AND HER PRETTY
LITTLE SHEEP, OR HARLEQUIN RED
RIDING HOOD, AND THE WICKED
WOLF OF WINDERMERE,

In which the following Artistes will appear :—

MISS MILLY HOWARD,	MR. HARRY WINDLEY,
„ TOPSY ANDERSON,	„ ALFRED ROUSBY,
„ FANNY ANDERSON,	„ FRED. IRVING,
„ NELLIE HARRINGTON,	„ JOHN N. GROUSE, &
LITTLE ESMERALDA &	„ GODDARD WHYATT,
EMMA.	

AND

AN ESPECIALLY ORGANIZED TROUPE OF

LONDON BALLET.

THEATRE ROYAL,

LEICESTER.

Lessee and Manager - - - Mr. E. CLINTON HALL.

LEICESTER

Amateur Dramatic Society,

MONDAY, DECEMBER 16TH, 1878,

In Aid of the Funds of the LEICESTER INFIRMARY

Under the following distinguished patronage :—

HIS GRACE THE DUKE OF RUTLAND, K.G.
THE RIGHT HONOURABLE THE EARL OF DENBIGH.
THE RIGHT HONOURABLE THE EARL HOWE.
THE RIGHT HONOURABLE THE EARL OF WILTON.
THE RIGHT HONOURABLE LORD JOHN MANNERS.

SIR BACH CUNARD, BART., M.B.F.H.	P. A. TAYLOR, ESQ., M.P.
	CHAS. MARRIOTT, ESQ.
SIR A. HAZLERIGG, BART.	H. PACKE, ESQ.
W. U. HEYGATE, ESQ., M.P.	J. COUPLAND, ESQ. M.Q.F.H
A. C. BARCLAY, ESQ., M.P.	ISRAEL HART, ESQ.
J. W. CLOWES, ESQ., M.P.	W. B. FARNHAM, ESQ.

SIR HENRY HALFORD, BART., and Officers of the
Leicestershire Rifle Volunteers.

Acting and Stage Manager..........Mr. GEO. MATT.

Hon. Secretary.......................... Mr. J. W. T. STEPHENS.

Hon. Treasurer.............................Mr. D. J. EWING.

STEWARDS :—

Mr. W. FAIRE.]   Mr. A. W. BOWMAR.

" Be not too rigidly censorious ;
A string may jar in the Best Master's hands,
And the most skilful Archer miss his aim."

ROSSCOMMON.

PRICES AS USUAL.

Box Office open on and after December 9th,
from 11 to 3 at the Theatre Royal.

The Performance will commence promptly at 7-30.
Carriages at 10-45.

PARSONS & CO., Printers, Station Square, Leicester.

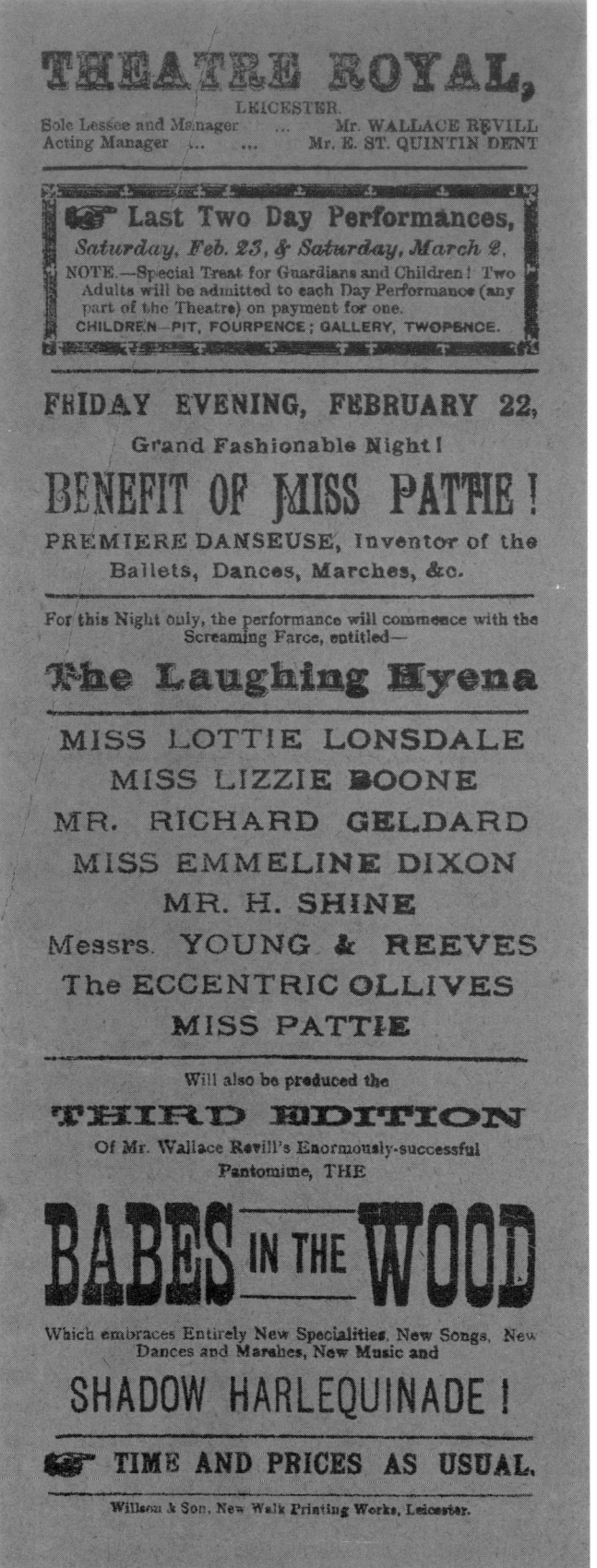

92   *Theatre Royal: Handbill for 1888-9. (R L C)*

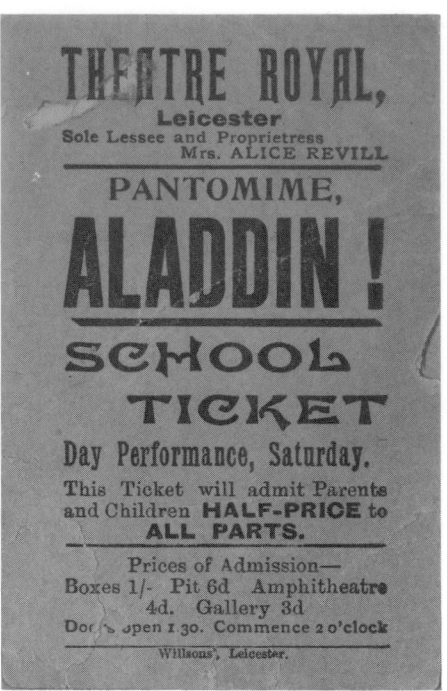

93   *Theatre Royal: School Ticket. 1898-9. (R L C)*

leaves the audience in fearful contemplation as to the ultimate destination of horse and rider. Nothing so exciting has been seen before on our stage.'

The race was probably accomplished by the use of treadmills and a moving panorama. Another spectacular production was *A Dark Secret*, which featured a regatta with a steam launch, canoes and a gondola punt.[7:34]

However, in July 1888, Captain and Mrs Kennion appeared in the Bankruptcy Court at Nottingham. She had disposed of her interest in the Theatre Royal, Leicester, in October 1887. While there she and her husband had paid the visiting companies 55% of the gross receipts. She stated that the last pantomime had not been a financial success, and she had lost between £1,600 and £1,700.[7:35]

In 1888 the theatre was sub-let to Mr Wallace Revill (fig.94), and the following year his lease was extended for three years. In a biographical article the writer pointed out that Revill had succeeded where others had failed, because he had not attempted to compete with the Opera House by producing 'high-class comedies and operas, or polished dramas.' He had given the patrons of the Royal what they wanted — 'broadly drawn and highly flavoured drama, in simple and broadly painted plays.'[7:36]

An example of this was the *Span of Life;* in a thrilling scene, the heroine and her hero-husband, who has rescued her from a band of Arabs, flee for their lives, but find the bridge spanning a chasm has been

94   *Wallace Revill. (W, Jan.22, 1892)*

95   *Lily Tuplin (W, Jan.11, 1895) (see also figs.96-98)*

destroyed. The Arabs are upon them. They give themselves up for lost. But the "Electric Trio", a group of acrobats whom they have befriended, seize one another and throw themselves across the gulf. So the heroine steps across the living chain as the curtain descends. The play was applauded 'to the echo.'[7:37]

So it was possible for both houses to prosper. Companies contracting to play with Revill could be offered special terms and a run of eight or more weeks, as he and his family controlled nine theatres. His pantomimes (fig.95-8) were always mounted in excellent style, the costumes being designed by his wife, who superintended their making. Revill's lease was extended several times, but in 1897, still lessee and only in his early forties, he died, and it was Colonel Winstanley who was to take the theatre into the twentieth century.

THEATRE ROYAL.

Leicester

Agreement made this *17* day of *March* 1894

Between WALLACE REVILL, Proprietor of the Theatre's Royal, Leicester, and St. Helen's, and *Miss Lily Tuplin*

The said WALLACE REVILL agrees to engage the said *Lily Tuplin* to perform to the best of *her* skill and ability *the part of "Cinderella"* in the PANTOMIME *Cinderella* at the Theatre Royal, *Leicester* at a weekly salary (from the production of Pantomime) of *Eight* pounds, shillings sterling, for the first seven performances in each week, and half salaries for all performances exceeding that number. Half salary *£4 - 0 - 0* for *7* days rehearsals, the first of which will commence on the _____ day of December, 1894, at 11 a.m. *This Engagement to be for the Run of Pantomime*

The said *Lily Tuplin* agrees to accept an engagement with the said WALLACE REVILL on the above terms, and undertakes to provide *her own Boots Tights Wigs & Dresses. Miss Tuplin takes Third clear Benefit during Run of Pantomime.*

The said *Lily Tuplin* further agrees to conform to the Rules and Regulations of the Theatre Royal, *Leicester* which said rules form part of this Agreement, a copy of which is on the other side hereof.

Wallace Revill

Please attach signature to the copy of Rules. |P.T.O.

I guarantee this Engagement to be for Eight weeks certain. Wallace Revill

96 *Theatre Royal: Contract for 1894. (Courtesy of the Trustees of the Theatre Museum, V & A)*

THEATRE  ROYAL.

Leicester

RULES AND REGULATIONS.

1.—All Artistes shall, within twenty-four hours after arrival in _____ *Leicester* furnish their private addresses to the Acting Manager.

2.—Notwithstanding anything contained in "The Employers Liability Act, 1880," or any Act continuing or amending the same, the Artiste shall not, nor shall the Artiste's legal personal representative, in case of the said Artiste's death, have any right of compensation or any remedy whatever against the Manager in respect of any personal injury which may be caused to the Artiste by reason of any defect in the condition of the ways, works, machinery, or plant connected with or used in or about the Theatre Royal; or by reason of the negligence of any person in the service of the Manager, at the said Theatre Royal, who has any superintendence entrusted to him, whilst in the exercise of such superintendence; or by reason of the negligence of any person in the service of the Manager to whose orders or directions the Artiste at the time of the injury was bound to conform and did conform, where such injury may result from his having so conformed; or by reason of the act or omission of any person in the service of the Manager, done or made in obedience to the rules or bye-laws of the Manager, or in obedience to particular instructions given by the management.

3.—No Artiste to sing or perform at any other establishment in _____ *Leicester* either prior to, during, or within four months after this engagement.

4.—Rehearsals shall commence at the time mentioned in the call; ten minutes being allowed (for variation of clocks) for the first Rehearsal, but not for any subsequent one.

5.—Any one absent from Rehearsal shall be liable to have his or her engagement cancelled, or to forfeit such portion of his or her salary as the Manager may think fit; and if the part should consist of one scene only, it should be considered as a whole rehearsal.

6.—All Performers shall attend such Rehearsals as the Management may deem necessary, during the run of the Pantomime, and any Performer disregarding this Rule will be subject to a forfeiture of one week's salary.

7.—For not being ready to begin at the time announced, or for keeping the stage waiting at any other part of the performance, to forfeit half-a-week's salary.

8.—Any person going on or off the stage at any other time or place, or in any other situation than that settled at Rehearsal, or leaving the stage before the proper exit, or for creating unnecessary noise or disturbance behind the scenes or in the dressing rooms, shall forfeit one night's salary.

9.—For non-compliance with the directions of the Stage Manager, a fine of five shillings will be enforced.

10.—No substitution of language, or of one song for another, or of one piece of music for another without permission, will be allowed. Any person thus offending will be subject to the forfeiture of one week's salary.

11.—Any person appearing in the Theatre in a state of intoxication may be instantly dismissed, or forfeit £1, at the option of the Manager.

12.—Assignments of copyright words and music must be produced to the Manager at or before Rehearsal. Performers singing or rendering copyright words or music without due authority, are to be liable to instant dismissal, and also to indemnify the Manager against all consequential loss, costs, damages, and expenses.

13.—No Drama, Opera, Pantomime, or any exhibition of any kind whatever, to be announced for a Benefit unless sanctioned by the Management, and any one issuing any bill or notice, without the previous sanction of the Manager, to forfeit one week's salary, and the Benefit to be declared void at the Manager's option.

14.—No auxiliary aid to be made use of for any Benefit unless approved by the Manager. The length and quality also of the performance to be by him decided.

15.—Any Performer or other person addressing the audience, or replying to any of their observations, without special permission, shall be subject to the cancellation of his or her engagement, or the forfeiture of one week's salary, at the option of the Manager.

16.—Salaries are not to be paid during a Performer's illness whereby the Management is deprived of his or her services.

17.—The Manager to have the power to cancel the engagement of any one engaged or employed by him, for using obscene, vulgar, or insulting language, or for indulging in unseemly conduct within the walls of the Theatre.

18.—Every person engaged as a Performer, or otherwise, to be paid weekly, according to the usual mode of play-house payment.

19.—No Performer or other person employed shall be entitled to be paid for any day on which the Theatre is not open for performance.

20.—Any person found smoking in the Theatre to forfeit a week's salary, and if the offence be repeated, the person so offending to be liable to the cancellation of his or her engagement, at the option of the Manager.

21.—No Artiste allowed to bring any person into the Theatre, dressing rooms, or behind the scenes, unless by special permission of the Management.

22.—It shall be at the discretion of Mr. WALLACE REVILL or his Manager to forbid any Spirituous Liquors being brought into the Theatre or dressing rooms.

23.—In case of Fire or other unforseen calamity, all engagements are null and void.

24.—No play, no pay.

I agree to conform to the above Rules, and accept them as forming part of my Agreement.

_____

N.B.—The Rules and Regulations will be Strictly Enforced.

97 *Theatre Royal: Contract for 1894. (Courtesy of the Trustees of the Theatre Museum, V & A)*

98   *Theatre Royal: Pantomime of 1894-5 (W, Jan.18, 1895)*

Fairs, Circuses & Amphitheatres

The circus was popular at the end of the 18th and through the 19th centuries, and in Leicester there were numerous sites where such shows were set up, some temporary, others more permanent. In 1793 Messrs Jones and Humphrey's new circus played in the Vauxhall Gardens presenting feats of horsemanship. At the same venue there was a 'GRAND ANIMAL EXHIBITION' followed by fireworks, after which the patrons moved into the Long Room for a ball.[8:1]

The Vauxhall Bowling Green in St Peter's Lane was chosen by Seignior Hengler, from the Vauxhall Gardens in London, for the first of his many shows in Leicester. Between 1806 and 1820 he and his wife and company appeared many times. The newspapers do not indicate if the performances took place in a building, but as they usually concluded with fire-

Mr. GEORGE WOMBWELL,

BEGS leave to announce to his numerous Friends and the Public of Leicester and its vicinity, that both his extensive Collections are joined together, &are now exhibiting in this FAIR; they contain the greatest number of Living Curiosities that were ever collected together since the days of Noah. It is impossible to give an adequate account of this splendid Collection in the limits of a Newspaper, as they would fill a volume.

First there is the great Male ELEPHANT, with his fine ivory tusks; two extraordinary animals from the interior of South America, such as have never been seen before in this country, the one a most beautiful animal stands about 18 hands, is called the Elaphus Camelus, the other the Paws or Vienna; these animals are allowed to be a perfect exhibition of themselves, they are covered with wool of the finest texture, and are altogether an admirable production of nature. A beautiful white Egyptian Camel; male and female Zebra; the Nylghau; the River Cow or Water Buffalo; two pair of Kangaroos; the Great Boa Constrictor Serpents; one of these is by far the largest ever seen in England, measuring upwards of 20 feet in length, and 36 inches in circumference; two fine Crocodiles, the largest ever seen in England; the grandest assemblage of Lions in the kingdom; the Cheetaah, or Hunting Tiger; noble male Panthers; a pair of Silver, or White Lions; a pair of Leopards, a singular instance of savage ferocity tranquillized into animal discipline—their gentle manners and sportive gambols with their keeper excite the astonishment of every beholder; they will not only suffer him to enter the den, and fondle with them, but by the word of command will jump over a stick, and through a small hoop, rise up and lie down, and a variety of tricks that will both please and entertain the audience; Striped, or Untameable Hyæna; Great Polar, or Sea Monsters; the Ursine Sloth, the only one alive in Europe; the Spotted, or Laughing Hyæna; Occlotor Tiger in miniature; pair of jackalls, or Lion's Providers; Spotted Cavies; Racoons; Civet, or Musk Cats; Cotimondies, or Ant Eaters; African Porcupines; Mococas; Agaties; Java Hares; pair of Ichneumans; pair of Horned Owls; with a variety of animals too numerous to mention.

Admittance—Ladies and Gentlemen, 2s.—Tradespeople, 1s.—Servants and Children, 6d.

The whole of the Collection is in such fine order, cleanliness, and condition, that the spectators are struck with astonishment, as it far exceeds any thing that human imagination can suggest. Mr. G. Wombwell is highly proud to have it in his power to say, his Collection is considered the first in the world; all others, when compared with this Collection, are mere shadows.

N. B. In order that the inhabitants may not mistake the Collection, the picture of the Elephant is to be seen outside.

---

works, they were probably out of doors.[8:2]

In 1818 there is mention of a New Circus with a Box and Pit entrance in Belvoir Street and a Gallery entrance in the 'Blue Lion' yard. Twenty years later Cooke's New Royal Olympic Arena was designed by Mr Harmston, the architect, with Boxes, Pit and Gallery. It had a 'splendid Ceiling,' with 'a massive candleabra, emitting hundreds of illuminated jets.' It was decorated with Banners of the Nations and Equestrian Emblems.[8:3]

In 1825 and 1832 Madame Hengler appeared at the New Cricket Ground in Humberstone Gate, and in 1835 a circus was set up there for the Michaelmas Fair. In the same year Batty's Circus Royal (fig.100), with its Boxes, Pit and Gallery used the site. This was probably a tent, as the review states that 'Every seat, every peg, and every foot of ground in all parts of the House … was occupied.' More than 2,000 spectators saw the show and hundreds were turned away.[8:4]

As part of this enthusiasm it was announced in 1839, that 'a splendid new Amphitheatre' was to be erected at the rear of the Royal Shakespearean Rooms in Humberstone Gate, which was to be similar to Ducrow's New Royal National and Olympic Arena in Whitechapel, London, of 1833-34 (figs.101-2). The Shakespeare Rooms were two large rooms which were to be converted into 'a SPLENDID SALOON for *Public Balls, Routes, Assemblies, Panoramas, Fancy Fairs, Auctions, &c.*' These were opened on Monday, May 13th by Professor Law and Mons. Buck, Magicians and Ventriloquists. There were four per-formances each day, with Boxes priced at 2s, Pit 1s, Gallery 6d.[8:5]

In October 1840, 'The circus in Humberstone Gate,' had 'for some time past resounded to the noise of preparation. DUCROW'S unrivalled stud' was to open on Monday evening, October 26th. The building is described in a Notice of Auction announced for Monday, May 17th 1841, which included

'The whole of the valuable, newly-erected, and capacious building known as the new AMPHI-THEATRE, the boxes of which will contain 450, the gallery 1,500 and the pit nearly 800 persons. The size of the stage is 70ft x 50ft, with large Horse Bridge at the back, and stabling for 100 horses under. The circus is 40 feet in diameter. The whole built in the most substantial manner, at an outlay of nine thousand five hundred pounds.'[8:6]

It was up for sale again on January 11th 1843, when the description varies only in the original cost, now given as 'upwards of Eight Thousand Pounds.' The announcement of the final sale on Wednesday, August 23rd 1848, however, reads

'*The Amphitheatre*, the largest out of London, brick built, the Stage 85ft wide, Walls 18 inches thick, the Building 100 feet long, 55 feet high, and will accommodate 3,000 persons, Stabling with Stalls for 30 horses, and about 300 square yards of ground at the back.'

It was opened in 1840 by Mr Monro, previously lessee of the Theatre Royal (p.52). On the opening night 'upwards of 1,300 persons crowded the Gallery alone

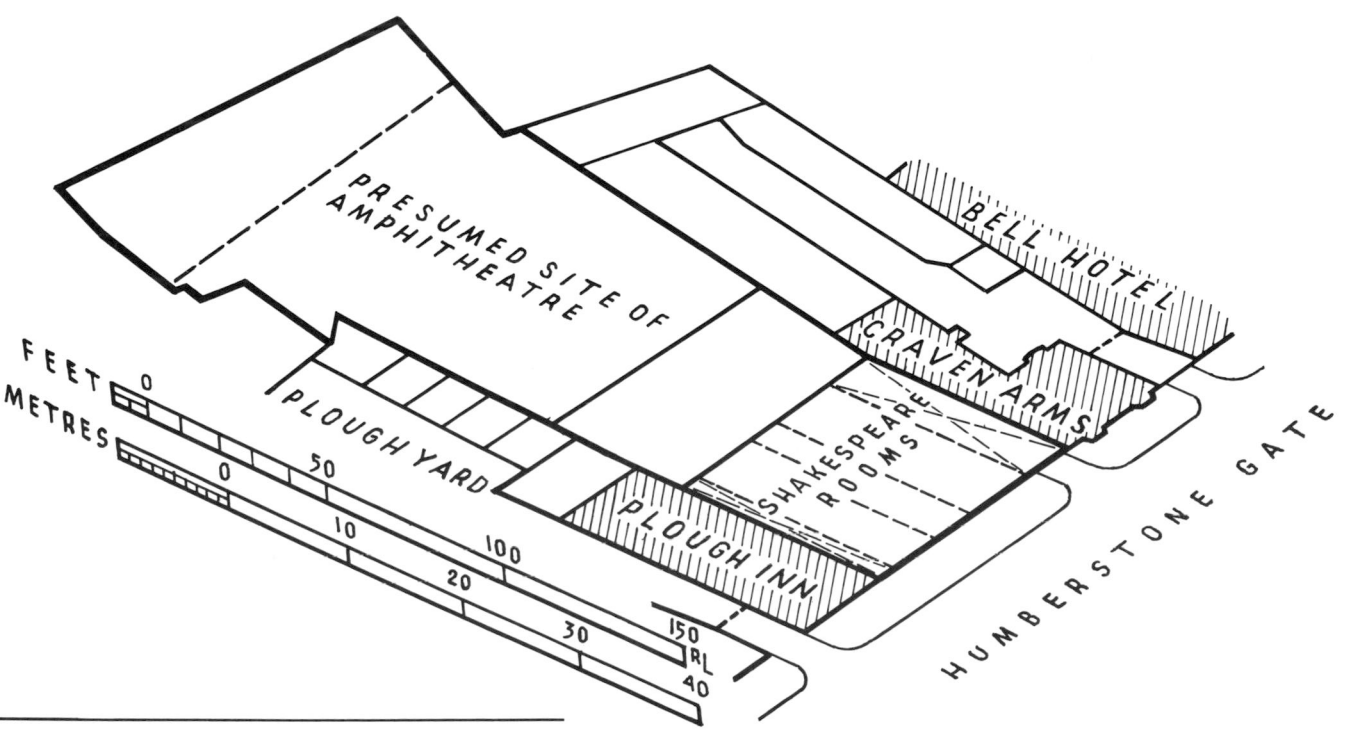

101   *Site of Amphitheatre in Humberstone Gate*

— a fact which triumphantly refutes the rumour so infamously circulated that the building is not sufficiently solid in its construction.'[8:7]

In 1841 Price and Powell's *Horses, Ponies and First Equestrian Company* appeared with Mons. Hengler, the great French rope dancer, comics, the 'best Ring Clowns in England and a troupe of Swiss Acrobats.' For the following month Ducrow's Establishment from Astley's announced *Mazeppa and the Wild Horse*,[8:8] but on Monday, November 22nd, Ducrow was informed by the Mayor that it was the intention of the Proprietors

'of the licensed theatre in Horsefair Street to lay an information against him, should he, not being an householder, nor having a settlement here, perform any play, tragedy, comedy, farce or interlude, &c. wherein there was dialogue, according to the terms of the act.'

The penalty for every such performance was £50. Ducrow's representative attended at the Bench at the Exchange where the situation was explained. As a result *Mazeppa* was performed without any dialogue,

the various portions of the spectacle being linked by recitative.[8:9]

On Monday, March 21st 1843, Messrs Hurst, Bostock and Jones performed a dramatic piece called *Hofer* in the Amphitheatre. Information was also laid against them to the magistrates by the proprietors of the Theatre Royal, and the case was proved. The penalty was a £50 fine or six months in gaol. The magistrates had the power to mitigate the term of imprisonment and decided upon two months, whereupon the representative of the proprietors withdrew the information, trusting that after what had happened it would serve as a caution to others.[8:10]

However, in 1862, Mr Charles Harrison, the then manager of the Theatre Royal, had to lay similar information against the management of the Temperance Hall (figs.103-4). This hall had opened in Granby Street on Monday, September 19th 1853, and was referred to in numerous advertisements as the 'NEW MUSIC HALL — LONDON ROAD.' It was mainly used for concerts, and the occasional panor-

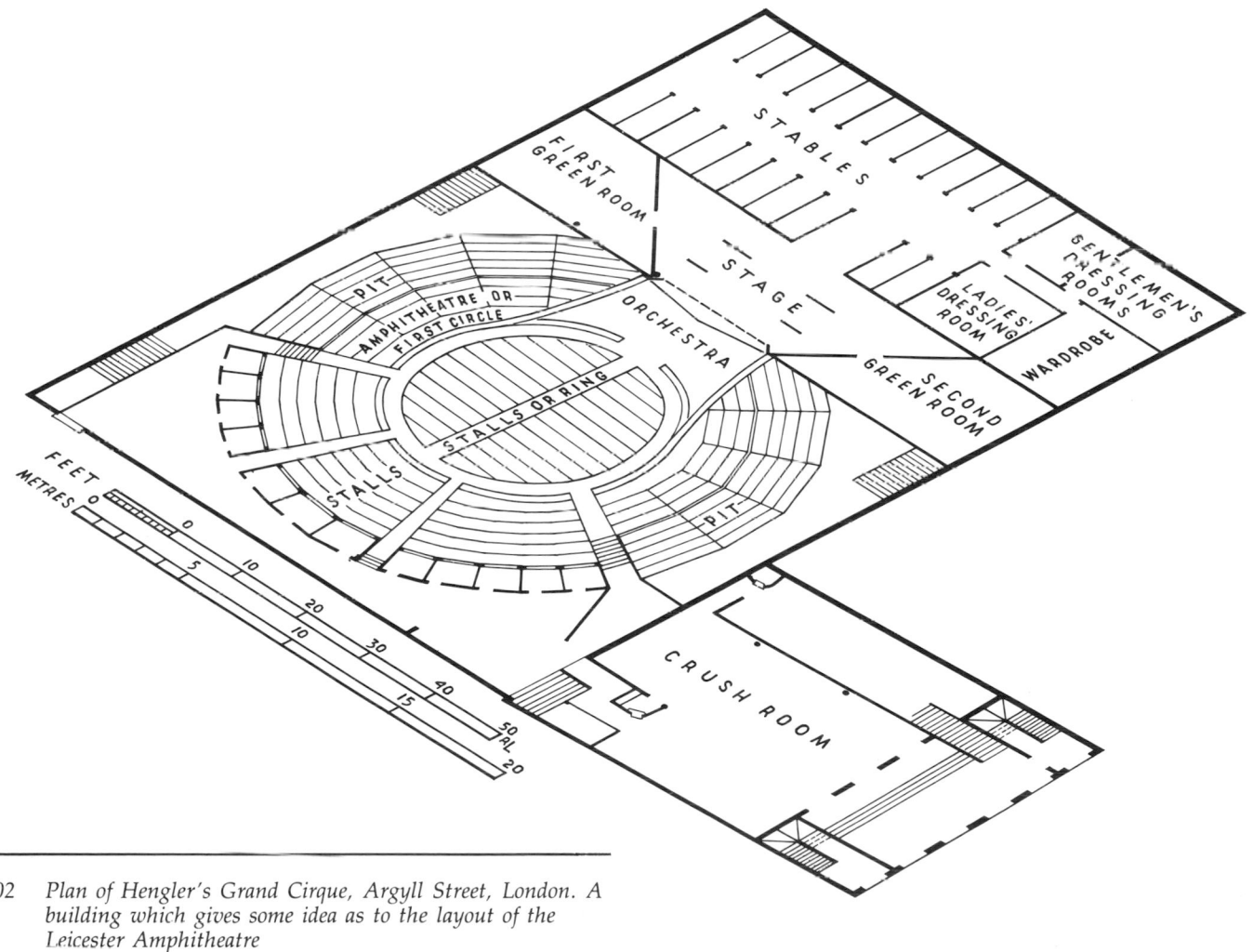

102   *Plan of Hengler's Grand Cirque, Argyll Street, London. A building which gives some idea as to the layout of the Leicester Amphitheatre*

ama, but Charles Dickens gave readings from his works there, Professor Pepper demonstrated his famous 'patented "ghost" illusion', and Charles Mathews, Jnr. presented one of his *At Home* performances. Mr Harrison complained that 'a performance of the startling drama "The Bottle" was being advertised for the 30th of August' although the Hall was not licensed for dramatic performances. A letter-writer suggested that the Temperance Society should apply for a licence, but Thomas Cook, a leading Director, replied that the 'Hall has already sunk to the low character of a common dancing saloon, and I should be sorry to see it enrolled as a licensed play-house.'[8:11]

In September and October 1843, Mr Batty presented his equestrian performances at the Amphitheatre. When he first appeared in Leicester he had only a performing black dog, but now his periodical visit was perhaps the greatest of the amusements to be offered to the townspeople. His wife resided in the town for a number of years and was buried in St. George's churchyard.[8:12]

In 1843 the boxes at the Amphitheatre, including two private boxes against the stage, had 'undergone a complete alteration. Instead of being left open to the ceiling as before, they are now completely boarded up and ceiled.' A principal box had been 'formed in the centre and made private for families and patrons of the Theatre', at an extra price. There were also centre boxes which each had a private door. The Pit had been freed from draughts, and a lounge had been made at the back of the pit seats.'[8:13]

In the following year, a Ball, for the Benefit of the Widows' and Orphans' Fund, was given by the Odd Fellows when 'The Pit and Circus' were 'Boarded over, thus forming one Grand Saloon.' This was repeated the following year, when it was described as 'the largest ball room in Leicester.'[8:14] In September

1844, the Amphitheatre is described as being
> 'wonderfully improved for comfort, the Pit passage being now covered over, and the Pit itself made warm and pleasant, all the openings at the back of the house are now closed, and a proper temperature kept up during the performance; ... refreshments are laid out in rooms contiguous to the boxes, and the pit is also supplied with every comfort.'

Arrangements had been made for country visitors to 'have supper or even beds supplied at the Waterloo Hotel, without the inconvenience of returning home the same night.' Following the 1848 sale the amphitheatre was demolished.[8:15]

W.F. Wallett, the famous clown (fig.105), who had given himself the title of the Queen's Jester, has already been noted (p.52) as manager of the Theatre Royal. In 1849 he opened a 'NEW CIRCUS' or 'Arena of the Arts', erected by Mr Herbert, with its Box and Pit entrance in Market Street, and its Gallery entrance in Bowling Green Street. In addition to this enterprise he was to appear in many circuses in Leicester and the county, such as Ginett's, Crouest's and George Sanger's. His farewell benefit in Leicester was at Crouest's Circus in 1890.
> 'Aged as he is, this veteran retains his power of quoting classic poetry, tickling his audiences with witty quip and crank, and doing, what few men in the present day can do — give the public an idea of what the cultured jester of old days was like. Every evening he has been vociferously applauded.'[8:16]

In 1863 Newsome's Circus in Queen Street was 'a capital erection of wood.... well lighted ... and fitted up in a neat and comfortable manner.' By October the building had been taken over by Pablo Fanques' Great Circus. Messrs Pinder 'erected a monstre hippodrome' in Rutland Street in 1866 'capable of

103   *The Temperance Hall, Granby Street. 1853. (L Me)*

104   *The Temperance Hall, Granby Street. 1853. (L Me)*

holding 2000 persons.' Three years later we read of Henry and Adams new circus building in Queen Street, certified by the Borough Surveyor as being perfectly safe. This was described as a temporary building (as were almost certainly most of the others) with a roof span of 62ft 10in. The ring was 44ft in circumference (sic), and the building was 105ft long by 85ft wide. It accommodated some 3,000, with stabling for 28 horses.[8:17]

The old Cattle Market Ground in Horsefair Street was the site of Stoodley and W. Batty Harmston's Circus in 1875; 'a commodious building' which was 'well warmed and exceedingly comfortable'. It was illuminated with gas and there was room for 1,500 in the gallery. In September 1882, John Sanger was about 'to erect a substantial building in Campbell-street, to be ready in November next.' This was a magnificent building in the 'continental style, brilliantly illuminated, warm, and uninflammable, and every mode of exit and convenience thoroughly perfected.'[8:18]

Three years later Campbell Street was the site for George Ginnett's Circus (fig.106),

'At an outlay never before attempted, has been erected the most substantial and handsomely appointed Circus building in England. The Proprietor has always been notorious for erecting a better class of building than any other Circus proprietor, thus studying the comfort of the visitors. The Reserved Seats are splendidly arranged with exquisite tapestry; the Second Seats are beautifully upholstered; the Third Seats are extremely comfortable; there is an extensive Promenade for all classes. The building has been erected by Mr W. Cox, Builder and Contractor, Leicester. The whole will be found, undoubtedly, the handsomest Circus ever seen in the Midlands. Private Boxes, to hold 5 ... £1 1s. Reserved Seats, 3s. First, 2s. Second Class and Promenade, 1s. Third Seats with a Spacious Promenade, 6d.'

It was lined throughout to prevent draughts, and was both commodious and comfortable. 'The outlets are capacious, and if necessary two thousand and five hundred people can reach the street in three minutes.' It was to be 'well warmed, and lighted with numerous chandeliers and gas jets. The Company will arrive on Saturday, ready for the opening night (Monday) ... Dress circles and boxes will be carpeted ... Mr J. Allen, the architect, has erected a very handsome building.'[8:19]

In 1889, Edwin Croueste erected a Grand Circus in Rutland Street (fig.107).

'The Hall is built throughout of corrugated iron lined with wood, and is 100 feet long by 75 feet wide. Mr Croueste has had experience of what the tastes of the Leicester people are like, and his arrangements show that he looks to the masses for

105   W.S. Wallett. (Courtesy of E. Arthur Crane)

his Chief Support, for while there is sitting room for only 150 in the boxes, the pit will hold 1500, and the upper promenade about 800. The ring is a full-sized one, 41 feet in circumference, (sic) and there are comfortable dressing rooms and stabling at the back for 13 horses.'

The roof was draped with crimson and white-striped cloth, and the walls with crimson and gold. The front of the promenade was in crimson and green, while the ends of the building were painted rose pink. The pillars were blue with the upper parts rose pink with a stencilled border. The boxes were papered with handsome crimson paper, with warm carpet to match. The ring was upholstered in crimson cloth, padded with green, with curtains to match, and the whole building was brilliantly lighted by a gas batten running the whole length on either side and four 20-light chandeliers over the ring.[8:20]

The Borough Surveyor was concerned that 'a wooden building of such a large area should be permitted even though of such a temporary nature,' and we are brought down to earth by his comment that 'Stabling for 12 horses is provided underneath the gallery, but it is not shown that any extra precautions will be taken to prevent effluvia rising into the Gallery above.' It was in this building, in 1893, that Mdlle Blanchard fell to her death from a trapeze into a net which did not break her fall.[8:21]

In 1840 the celebrated Lion Tamer, Van Amburgh, with his lions, tigers and leopards, had played on the Cricket Ground, where 'A handsome and Commodious PAVILION' was erected. For his return visit in 1843 he announced that a Grand Procession 'will arrive in Leicester from Lutterworth on Monday 22nd at 11 o'clock.' The menagerie processed along Oxford Street to High Street, through the Market Place to Belvoir Street, then via Granby Street and Humberstone Gate to the Pavilion. It was standard practice for circuses to parade through the town, and when his show appeared at the Amphitheatre in 1845, 'the procession was a long and imposing one, ... The Elephant, ... attracted great attention. The cavalcade filled nearly three sides of the market-place. A vast

concourse of spectators ... followed the moving panorama as it traversed street after street.'[8:22]

The Pleasure Fairs took place in Humberstone Gate until the end of the 19th century. As well as menageries, panoramas, swings, and merry-go-rounds, the drama was present in the form of marionette and theatrical booths, composed of wooden trestles, poles and canvas. One of our earliest references to what was presumably a booth theatre at the Michaelmas Fair, refers to a performance of *Othello* at 'Holloway's Show', when the Moor is described as being 'attired as a Scotch Highlander ... in Kilts.' We are told the company was 'performing no travestie, but the original play.' The five acts, however, were 'dispatched in five and twenty minutes.' In the same week, by comparison, the Othello at the Theatre Royal (p.9) 'appeared in a cocked hat, powdered wig, laced coat, white cord smalls, and Hessian boots.'[8:23]

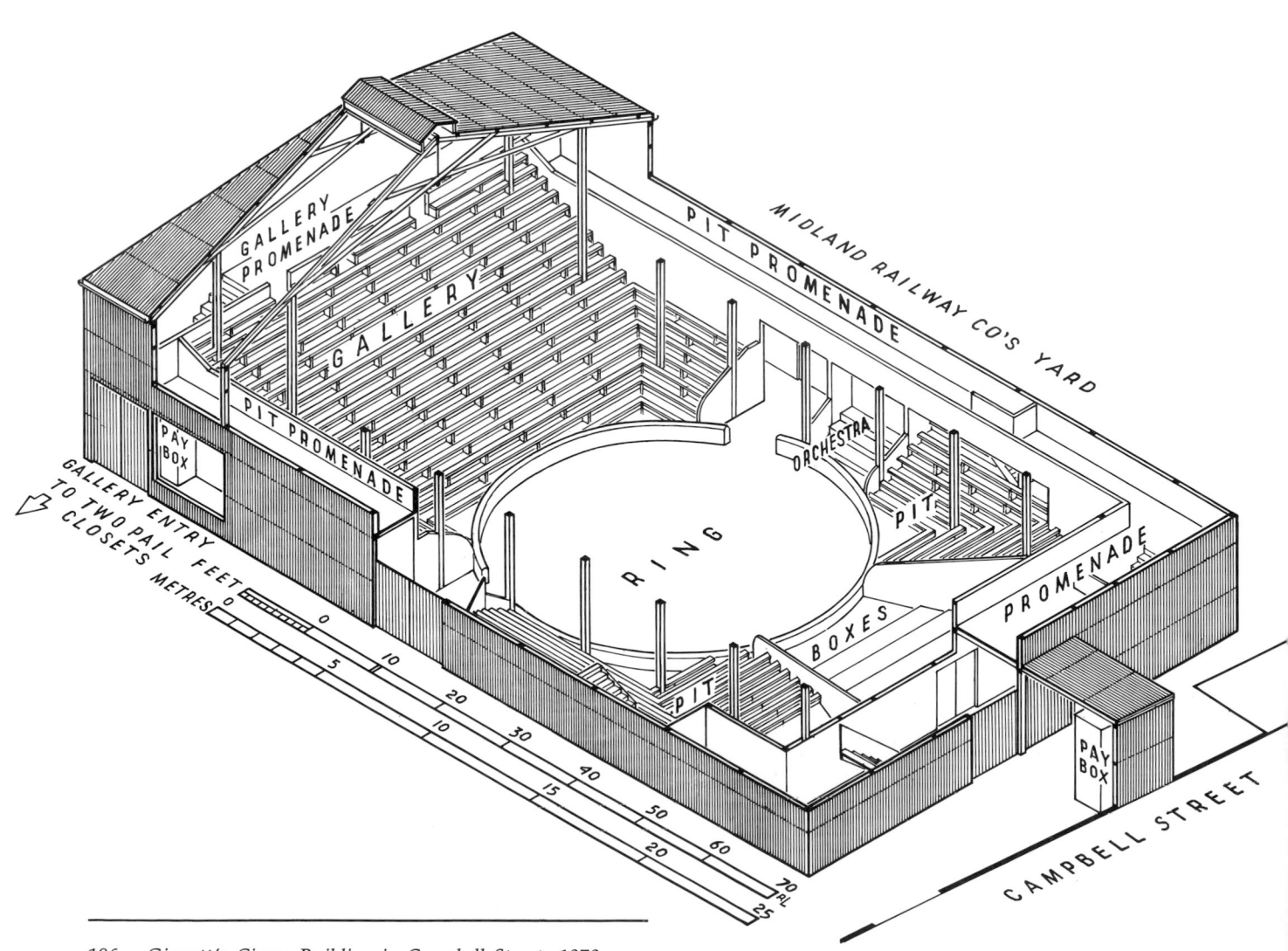

106   *Ginnett's Circus Building in Campbell Street, 1878: reconstruction based on original drawings.*

In 1840 one of the booths was the 'Queen's Theatre', its 'corps dramatique' being represented 'By three pigtails and clowns attached to them, two pale gentlemen in tights and tinsel, with three young ladies to match.' When the curtain dropped at the close of the 'brilliant season of four days and a half,' Mr Twitchem, the spirited proprietor, addressed the supporters of 'legitimate drama', which he described as the 'best done in Town between four poles.' 1854 was to see three booth theatres — Frederick's, Noakes's and Rayner's, all charging one penny for their performances. In 1858 the dramatic talent consisted of

'the *Murdered Boatman, The Robber of the Rhine* and *The Hag of the Tomb*. With all the terrors of blue-fire and gunpowder, and most unpardonable liberties taken with *Othello* and *Richard III*, who, each in their turn, held out pressing invitations to "pay their pennies and take their places".'

In addition to appearing in Humberstone Gate Sammy Rayner also had a site at the corner of Queen street, where you could 'see Maria Marten, ... and have a plate of hot peas — all for threepence.'[8:24]

In 1862 there were two 'Thespian temples', where 'genteel comedy' and 'heavy tragedy' could be enjoyed in full perfection at the nominal price of one penny. At the Michaelmas Fair in 1870 at Holloway's Theatre the proprietor was inviting the crowd to 'walk up, walk up; gallery only threepence.' In the county similar activities accompanied the Statutes Fairs 'when manservants and maidservants sought fresh employers by exhibiting themselves in rows down the side of the street.' At Ashby 'A spacious area was selected in the Market-square, and a wooden erection with canvas roof was speedily put up. ... A large platform was put up in front of the theatre, and on this the actors and actresses showed themselves. ... The play selected for the edification

107   *Croueste's Circus Building in Rutland Street, 1889: reconstruction based on original drawings, but omitting the cloth draperies and gas battens described in the text, which must have constituted something of a fire hazard*

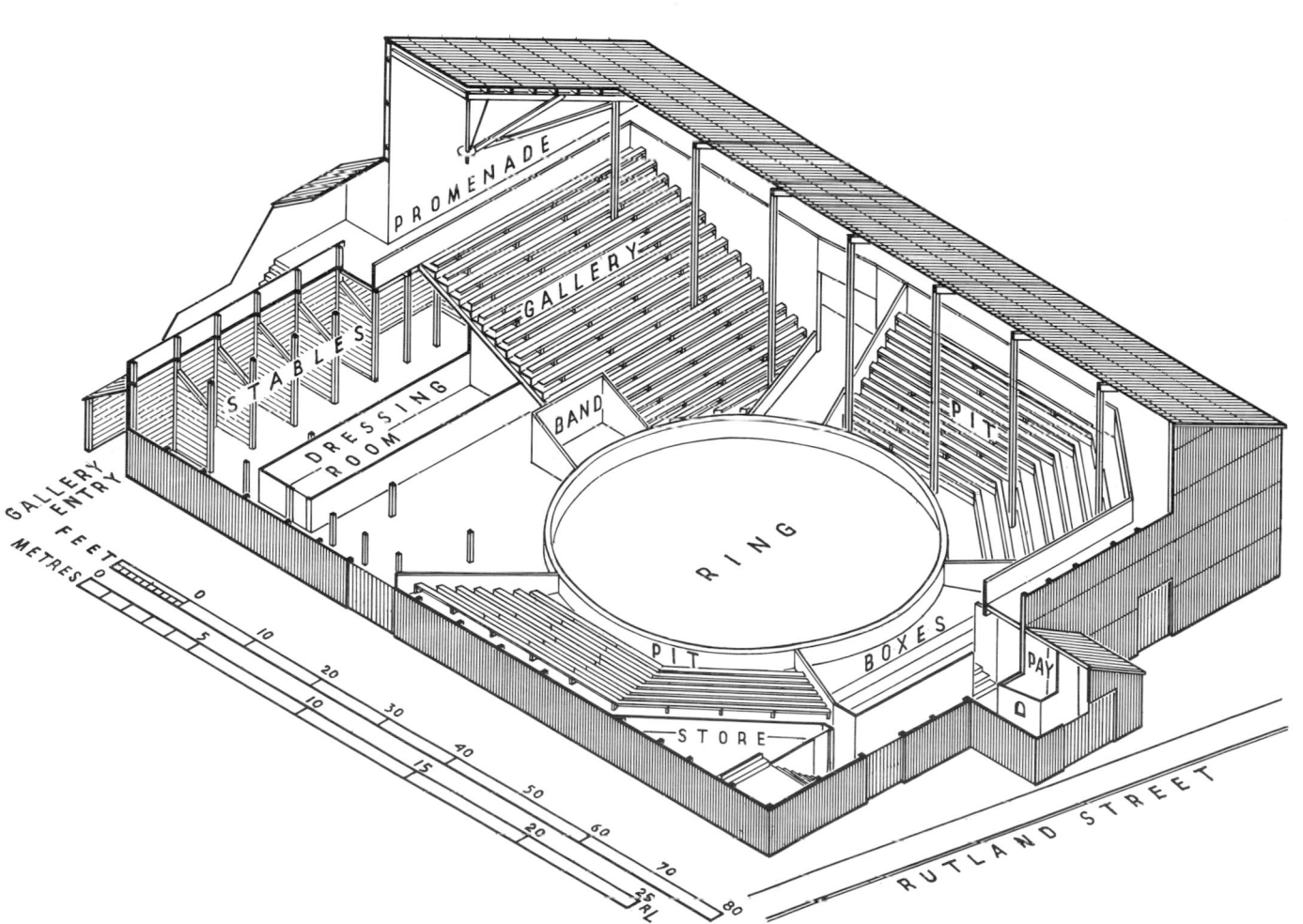

108   *Harry De Marr's* Two Little Vagabonds *company. (T.R. Miller)*

of the patrons of the drama was the "Idiot Witness", which hugely delighted the audience. ... But the biggest draw in the Statutes was the boxing booth.'[8:25]

Travelling troupes still toured the country, and on one occasion at Market Harborough in 1839, a company of strolling players issued bills for a performance, some of them expressing regret that part of their scenery had not yet arrived. They promised to perform the following day, and many bought tickets, but 'The gentlemen of the sock and buskin' did not make their appearance.[8:26]

Harry De Marr was the proprietor of a travelling theatre which toured the country at the turn of the century, and c.1904 was playing in Hinckley, where they always did well (fig.108). The company consisted of the De Marr family and members of the Miller family, who eventually settled in the town. The theatre was fitted up from wooden panels, bolted together and covered with a canvas roof. The stage was built from rostrums, and there were four rows of chairs at the front, behind which were benches. The theatre moved from place to place by train, being taken to the sites on flat railway drays. An undated cutting from the *Hinckley Times* gives details of a performance of *Dick Whittington* on the site of the Borough Theatre, in which Mrs De Marr played Dick and Miss Vinnie Miller 'made a piquant and dainty Alice.' Mr T.R. Miller and his family are today actively concerned with the Concordia Theatre.[8:27]

Even as late as the 1920s touring theatrical booths were found. About 1923 Billy Holloway and his wife, brother, son and daughter, and a gentleman named Sam Payne, were performing in the county at such places as Mountsorrel, Hinckley, Earl Shilton, Barwell and at Ellistown, where they arrived in their caravans and lorries and set up their theatre in a field. Known locally as the Blood Hut, it was part panel and part canvas, some twenty feet wide, with a stage at one end, with small wings at either side for the scenery. A caravan at the back served as a dressing room. In the auditorium were four or five rows of stalls, which had probably been salvaged from some music hall or cinema; once they had been upholstered, now they were merely covered with cloth. Behind were rows of pit benches covered with American cloth. The gallery, carried on some scaffolding, had from six to eight rows of planking, each row seating fifteen people. In all the house held about 200! A generator, which thumped its way through the performances, lit the bulbs in the house and on the front of the building.

There were fortnightly changes of programme, announced on long bills displayed around the area. Each performance started with variety turns, followed by a drama, *Maria Marten*, *The Wild Man of Borneo* or *The Sign of the Cross*, finishing with a jig. Billy Holloway, a clean shaven, rather florid, stout man

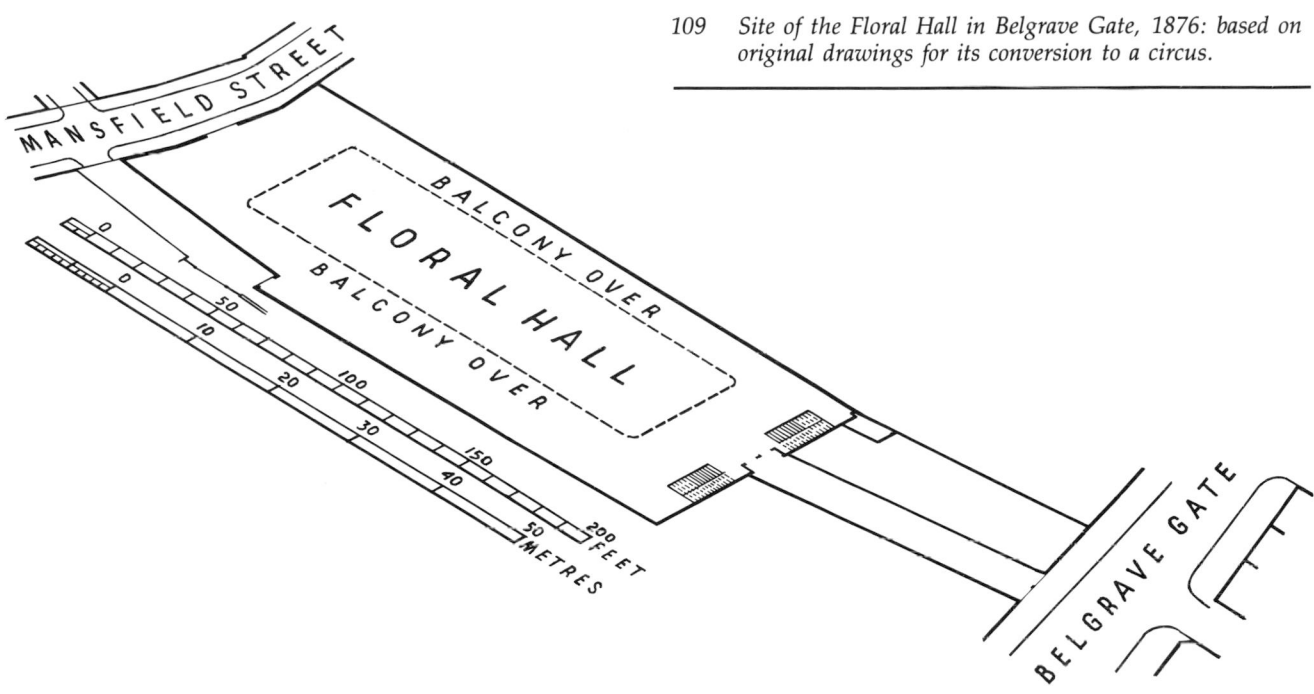

109 *Site of the Floral Hall in Belgrave Gate, 1876: based on original drawings for its conversion to a circus.*

always played the hero; his brother played the villain. The audience was expected to participate with hisses, boos and cheering. Mrs Holloway always had to finish her parts early, so that she could serve fish and chips, which she prepared in a hut outside, to the departing audience. People walked to Ellistown from the surrounding villages to sample these delights.[8:28]

In March 1876, a company was formed for the purpose of establishing a 'FLORAL HALL SKATING RINK', which was to become a 19th century equivalent of the present Granby Halls. A site was obtained between Belgrave Gate and Mansfield Street (fig.109) on which it was proposed 'to erect an extensive building ... affording on the ground floor the finest covered skating area in the provinces.' The hall (fig.110) was 212 feet long by 83 feet wide. There were broad stairs leading to extensive balconies, supported by iron columns, running the length of the building, which were to be used as promenades. On the left , in the centre of the hall, was the orchestra, with six private boxes opposite. The roof was curved, and composed of wood and glass, with wooden arches. There was a side aisle with a glass roof, which it was suggested could be used as a picture gallery.

'It was originally intended to open the hall as a skating rink, but owing to the difficulty of obtaining roller skates ... the company resolved upon having the hall fitted up as a circus. ... Seats have been arranged round the ring, gradually sloping up to the balconies at the sides. The first seats are

110 *Interior of the Floral Hall. (W, Dec.2, 1892)*

those rising to the balconies, which accommodate about 600 persons. The immense amphitheatre gallery is entered from Mansfield-street, and alone will seat about 2,000. It is estimated that no less than 5,000 persons may witness the perform-ances.'

It was opened on Friday, December 15th with a concert under the direction of Mr Henry Nicholson and on the following Monday the 'GRAND CIRQUE and HIPPODROME' commenced. By now the management had 'enlarged the Gallery, and erected a New Balcony on the Promenade, which will add 1,000 additional seats.'[8:29]

Wallett appeared here in 1877, and there were the usual equestrian shows of *Dick Turpin's Ride to York* and *Mazeppa.* By February 1878, it was being used as the 'NEW THEATRE OF VARIETIES', when it had been 'Re-decorated and Re-embellished,' with a 'Magnificent Stage, Scenery and Appointments.' Acts then included 'Blondin and Blanche on the rope' and 'Little Bob's Dive of Seventy-five feet, From the Roof to the Platform.' As the roof was only 49 feet at its highest point, this seems something of an exagger-ation. In May we read that 'the undertaking had not been a financial success ... owing to the slackness of trade,' and by September it was being converted into a 'FLORAL BAZAAR and MARKET. The Promenade or Gallery will be continued round the building, and there will be a public thoroughfare through the building into Mansfield-street.'[8:30]

In September, 1879, the Floral Hall was eventually opened as a Skating Rink, but Promenade Concerts and Dancing were still introduced, and in 1880 there was an Industrial Exhibition. In 1884 it was once more adapted for use by Hengler's Circus, with Wallett again appearing. Sunday gatherings, The Mayor's Promenade Concerts, Exhibitions, Newsome's Hippodrome and Circus, a Venetian Fete, Hamilton's Diorama, An Irish Fancy Fair, a Roman Catholic Bazaar, Bicycle Racing, and Boxing were all accommodated. In 1887 John H. (Jubilee) Clarke took over the management and organised a 'giant show ... known as the Jubilee Exhibition.'[8:31]

On Monday, August 20th 1888, he transferred his mammoth open air show *Clarendonia* from the then open Clarendon Park to the Floral Hall. In 1889 it was again a circus, and in 1890 Madame Patti, being indisposed, failed to appear. By 1895 it was once again a Skating Palace, and in the same year it housed Madame Tussaud's Waxworks. In January, 1900, it was sold to the owners of the new Palace, Theatre of Varieties, which was soon to rise on the site. It closed with 'Mr Jubilee's ... Red, White and Blue Exhibition,' intended to strike upon the 'patriotic sentiment which is rampant in the town just now.'

Its passing was deplored, as it had been in great demand for bazaars, dog and poultry shows, public meetings, and brass band concerts. 'How shall we get cheap Sunday evening concerts? Where will our new Municipal Orchestra play at paying prices? and how will any substantial portion of political Leicester ever be able again to listen to the great statesmen of the country? The demolition of the hall will leave a blank which it is almost appalling to contemplate.'[8:32]

Music Halls & Variety Theatres

Entertainment was also provided in the Club rooms of many taverns, such as the Black Lion and the Old Cheese, which Mr William Paul (fig.111), as landlord, took over on March 10th 1863, where he ran a 'free and easy' (fig.112). But what seems to be our earliest notice of a Music Hall dates from September 1862,

'THE ALHAMBRA MUSIC HALL (LATE CIRCUS) BELGRAVE GATE. Proprietor. Mr Dan Cooke. The above place of amusement, tastefully decorated and fitted up at an enormous expense, thoroughly waterproof in all parts, is OPEN EVERY EVENING at Seven o'clock, commencing precisely at Half-past ... Private Boxes, 1s. Orchestral Stalls, 6d. Pit, 4d. Gallery, 2d.'[9:1]

In 1861 this building had been advertised as 'STEVEN'S NEW CIRCUS — FLEUR-DE-LIS GROUNDS, BELGRAVE GATE', when Mr Stevens had engaged Mr and Mrs Palmer from Astley's. It was 'a large wooden building ... capable of holding upwards of 2000 persons' which appears to have been owned by Edwin Croueste (p.83). On Monday, September 2nd, Steven's son, 'a little boy of fourteen years of age', whilst playing the part of a monkey, 'went rather too high on the rope, so that his "cotton hair" caught fire from the gaslights', and he died the following day.[9:2]

In 1862 Messrs Forbes and Barnett of Newcastle-upon-Tyne had advertised that they intended, on Tuesday, May 12th, 'opening the New Hall' (now the Central Library), built in Wellington Street in 1831, 'as a first-class music hall for the people, similar in character to the Alhambra and other metropolitan music halls. The entertainment will be... constantly changed. An Enterprise of this class has long been

111   *William Paul, (M J, Oct.15, 1880)*

112   *A 'Free and Easy' as seen by the Temperance Society. (T C, Jan.13, 1882)*

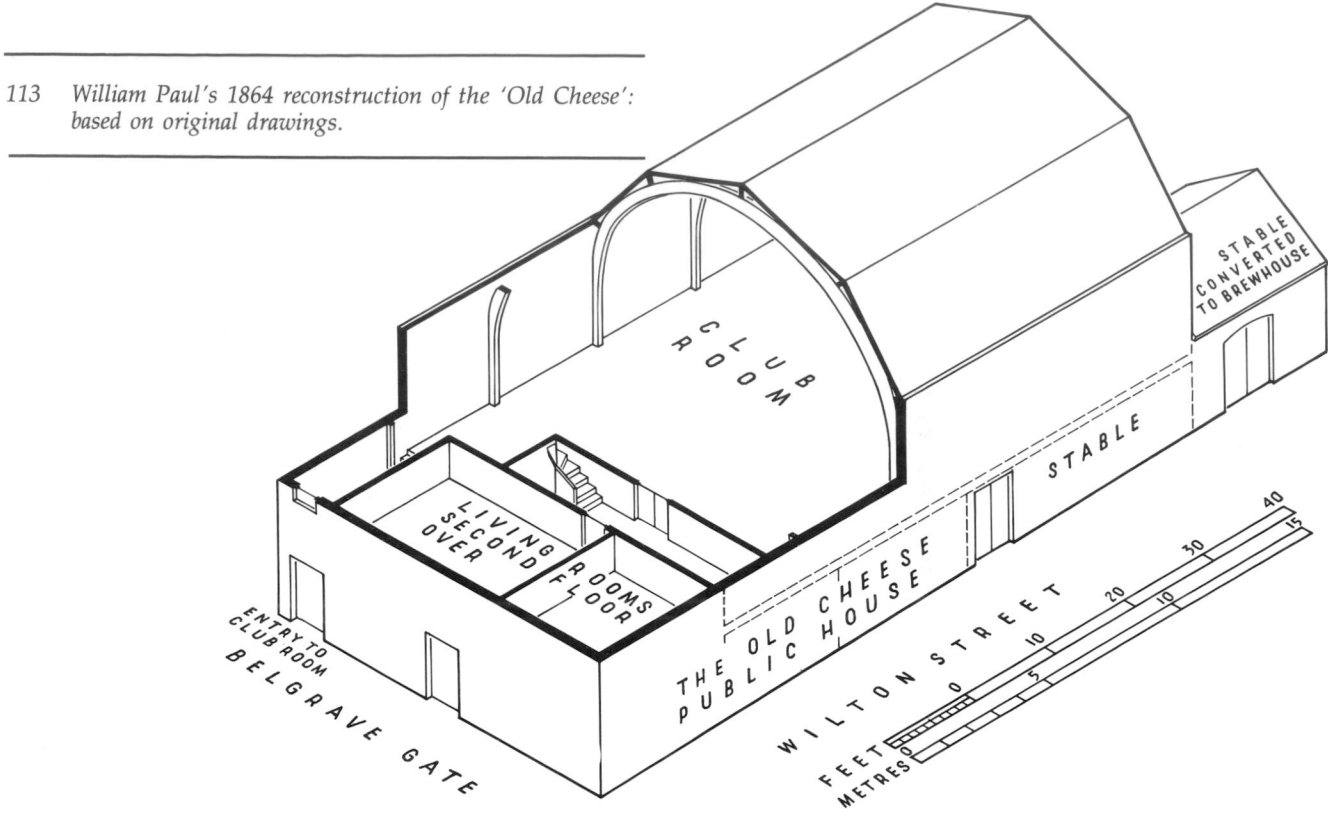

113   *William Paul's 1864 reconstruction of the 'Old Cheese':
based on original drawings.*

114   *Paul's Concert Hall of 1876: based on original drawings
submitted for approval, but perhaps not put into effect in
its entirety.*

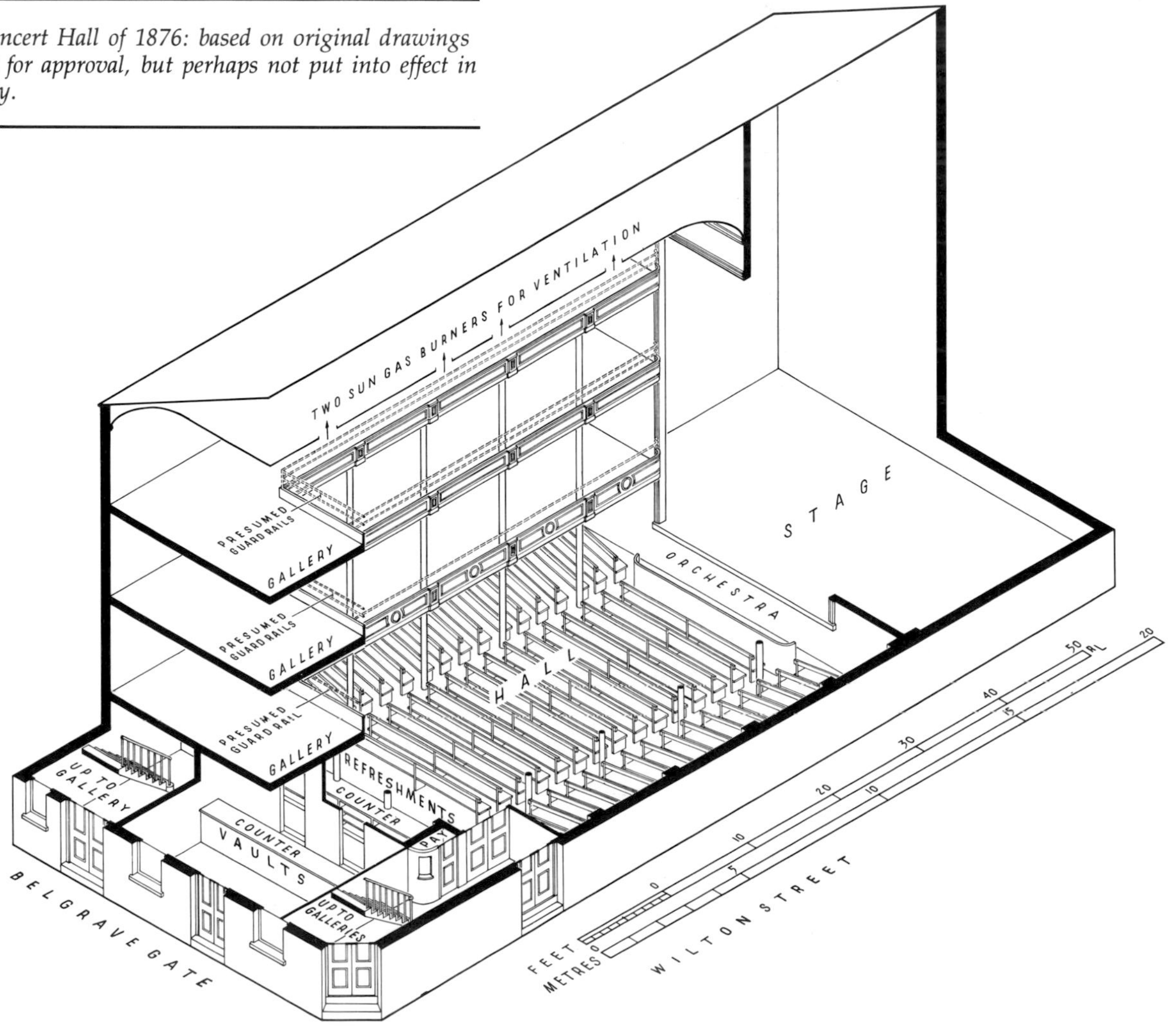

wanted in Leicester.' It was advertised as a 'FIRST-CLASS CONCERT HALL. Admission 1s 6d and 3d.' (This hall should not be confused with the New Lecture Hall in Wellington Street — opposite East Street — which opened with 'A Grand Concert, directed by Henry Nicholson' on Monday, September 29th 1873.)[9:3]

The opening of the Alhambra led the *Journal* to comment on

'the numerous concert halls which have of late years sprung up in the metropolis and all the large towns. The demand for this kind of amusement is still a growing one, and seems to satisfy a certain class of persons who, although not caring to visit a theatre, are desirous of witnessing an entertainment akin to it. Leicester as yet has been without an amusement of this character; several attempts on a minor scale have been made, but hitherto, from various circumstances, they have always failed. It has remained for Mr Dan Cooke, the spirited proprietor of the "Alhambra", in Belgrave Gate, to inaugurate the opening of a concert hall here. ... The building ... has been ... newly fitted up through-out; a commodious stage, pit, gallery, and boxes have been erected; and a numerous company consisting of solo comic singers, pantomimists, ballet actors, and the usual concomitants to be found in a concert hall.'[9:4]

In 1864 William Paul reconstructed the Old Cheese, with an enlarged club room at first floor, and an entrance direct from Belgrave Gate (fig.113). There is a certain degree of confusion regarding the names by which Paul called his place of entertainment. In 1870 the public house was referred to as the Prince of Wales, while the hall itself was called the 'Midland Music Hall'.[9:5]

In 1869 Paul also ran another hall, confusingly called the Alhambra, but in this instance in Queen Street — Southampton Street. This had earlier been occupied by Messrs Henry and Adams Circus. As there are unlikely to have been two Alhambras open at the same time, it is reasonable to assume that the Fleur-de-Lis Alhambra had closed. Paul opened his on September 13th,

'sometime before the doors opened the neighbourhood was thronged with people anxious to be present at the 1st entertainment, and nothing could exceed the heartiness of favour with which each new *artiste* was greeted and applauded. Probably there were 2,000 persons present. ... The stage is very lofty and wide, is well built, and fit for any display, either in ballet, horsemanship, or anything else it may be devoted to. It is the work of Mr James Paul, who has also supplied the machinery. The drop scene is by Mr W. Pennington ... He and Mr Graves have jointly supplied the other part of the scenery.'

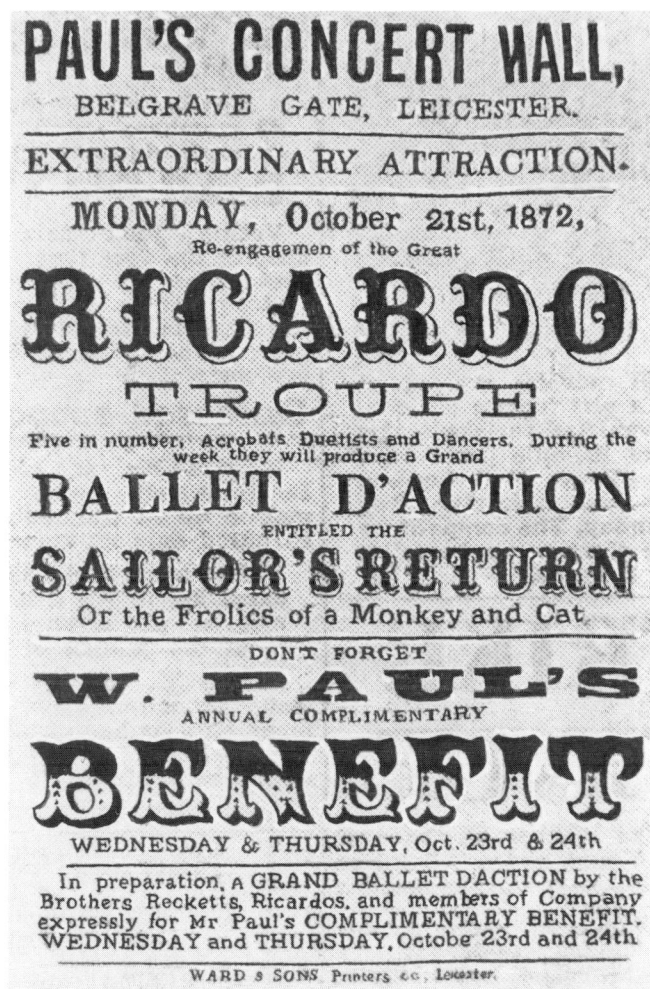

115   *Paul's Concert Hall, 1872. (L Ma. Feb.25, 1959)*

It would seem that Paul each week transferred the Alhambra's cast to the Midland, and with this double exposure it is not surprising that it is not advertised after 1870. In 1873 we learn that the 'Alhambra Music Hall, proprietor Mr Sweeny, is again closed down, and the company disbanded.'[9:6]

In 1875 a sale was announced of

'All that extremely Valuable OLD LICENSED PUBLIC HOUSE known as "THE PRINCE OF WALES". ... with the large CONCERT HALL attached thereto, now and for many years past occupied by Mr W. Paul. The premises comprise a Fine Concert Hall, 63 feet by 38 feet, with excellent Refreshment and Supper Rooms underneath.'[9:7]

Presumably the property was now bought by Paul, for in October 1876, he announced his intention of enlarging the building to accommodate about 1,500 people, and submitted plans which were approved on November 17th (fig.114). Strangely the *Advertiser* of the following day tells us that the alterations were already so far advanced that the hall now had to be closed.

'The whole of the block of buildings which stands on the site will, with the exception of the side walls, come down, and the body of the hall will in future be level with the ground. The stage, which now stands very nearly in the corner, will be placed more to the Wilton-street side of the building. There will also be a large promenade and refreshment bar upstairs,' and 'a refreshment bar downstairs. The entrance will be from Belgrave-gate as heretofore; but in future there will be two doors' one 'on one side of the hall, and the other on the corner of Wilton-street. The whole of the alterations will not be completed until the Summer months, when the roof will be raised much higher, and another gallery erected.'

Unfortunately the description does not accord with the drawings, which show three galleries, as against the two which would seem to be suggested above. The work does, however, seem to have been carried out in a piece-meal fashion, presumably so that the hall would not be out of commission for a lengthy period at any one time. In 1878 Paul advertised

'the Wonderful, Astounding, and World-famous ELECTRIC LIGHT! ... All should see this the Greatest Scientific Achievement of the present day.'[9:8]

In February 1882, it was announced that Mr Key, lessee of the Theatre Royal, had bought the premises and proposed to pull the whole block down, but in May we are assured that 'Mr Paul ... remains THE SOLE PROPRIETOR OF THIS HALL.' In July further alterations, or perhaps a continuation of the previous work, were put in hand. These necessitated the removal of the old roof to be replaced 'by a new one of pine placed four feet higher, ... ventilators have been provided in addition to the ordinary wall ones. ... Alterations have been made to the stage, and ... the seats will be re-arranged.'[9:9]

In September it was advertised as being 'The only Music Hall in Leicester' and we are told 'This hall looks very cheerful now. There has been a complete renovation within, all the seats are re-covered, the galleries are re-decorated, and the stage is fitted up with an entire fresh set of scenes, from the brush of our clever townsman, Mr Graves, not the least attractive being the new drop scene "The Lake of Como".' During these alterations a fire broke out in the roof, but was extinguished without too much damage.[9:10]

In spite of the strength of feeling against public houses and their music halls on the part of the Temperance Movement and members of the Church and Town, Paul was to become a very respected man. This was largely due to the excellent way in which he ran his establishment; there was never any trouble in the audience, nor impropriety in any of the Acts he engaged. These included Chirgwin — the White-eyed Kaffir, Harry Liston and the young Vesta Tilley. Performers were warned 'Amateur singers and professionals also, will do well to avoid carefully certain songs.'[9:11]

Wallett was a personal friend of Paul's and often took the chair. As an old man of 74 he gave a humorous address at Paul's benefit in 1881. In addition to presenting high-class entertainment for those who had little to spend, Paul was a benefactor to the elderly. Every Christmas he provided a dinner for some 100 old people in the Saloon beneath the Concert Room, after which they were entertained

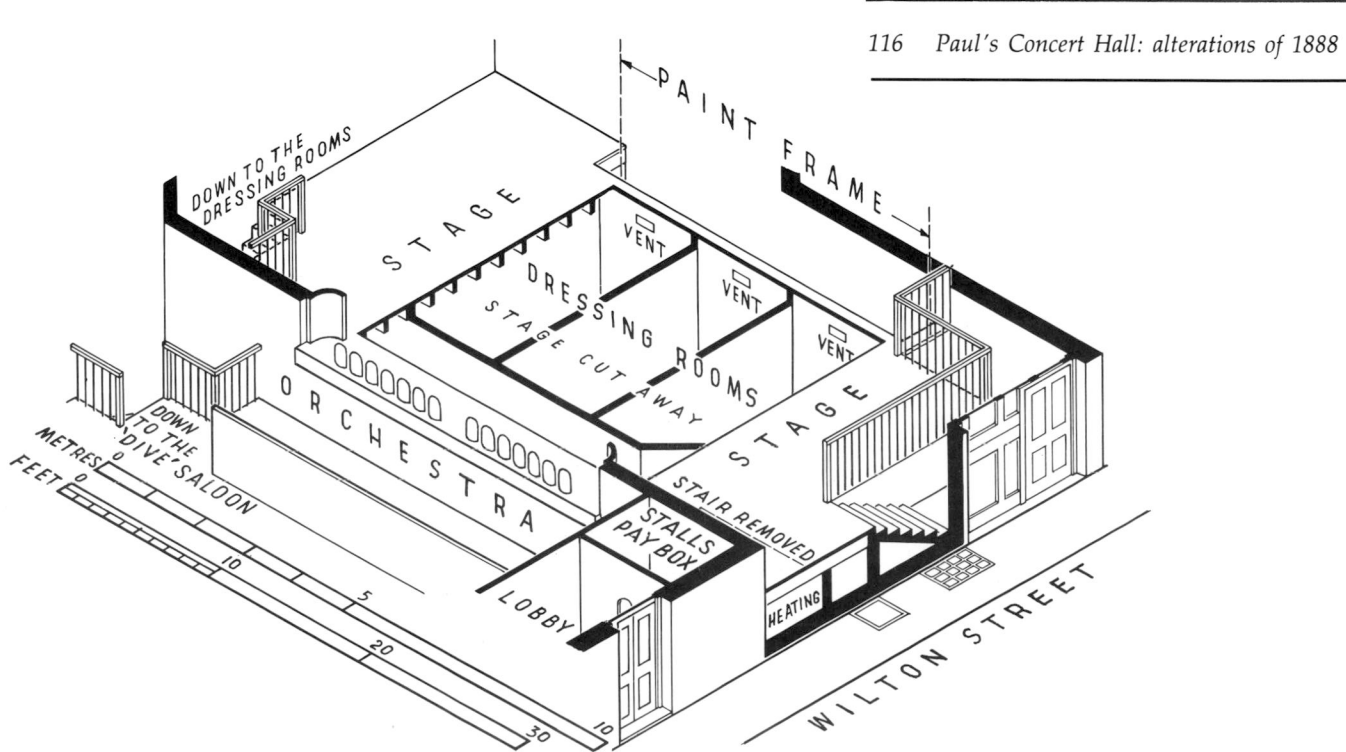

116   *Paul's Concert Hall: alterations of 1888*

upstairs, and when leaving each was given 1s. This annual treat was carried on by his son, and in 1886 'at the upper table, dined many magistrates, Town Councillors, and gentlemen of the Press.' The elderly 'who had been regaled "upstairs" because they could not be carried down — and others who were bed-ridden at home had their dinners sent to them.' They also received their shillings.[9:12]

William Paul died in November 1882, and the management was taken over by 'Mr James Paul, on behalf of the widow and family.' In 1885-6 prices are given as 'orchestral stalls [which were approached through the Saloon Restaurant] 1s; Body of Hall and Side Balcony, 6d; Centre Balcony, 9d; 6d at 9 o'clock.' Prices which would seem to suggest that there was only one balcony at this time.[9:13]

In May 1888, Will Till and Harry Champion were billed to appear, but on June 6th the building was put up for sale 'by Messrs H. and F. Tarratt. Included with the sale were all the trade fittings, &c. valued at about £500. The first bid was one of £5,000, this was increased to £6,100, but beyond this figure no one would go, and the property was knocked down to Mr

Lovejoy, proprietor of the Peckham Music Hall, London.'[9:14]

As part of their new duties the Magistrates had included Paul's in their survey of structures, and they required a number of alterations to be carried out. These included the provision of new dressing rooms beneath the stage (fig.116), and the construction of concrete stairs leading to a new Scene Door and Artistes Exit to Wilton Street. The work necessitated the removal of a mezzanine floor beneath the stage.[9:15]

The Borough Surveyor's efforts 'on the score of safety in the case of fire' were promptly rewarded by the only theatre fire in Leicester; apart from a small fire in the Theatre Royal gallery in 1956.

'Paul's Theatre of Varieties, the well-known place of amusement in Belgrave-gate, Leicester, was completely burnt down on Thursday morning.' February 28th 1889. 'The flames continued to rage furiously, and by eight o'clock the large gallery part was burnt to the ground, and nothing but the bare shell of the other part was left standing.'[9:16]

In 1862 a Gladstone Hotel and Concert Hall was

117   *The Gladstone Hotel and Concert Hall, 1862: based on original drawings.*

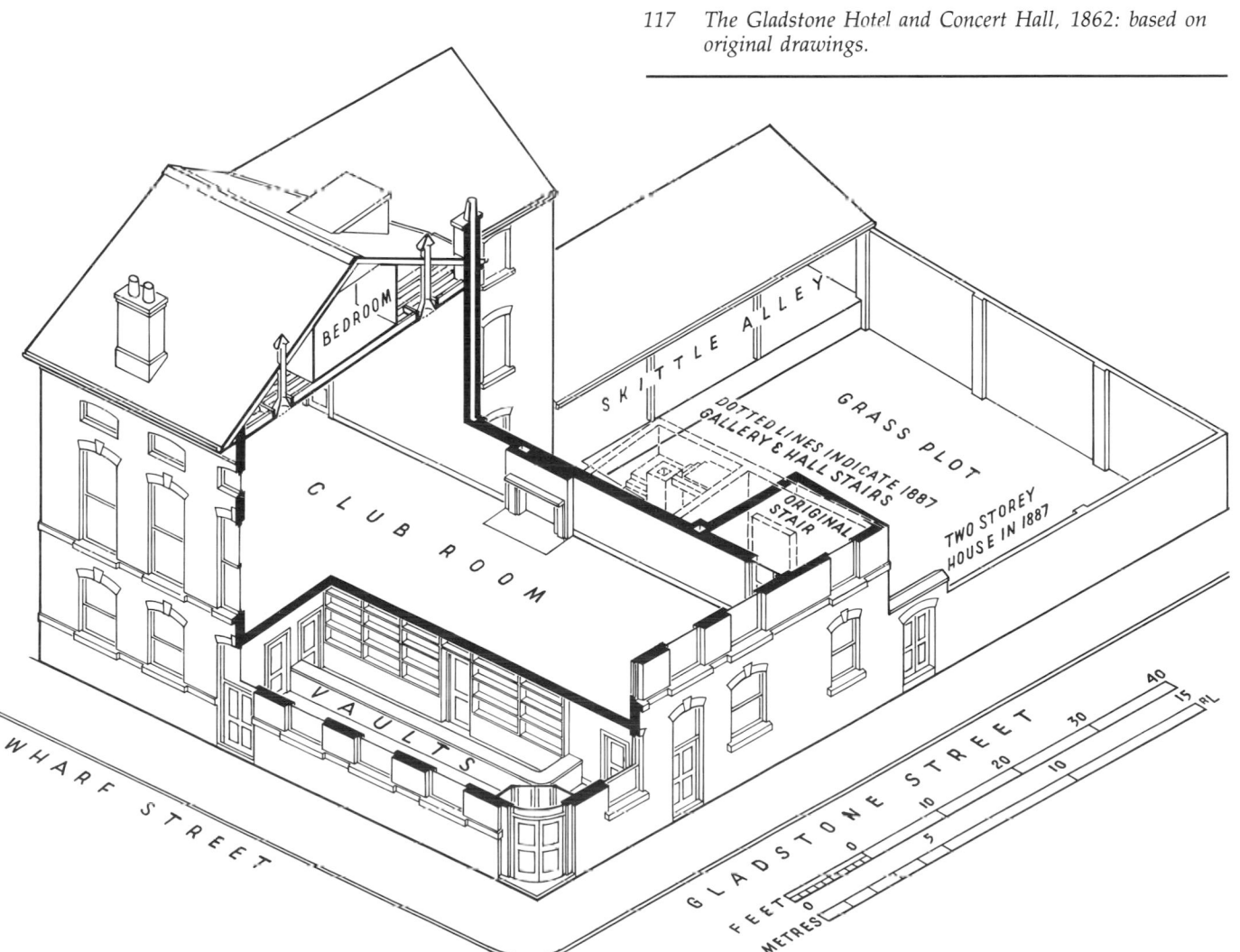

118   *Social cartoon showing 'The Green Man Inn', with the statue representing Sam Torr's song 'On the back of Daddy, Oh!' on the parapet. (T C, Nov.25, 1881)*

119   *Sam Torr. (Howell and Ford)*

erected on the corner of Wharf Street and Gladstone Street for a Fred Bakewell (fig.117), and occupied by a Mr William Cooper, who had run a free and easy at The Barrel, subsequently known as The Tower Vaults. By 1866, however, it appears to have been owned by a Mr Samuel Sweeney. On his becoming bankrupt it was put up for sale on Wednesday, November 28th under the title 'SWEENEY'S NEW OXFORD MUSIC HALL' with

> 'The whole of the BOARDING, SCANTLINGS & FITTINGS of the Gallery, containing several hundred feet of timber, iron pillars, beautifully painted scenes and side wings, all the seats, tables, and other valuable fittings of the Music Hall, beer engine, liquor fountains, several hundred glasses, one ring 36-light gas burner, sunlight, ventilator, &c, complete, gas chandeliers and brackets.'[9:17]

On August 20th 1867, the Oxford Music Hall was again for sale when it was described as 'that Commodious three-storey Spirit licensed BUILD-ING, with two Front Entrances, one of stone, and a stone staircase, Two spacious and lofty CONCERT ROOMS ... known as THE OXFORD MUSIC HALL.' Sweeney's management was followed by that of a Mr Cleaver, who was in turn succeeded by Mr Coverdale — previously a 'Chairman' at Paul's Concert Hall. In 1869 it was rented by the Hallelujah Band for religious services, and in 1874 'The Gladstone Hall ... originally a Concert Hall and drinking Saloon, is now used for mission work under the title of the Gladstone Hall Ragged School.' The Mission had taken the Hall in 1872 on a seven year lease. By July 1880 it had once again become the

> 'GLADSTONE MUSIC HALL. This Hall, originally built for the purposes of a Music Hall, and fitted with Stage and all appliances, has been

redecorated, and brought again into use by Mr Charlestone, who opened last Saturday. Scenery and Decor. W. Laffar — late Theatre Royal.'[9:18]

In 1881, Sam Torr was the proprietor of the Green Man also in Wharf Street (fig.118), to which he invited 'his old and new acquaintances to his select HARMONIC MEETINGS nightly. Chair will be taken at Eight o'c by the Leicester favourite, WILL ADDISON.'[9:19] But on Monday, September 3rd 1883, he opened the Gladstone Hotel as The Gaiety Palace of Varieties (figs.119-21), with Vesta Tilley topping the bill.

> 'The body of the hall contains a bar, and for the accommodation of the audience numerous tables and chairs are provided. A select area near the orchestra and the chairman's seat of honour is reserved for about 50 persons. About 200 persons can be seated in the body of the hall, while a promenade gallery upstairs will hold a similar number.'[9:20]

On Tuesday, May 5th 1885, the Gladstone was put up for sale by the owner, Mr Thomas Ridge of Nottingham, but was withdrawn. It was then described as being '45 feet long by 31 feet wide, is tastefully decorated and fitted with Gallery and Two Refreshment Bars, and capable of seating over 500 people.' Sam Torr and Thomas Ridge were respon-

120   *The Gaiety Palace of Varieties, 1883 (Howell and Ford)*

121   *The Gaiety Palace of Varieties: showing alterations to the original concert hall. (Howell and Ford)*

sible for presenting the Leicester-born Joseph Merrick — the Elephant Man — at the latter's Nottingham music hall, and it may therefore be assumed that he would also have appeared at the Gaiety.[9:21]

Numerous public houses had concert rooms, such as the Champion, Humberstone Gate where, in October 1881, Martin Hogan, of Sam Hogan's Minstrels, was appearing as 'Pianist and Tenor Vocalist'. In his younger days, Dan Leno, tramping the country with his father and mother, had appeared at Paul's, the Rainbow and Dove, the Antelope, and the Barley Mow. The Magazine Hotel in Newarke Street was advertised as 'open to the public on Saturday and Monday evenings for MUSICAL ENTERTAINMENTS.' It was to be sold by auction in 1886, and in 1887 a licence 'for dancing, singing and music' was refused. In this year the Magistrates at the Brewster Sessions refused many licences where music or 'free and easies' were proposed, opposition to licences being made by solicitors representing the Temperance Party. Entertainment was also provided in the Working Men's Clubs, and in 1896 we are told that 'on two nights of the week music hall artistes gave turns at' the Bond Street Club.[9:22]

The Gaiety was on the Borough Surveyor's list of places requiring attention, and here new staircases and lavatories were installed (fig.117), but a licence was witheld in 1888 by the magistrates until two other requirements had been met, namely 'the

removal of a loft and the provision of an iron curtain'. The proprietors from 1889 were Mr Fred Reeves and Mr Hal Verdo, who 'engaged the services of Mr James Paul' as acting manager until his death in 1891. Later in the year the artistes included Nan Torr and Ada Wallett.[9:23]

In April 1892, drawings for the rebuilding of the Gaiety Music Hall were submitted by W. Hancock, a London architect, on behalf of Messrs Langmore and Bankart of Leicester, and approved (fig.122), but no mention of any alterations is made in the press. By 1895 the building had become the New Empire Theatre of Varieties. In 1901 it reopened on April 1st as the Royal Empire Theatre, under the lesseeship of Mr Cecil Gray, in the second week one of the turns was Arthur Prince, the ventriloquist. Gray had installed a 'rich and costly' new curtain, and intimated that he intended 'purchasing adjoining property and shifting the stage from its present position to the side of the building,' to provide additional accommodation. This does not appear to have been done, unless it was at this time that the 1892 proposals were carried out![9:24]

On Wednesday, January 1st 1890, the foundation stone of the new Prince of Wales Theatre of Variety was laid by Mrs Lovejoy, and the theatre was opened on Bank Holiday Monday, August 4th (figs.126-7). It was designed by Mr Harry Percival 'in the renaissance style, in red brick and stone dressings, and cost

123   *The Gaiety Music Hall in 1985. (Photo: R L)*

124   *The Interior of the Gaiety Music Hall in its final form as the Hippodrome of 1927. (R O)*

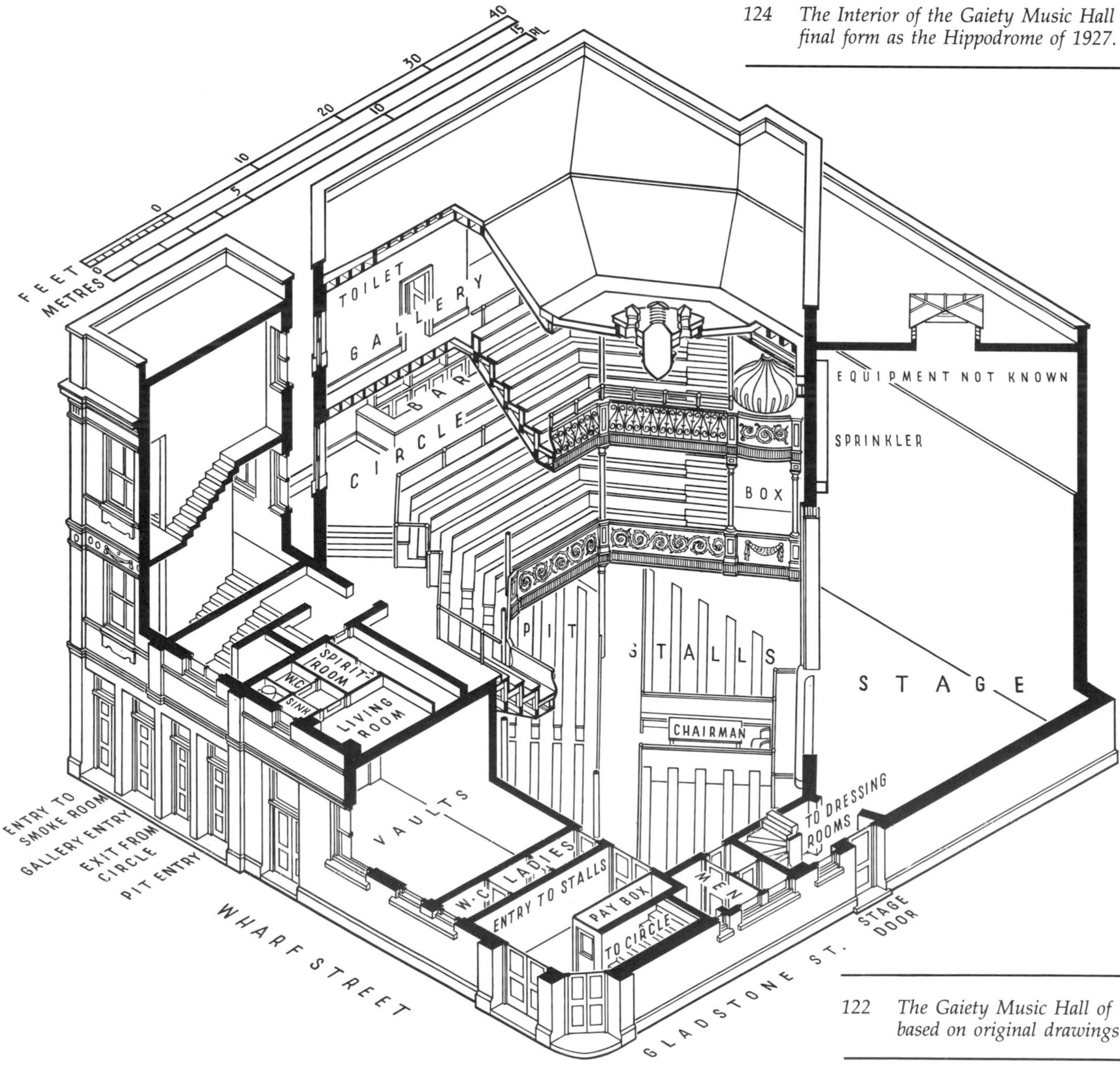

122   *The Gaiety Music Hall of 1892: based on original drawings.*

£10,000.' The contractors were George Duxbury and Son. As might be expected in a building replacing one destroyed by fire, 'The utmost care has been taken to render the building fireproof.'[9:25]

From a spacious entrance hall 'there are four fire-proof staircases, each 4ft.6in. wide — two down to the stalls and pit, and two up to the circle and gallery.' The stage was 'divided from the auditorium by an 18in. wall, carried up 12ft. above the flat roof of the auditorium. All the openings in this wall are fitted with wrought iron self-closing doors. The pro-scenium opening is 21ft. square' and 'is fitted with a green baize curtain, over which is fixed a wrought iron perforated pipe. The curtain can be saturated with water in a few seconds by turning a handle on the stage, ' ' and by means of patent sprinklers a perfect flood could be poured on the stage if neces-sary. ... A full house could be emptied under two minutes, but it seems that fire is almost impossible in this building.'

The roof over the stage was raised high enough to permit the scenery to be taken up without rolling. On the roof was a large exhaust ventilator, 6ft square. There were six well-lighted, ventilated fire-proof dressing rooms over the prompt side of the stage, and flanking the auditorium, fitted with hot and cold water and lavatory accommodation. On the opposite side of the auditorium, was a room for the scenic artist. A stone staircase, enclosed by brick walls, led from dressing rooms direct to the street, with an additional exit direct to the gallery.

An orchestra well for 20 musicians was sunk partly beneath the stage, with seating in the Pit, Stalls and two Stage Boxes for 355; in the Circle and six Private Boxes, 405; and Gallery, 500; making a total of 1260. The Stalls and Circle had folding seats upholstered in blue plush, and the curtains and hangings to the eight Private Boxes were in gold plush. Every person had an uninterrupted view of the stage, even from the refreshment saloons which were at the back of the auditorium, their floors being raised high enough to give a good view of the stage to any person standing there. Adjoining the orchestra was a central table and seat for the chairman. In line with contemporary views regarding theatre safety, the Pit was sunk so that the lower tiers of the Circle were at street level, thus reducing the length of any exit stairways.

Each part of the house was provided with the most approved lavatory accommodation, well lighted and ventilated. The auditorium was heated by hot-water pipes, and there were a number of fresh-air inlets. The vitiated air being extracted by six exhaust ven-tilators at the rear of the Circle ceiling, and conducted in tubes up to the cowl on the roof. To assist ven-tilation and carry away the smoke, the corona around the sun burner was exceptionally large.

'The electric lighting ... consists of 46 incandescent

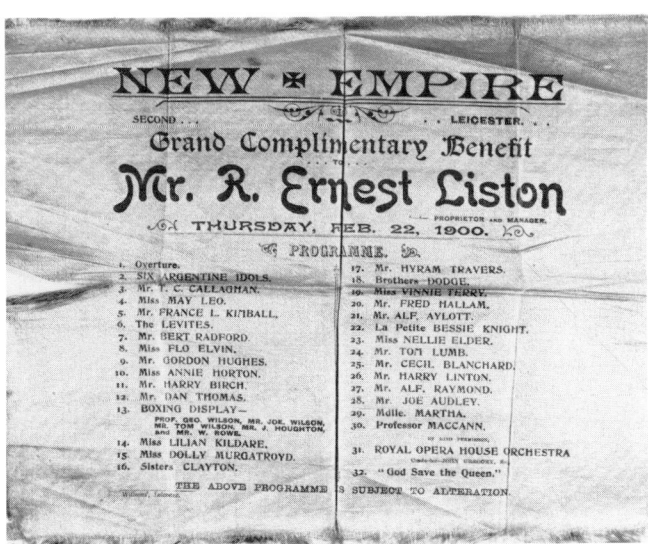

125   *Programme for the New Empire (late Gaiety Music Hall), 1900. (R O)*

lamps of 16 candle-power each inside the hall, and one arc lamp of 1,500 candle-power which illumin-ates the outside of the building. These are supplied with current from 26 accumulators, charged by a Castle dynamo driven by an engine by Messrs. Crossley Bros. ... The main controlling switch-board is situated in the engine-room beneath the stage.' 'The gas arrangements' on the stage 'are of the most approved type. The patent system adopted is that of Mr J. Tollerton of Leeds.'

By May 1893, the theatre had been purchased by Captain Orr Gray, who renamed it the New Tivoli, Theatre of Varieties. In 1896 drawings were sub-mitted by Mr Percival showing proposals for remov-

127   *The Prince of Wales Theatre of Varieties in 1915. (R L C)*

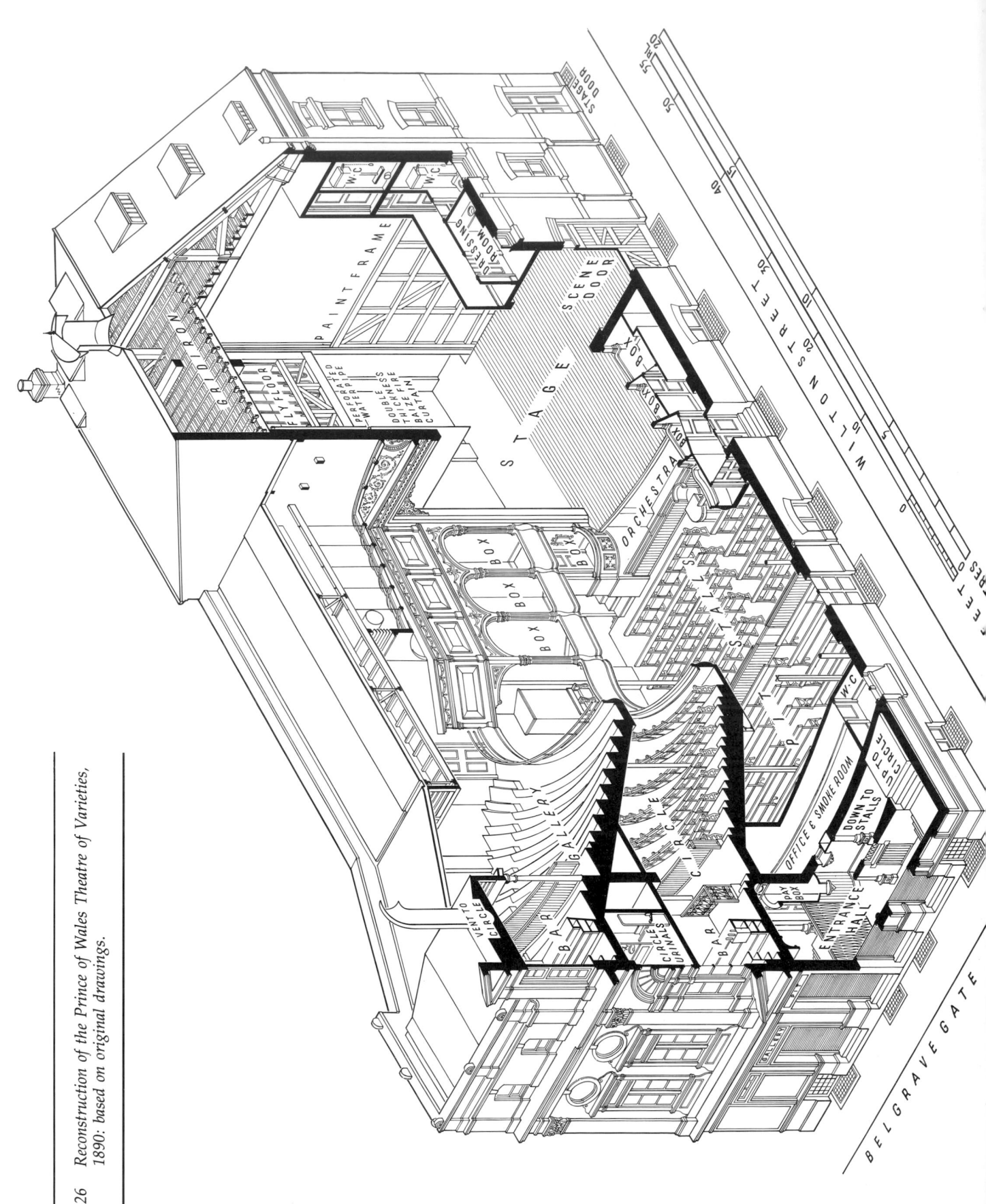

126 *Reconstruction of the Prince of Wales Theatre of Varieties,*
1890: based on original drawings.

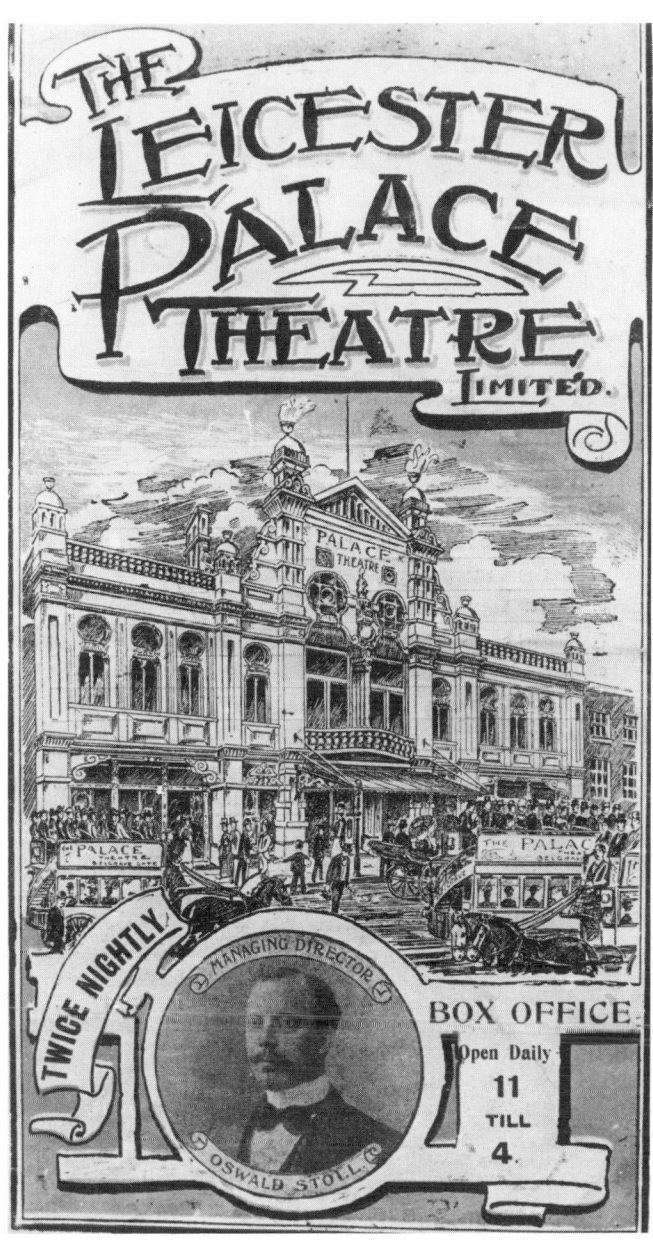

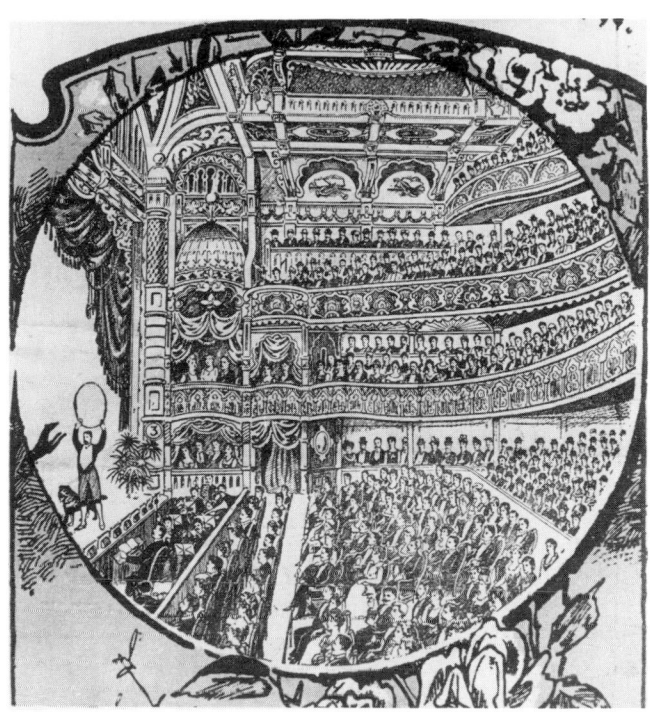

129   *The Palace Theatre, left and above. Programme illustrations. (L C I C)*

ing the Refreshment Bars in the Pit and Circle to the adjoining premises, which would have permitted the introduction of five extra rows of seats in the pit and some thirty extra tip-up seats in the Circle. In the same year *The Cinematoscope* was being advertised, but it was not until 1910 that the authorities were requiring the installation of a fireproof enclosure for the projector, constructed of sheet iron and ventilated by a 12 in diameter galvanized iron pipe from the open air in the adjoining premises, which suggests that the proposals noted above were not carried out. Both this, and the enclosure which it replaced, were sited centrally at the rear of the pit, beneath the overhanging circle.[9:26]

It is interesting to note that it was only at the Gladstone and Gaiety halls that we find tables and chairs being provided for the audience (fig.121), which is the generally accepted pattern for a music hall

derived from the pub 'free and easy'. The majority of Leicester halls were based more on the concert hall with rows of benches, perhaps with shelves on their backs for drinks. Bars were so arranged that clients standing at them could still view the action, and waiters serve the seated patrons. A practice which was discontinued at the Pavilion (p.105) when Joseph Lawrence became manager, circa 1903. About this time the hard benches were replaced by more comfortable seats.[9:27]

The Leicester Palace, Theatre of Varieties (fig.128-32), erected on the site of the Floral Hall in 1901, was designed so as not to 'be like the common music halls. It will not be possible to sit in the theatre and drink. I believe the management does not care much whether it gets a licence for the theatre or not, as it believes in making its money out of the payments made at the doors rather than from the bars.' Nevertheless bars were included, but these were 'like the theatre bars which we already have, namely, where men only can get what they want to drink, out of sight of the audience.'[9:28]

'The building, which has a holding capacity of 3,500, has been erected for the Leicester Palace Theatre, Limited, for which that Napoleon of managers, Mr Oswald Stoll, is the managing-director.' The theatre was designed by Frank Matcham, in the 'oriental' style, and built by George Duxbury and Son at a cost of about £50,000, although Matcham quotes a figure of £25,000 in the company

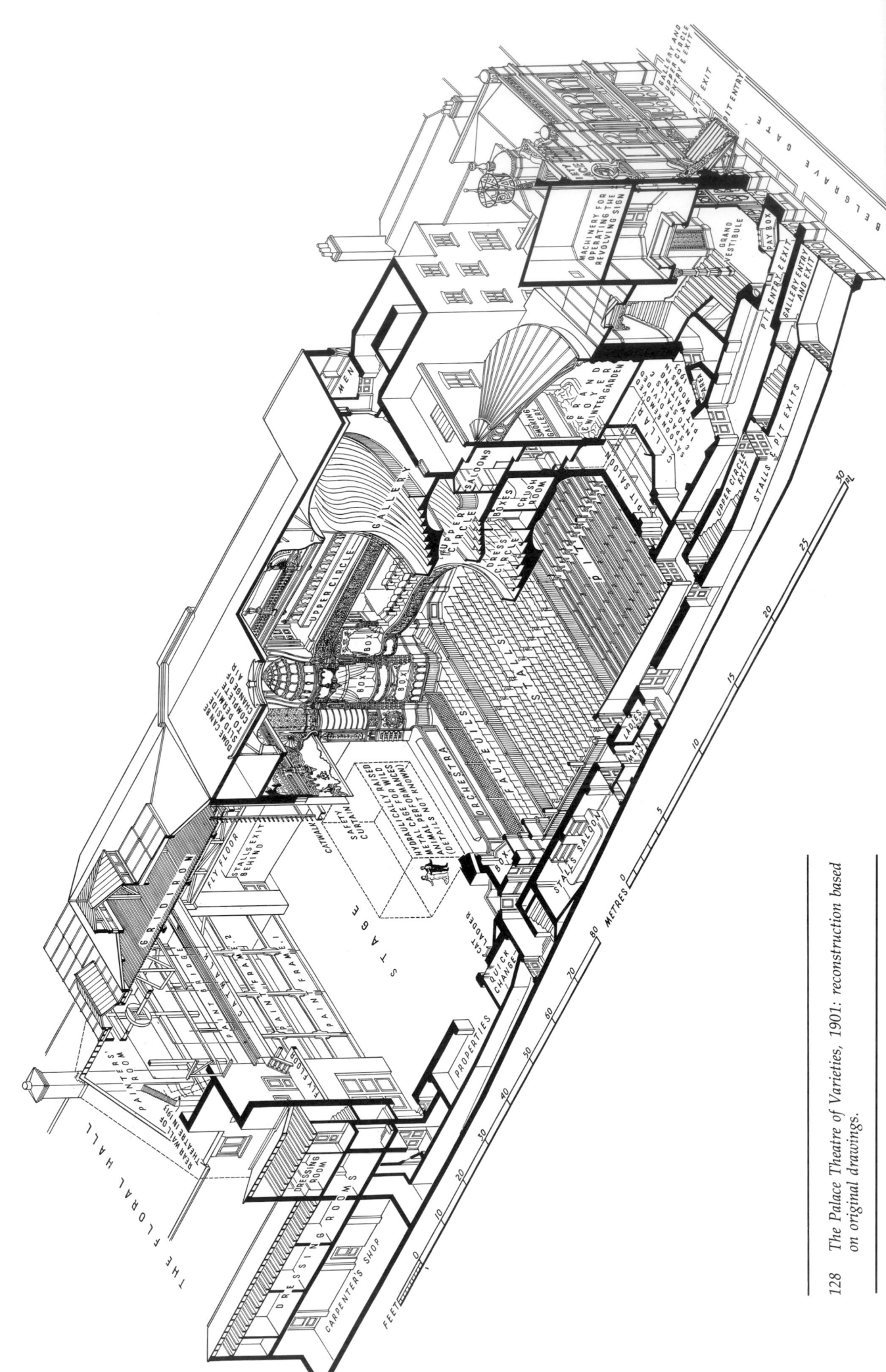

128 *The Palace Theatre of Varieties, 1901: reconstruction based on original drawings.*

prospectus. Here he also mentions that the theatre will cover 'only a portion of the site, there being sufficient ground remaining to form a Minor Floral Hall, at a very small outlay, as the present roof and entrances from Mansfield Street can be retained.' A suggestion which was carried out. The Palace was opened on Monday, June 17th 1901,[9:29] when it was described as 'a three-tier theatre'. On the ground floor there were

'three rows of fauteuils, furnished with luxurious armchairs; twelve rows of stalls, with similar seats; and twelve rows of pit, having continuous seating upholstered in velvet, the floor being covered with thick velvet pile carpet and linoleum. At each side of the stalls there are raised promenades, with Orientally designed railings. ... The large grand circle contains six rows of tip-up seats. At the rear of these are seven handsomely decorated private boxes, ... approached through a long and richly furnished foyer. At the ends are open lounges giving a splendid view of the stage. Wide promenades are continued along the sides, with staircases at the end leading to six handsome private boxes and to the fauteuils.'

'The upper circle is over the grand circle, and is well set back from the front, with plenty of height to the ceiling. ... Promenades are continued round the sides, which are open to the main ceiling, the gallery being kept at the rear over the upper circle. There are four handsome saloons, one at the back of the pit and one at the side of the stalls, and one over this for the grand circle and fauteuils. The upper circle and gallery have a fine saloon divided, with easy access. ... Gold and colour are effectively introduced ... The upholstery, curtains, carpets and tableau curtains are all of one tint, that of copper.'

'Two separate entrances and exits have been provided in every part of the house, and so that the interval between two performances can be reduced to a few minutes, large waiting rooms have been provided, and the money for the second performance can be taken before the first is finished. The principal entrance is through ... a large vestibule, with a balcony round it, ... A wide marble staircase, ... leads to a crush-room, or waiting room, which is half circular, with a glass and iron-domed roof, the whole being fitted up as

130   *The Palace Theatre, Interior in 1959. (Photo: Fisher and Potter)*

132   The Palace Theatre. Detail of proscenium arch. (Photo: T. Buckeridge)

131   The Palace Theatre. Prompt side boxes. (Photo: T. Buckeridge)

a winter garden, with rockeries, fountains, and dripping wells, having ferns and palms, and is lighted by small electric lights placed in the crevices. A rustic smoking balcony overlooks this crush-room,' described by one reporter as 'the Aladdin's cave at the entrance.'[9:30]

'The stage ... is divided from the auditorium by an asbestos fireproof curtain, and hydrants, fully equipped, are provided at all desirable points. In the centre of the stage is a wrought-iron cage, which can be raised or lowered at will by hydraulic power, so that an immediate safe enclosure for wild beast shows can be obtained. The dressing-rooms are situated in a block of buildings to the left of the stage, and are fitted up with all modern requirements, being heated by hot water and lighted by electricity.'

'The building has been erected on fireproof principles, and the walls, floors, ceilings, and roofs of the entrances and auditorium and the three tiers of galleries are all constructed of steel and concrete.' The galleries being 'carried by long girders running the whole width of the theatre without columns, so that there is no obstruction to the view. Another feature is that the ventilation has received special attention, fresh air being brought into the building through tubes and extracted from the ceilings. There has also been constructed in the centre of the auditorium a large sliding roof.'

This was opened, weather permitting, between performances to clear the air, and in summer-time its use made it possible to advertise the theatre as the coolest place in town.[9:31]

As noted above the theatre was designed to be used on a Twice Nightly basis, and improvements were made to the second house stalls, pit and upper circle waiting accommodation in 1903, while waiting rooms for gallery, amphitheatre and upper circles were added in 1913, with further waiting rooms at the side in 1938. The early performance commenced at 7 o'clock, and terminated at 8-50. The late performance commenced at 9 o'clock and finished at ten minutes before eleven. Private Boxes were priced at 10s 6d, 7s 6d and 5s; Fauteuils, Numbered and Reserved, 2s; Grand Circle, Numbered and Reserved, 1s 6d; Stalls, Richly carpeted and fitted with Tip-up Seats, 1s; Pit, Upholstered Seating, 6d; Balcony, Upholstered Seating, 4d; Gallery, 3d.[9:32]

Theatres & Music Halls in abundance

The Opera House proved successful under the management of Winstanley, during the last years of the 19th and the beginning of the 20th centuries. In the pantomime of 1896-7, Mr R.W. Paul introduced the *Animatograph*, which had been shown at the Alhambra, London. This, taking the place of the transformation scene, was a series of moving photographs.' The scenes on Black Friar's Bridge, the unloading of a boat at Brighton and the view of a sea cave on the coast of Galicia ... the waves rolling ... splashing upon the rocks and receding in masses of foam, is simply wonderful.' The houses were overflowing and previous records were broken. In *Robinson Crusoe* the following year the scenes shown included views of 'Granby-street and the Clock Tower, Leicester. The meet of the Quorn Hounds at Kirby Gate and Gartree Hill, and scenes from the Queen's Jubilee Procession.' The local views 'excited much interest'. In this pantomime the star and 'vampire' traps were cleverly used, and there was a flying ballet with dancers on wires. (A vampire trap was similar to a grave trap, but had hinged and sprung sections of the stage floor through which a performer could dive.)[10:1]

Leicester had been entertained by many farcical comedies, and the *Wyvern* had commented in 1894 that 'the intellectual section of the community do not now-a-days have many inducements held out to them to attend the play. Light dramatic farce almost entirely rules the roost.' In the last years of the decade musical comedies took the place of farces; the Carl Rosa and D'Oyly Carte Opera companies continued to pay their regular visits to the town, and the Amateurs gave their yearly presentations. The few dramatic productions were of the type that had previously been presented, while Mr and Mrs Kendal, Osmond Tearle and Frank Benson gave plays from their repertoires. When J.M. Barrie's *Little Minister* was produced in 1898 the house was well filled and the audience enraptured.[10:2]

The Royal continued to supply the farces that the patrons enjoyed, particularly those who frequented the pit and gallery. Melodramas, such as *The Trail of the Serpent*, *Two Little Vagabonds*, with its spectacular flood scenes, *The Secrets of the Harem* and *Greed of Gold* all played to crowded houses.[10:3] Pantomimes at Christmas provided good entertainment. In 1896 'every available seat' was 'occupied long before the raising of the curtain' for the Pantomime *Robinson Crusoe*. On Monday, January 24th 1898, *Little Dick Whittington* was patronised by the Fosse Football Club, which later became Leicester City Football Club, and for the opening of *Aladdin* in December 1898, the theatre was 'beseiged by a huge crowd, and at six o'clock there was not a single vacant seat in the house, not even for a pressman.'[10:4]

After the death of Mr Revill, his wife continued to manage the theatre (fig.93). Early in 1900 John Jubilee Clarke applied for the lease, but the view of the proprietors was that it 'cannot be entertained for the present.' With rent owing, an extraordinary special meeting of the proprietors was held on March 21st 1900, to consider selling the company's property by auction. This notice, however, was withdrawn, and in May it was agreed that Mr Revill's executors be permitted to sub-lease the theatre to Colonel Winstanley, subject to his 'undertaking not to close the theatre for more than six weeks in any one year and to carry on the business ... in a similar way to the late Mr Revill.' In 1901 Winstanley was granted a lease provided he spent £70 yearly on internal decorations. Jubilee Clarke now became his house manager.[10:5]

By 1900 the Gaiety had become the New Empire Palace of Varieties. In addition to music hall turns, patrons could see the *Bio-Tableau*, which showed incidents from the Boer War 'taken on the spot', as well as equally sensational films.[10:6] Arthur Stevens, writing in the *Guardian* about a visit to the gallery contrasts the performers with those of thirty years ago, when

'doubtful jests and questionable songs ruled the roost, but now thanks to the good sense of the managers of such places, nothing is to be seen or heard which will not pass muster.'

He writes of an appreciative audience, and gives us a sketch of his neighbours:

'What do you think of them? said the little man on my left, ain't they good? I reckon they're the best we've had in Leicester for a long time, and I ought to know! I never misses a Friday night at a 'all and haven't done these fifteen years. I gets paid on a Friday, and I allus reckons a tanner for amusement, threepence to come in and the other for two drinks when I gets out.'

The courting couple on the other side were tired perhaps of 'living on love' for 'The blushing swain produced a greasy paper parcel from his overcoat and

unfolding it, presented to my gaze a semi-cold colla-
tion of fish and chips.' Such was the delights of a
night in 'The Gods'.[10:7]

In 1916 the theatre was being advertised as The
Empire, presenting films and variety. In 1921 plans
submitted for official approval show the Vaults
replaced by an entrance hall and crush room. At
ground level the Smoke Room and Bar were removed
to make room for additional seating and a projection
room. The screen is shown as being directly behind
the proscenium opening. At first floor level the
original living rooms were turned into stores and
offices. The following year these were also removed
to provide more seats. Now a cinema, the building
was called the Hippodrome, and was again altered in
1927, when the stage and ground floor projection
room were removed, together with the crush hall,
making the greater part of the ground floor available
for seating. The proscenium opening was removed
and the upper floors opened out to give better sight
lines to the screen, which was now set in the rear
corner of what had been the stage (fig.124). A new
projection box and winding room were constructed at
second floor level.[10:8] The cinema finally closed in
the late 30's.

The Prince of Wales in Belgrave Gate had been
opened by Mr A.F. Lovejoy on August 4th 1890 with
a marvellous array of talent. However, by October
prices, which ranged from 6d to 2s, were reduced and
half price was in operation for the stalls and circle
from nine o'clock. In December the *Journal* commented that

> 'The music halls are now in full swing and the
> proprietor of the above has no cause to complain
> of lack of patronage. Now that he has placed his
> rates of admission within easy reach, the place has
> been rendered cheerful by good attendances.'[10:9]

133   *Royal Opera House Playbill of 1901 on wall of The
Saracen's Head. (L Me)*

134   *Tivoli (Prince of Wales) Playbill of 1899. (R O)*

In 1896 the advertisements for the house were being put out under the name of the Tivoli, when we are informed that patrons' cycles could be stored 'free of charge' during the performances. In 1898 a petition was presented for the compulsory winding up of the Tivoli, Leicester, Ltd, and in 1899 it was still called the Tivoli, but now the proprietors were Messrs Dew and Stacey (fig.134). By 1901, however, it had been renamed the Pavilion, under the management of the Macnaughton (Macnaghten) circuit. The fare offered ranged from sketches to variety and revues, while weekly episodes of films ensured patrons' attendance in the following weeks. Gracie Fields appeared here in the revue *It's a Bargain* in June 1916, returning in November of the following year. Houses were good and the theatre was popular. In 1929 the Walkley Healey Repertory Company came for a three week season, but stayed for eighteen months. There were two plays a week, performed twice nightly at 6.40 and 8.55 with a matinee on Thursdays.[10:10]

The 'Old Pav' as it was affectionately called was pulled down to make way for a road widening scheme. At the last performance on Saturday, November 29th 1930,

'People who had paid for the privilege sat in the orchestra seats and on the stage, and as "Auld Lange Syne" was struck up, they came forward and linked arms with their favourite actors and actresses ... Almost every square inch of floor space was occupied by theatre "fans" wanting to pay their respects at the "death" of the old place, and although a general atmosphere of cheeriness prevailed, there was pathos in the air as well.'[10:11]

The opening of the Palace Theatre of Varieties with its comfort, magnificent decoration and a nationally known management cannot but have had an effect upon the halls already in existence. On the opening night the Peerless Sandow topped the bill, with Charles Coburn — The Man who broke the Bank at Monte Carlo — among the many artistes who appeared, together with a series of animated photographs on the American Bioscope. The house was crowded, and Sir Oswald Stoll appeared on stage and, after thanking the audience for their attendance, said that 'the directors would try to make Leicester proud of the Palace.' For the second house of the evening 'There were fierce struggles to get to the pay box ... and many had to be turned away.'[10:12]

Among the artistes to top the bill during 1901-2 were C.H. Chirgwin — the White-Eyed Kaffir, Miss Florrie Forde, Bransby Williams in his characters from Dickens, Gus Elan — famous for his Cockney songs, Harry Champion of 'Boiled Beef and Carrots' fame, Vesta Tilley, Lily Langtry and Eugene Stratton to name but a few. 1903 was to see Marie Lloyd on the boards, she played to crowded houses, as did Arthur Rigby with his company — Rigby was later to move

to America and feature in films. Marie Kendall was a comedienne of whom the *Guardian* commented she 'won her way to the hearts of the audience.'[10:13] Leading artistes paid regular visits to the house, Bransby Williams, for example, appeared nineteen times between 1901 and 1930.

Fred Karno's troupe of comedians was another act with regular dates. It was in one of Karno's companies that Charlie Chaplin made his appearance in Leicester in 1909, in a comedy sketch called *The G.P.O.* The leading comedian was Fred Kitchen. At Karno's request, Kitchen wrote a small part for Charlie as a tryout, but he returned him to Karno with the comment that 'he did not come up to expectation.'[10:14] In 1910 Chaplin went to the United States with one of Karno's troupes, where he was soon to become a cinema star.

When George Robey, the Prime Minister of Mirth appeared, it was said of him that he was 'difficult to beat for excellence, nothing dims the bubbling brilliance of this comedian.' He was still displaying his talent when he appeared in 1951 with Hetty King — the male impersonator, Wee Georgie Wood and Albert Whelan, all stars of the music hall in its heyday, in *Do You Remember?*[10:15]

It is only possible to name a few of the artistes who appeared at the Palace, which was a No.1 date, so the audiences were able to enjoy all the skills which the top liners could present; there were comedians, jugglers, acrobats, trapeze artists, dancers, singers, magicians and equestrian acts. In December 1908, Fred Ginnett's company were presenting an improved edition of *Dick Turpin's Ride to York* (fig.135), which had enthralled people in earlier times. Mr Courtice Pounds and his sister Louie appeared in a musical sketch. He was 'acclaimed the most versatile star of the day.'[10:16]

Mrs Courtice Pounds was eventually to settle in

135   *Main Entrance to the Palace Theatre. (L Me)*

Leicester at 57 Princess Road, and her home was the 'theatrical digs' for most of the stars visiting the town. As performers from the halls and theatres were constantly moving, and had to fix up 'digs' for each week, most of them carried an address book of theatrical landladies, with remarks beside the names, such as 'home from home' or 'never again'. In 1921 the *Mail* was complaining that there was 'not much choice for professionals fulfilling engagements in the City.'[10:17]

It was quite usual for a short play to be one of the items in a music hall programme. Seymour Hicks and Zena Dare, both to become famous theatrical personalities, appeared here in such a turn. Another very popular turn was of the type of *The Gathering of the Clans* in which a hundred Leicester juveniles performed. The review said it was 'a very pleasing production ... with elaborate, spectacular effects which reflects very creditably upon those responsible for training the youngsters.'[10:18] Local youngsters were often used in this way, thus ensuring good houses.

As mentioned earlier a further feature of the programmes was the American Bioscope which showed short films and weekly news items. In 1901 the people of Leicester were able to see the funeral of McKinley — the President of the United States. In 1909 'excellent views of the Fosse and Watford Cup Tie' were shown, and in August Bleriot's flight across the English Channel was screened.[10:19]

When artistes who are at, or near, the top of a bill are displaying their talents, it is all too often forgotten how many years of hard work have gone into perfecting their craft (p.95). When W.C. Fields appeared in 1911, the paper reported that he was 'the originator of the "silent eccentricity" in juggling ... it took him many years before he mastered his task.' He made a return visit in 1913, but later he went to Hollywood and became one of the foremost comedians of the great days of the films. Another actor who made his mark in Hollywood was C. Aubrey Smith, who appeared at the Palace with Lilian Braithwaite in *Instinct* in March 1913.[10:20]

The Palace patrons enjoyed spectacle and Albert Hengler provided this in full measure when he presented *Mexico*, in February 1912, in six magnificent scenes. The reviewer was to comment that it was 'a marvel of stage management, chock full of excitement and interest, and capably acted.' The high spot was 'the explosion and bursting of the dam into which the refugees leap on horseback, and make good their escape' (fig.136). The show held the boards for a fortnight and played to crowded houses nightly. It returned the following year, when on the Saturday evening, the two big water tanks overturned, flooding and damaging the stage and almost drowning the orchestra.[10:21]

136   *The sensational water spectacle* Mexico, *with the famous plunging horses. (L Ma, Feb.17, 1912)*

When war was declared in 1914, Oswald Stoll 'expressed his intention to "carry on" as usual.' He also made arrangements for any news of importance to be shown on the screen immediately. Although variety continued, the war years were to see the introduction of revues. These were performed by variety artistes touring as a company, and were bright and sparkling with choruses of dancing girls; just the entertainment needed to encourage people when news from the front was not good. Even so, by the Spring of 1916 business, all over the country, was poor. It was not helped by the introduction of an Amusement Tax to help with the cost of the war. The tax was levied on all admissions, and inevitably put up the price of seats. In 1917 the Amusement or Entertainment Tax was exempted on seats which were given free at a music hall or theatre to wounded servicemen: the management, however, still had to pay tax on all other complimentary tickets.[10:22]

Many of the music hall performers went into the Services and booking a programme for each week became increasingly difficult. Nevertheless the Palace remained open and provided entertainment of a high class. After the war the performers started to pick up their careers again. Many joined together to form companies such as *Splinters*, where all the girls were boys. There was a longing for bright, well-dressed shows. Gracie Fields starred in *Mr Tower of London* in 1923, and 'charmed and captivated all hearts.'[10:23]

Variety continued to interchange with revues and even the occasional play. Cedric Hardwicke performed in July 1926, and George Formby — Senior and Junior — appeared in *Seeing Life* in December, while July 1927 saw Tommy Handley in *The Disorderly Room.* In 1931 the Palace went over to films which continued until 1937. Then the stage was reconstructed to bring it into line with the Coliseum and other Stoll theatres; a revolving stage being built in a great circular pit (fig.137). Wednesday, December 15th was the opening night of the spectacular, '*St Moritz* on the revolving ice stage.' It ran until the 19th February, to be followed by *The Merry Doll*.[10:24] However, little use seems to have been made of this revolve as a short variety season followed, and by June 1938, films had returned and continued until 1946.

Twice nightly programmes were re-introduced. Max Miller (fig.159) was a popular performer, while Eric Barker, Pearl Hackney and Terry Thomas appeared together in one bill. Don Ross brought his Circus, and Peter Sellers, the resident comedian of the radio show *Variety Bandbox*, appeared in 1950. In the following year Buster Keaton appeared 'in Person', Bela Lugosi played in *Dracula*, and February 1953, saw Jimmy Young — The King of the Discs. On March 30th 1952, there was a special performance in aid of the Comforts Fund for the Royal Tigers in Korea. Stars such as Petula Clarke, Frankie Howerd, Jimmy Jewel and Ben Warriss, Ben Lyon, Teddy Johnson and Jack Warner all gave their services, and were supported by the Leicester Choral and Dramatic Society and the Band of the 5th Battalion, Royal Leicestershire Regiment, with Richard Attenborough as presenter.[10:25]

In Loughborough, following the closure of the Sparrow Hill Theatre, drama was presented in the Corn Exchange in the Town Hall, or in travelling theatres like the Royal Albion Theatre which performed on The Green at Ashby in 1869 (fig.138), or The Temple of Varieties which Sam Jones set up on the Loughborough Ashby Road in September 1882. Here he presented *Macbeth* on Friday 29th followed by *Diavoletti* on Saturday; *Faith, Hope and Charity* on Monday; *Cast on the Mercy of the Waves* on Tuesday, with *Bottle* on Wednesday and *Ticket of Leave Man* on Thursday.[10:26]

By 1896 a more permanent theatre was erected in Ashby Road adjoining the Gas Works. This was similar to the circus buildings noted earlier in being 'substantially built of wood and corrugated iron.' The New Theatre was leased by Kate Howard, with George H. Willmot as manager. It should have opened on Monday, September 14th, but the opening was postponed to the following day, 'when the first performance was given, there was considerable delay in consequence of the backward state of the

137   *Demolition of the Palace Theatre, showing the pit constructed in 1937 for the revolving stage. (Photo: G. Pearce)*

building, and it was midnight before the curtain was finally lowered.' Sydney Vereker's No.1 company presented *Jack of Hearts*, which was enthusiastically received by a crowded audience.[10:27]

The first season included Ben Greet's Company in *The Sign of the Cross*, Miss Verner's Company in *£1,000 Reward, or The Secrets of London*, Fred Connynghame's Company in *Phantoms*, and Mr Abud's production of *Trilby*. The *Journal* was to note the

'Best seats poorly patronised, and it is becoming evident that want of support on the part of the gentry of the neighbourhood will lead those in charge of high-class plays and players to steer clear of Loughborough.'

Loughborough Amateur Operatic Society, however, played *The Sorcerer* for three nights in December to crowded houses. In 1897 a pantomime, *Red Riding Hood*, was presented, while Mr Herrick — a Leicester man — brought his company in *The Streets of London*, and the Neilson Grand English Opera Company also appeared.[10:28]

The first season was sufficiently successful for Kate Howard to purchase extra land and extend the building in 1897. Originally the accommodation consisted of Orchestral Stalls (2s 6d), Pit Stalls (2s), with a balcony approached by stairs at the rear of the Pit (6d). This was subdivided into Centre Balcony (1s 3d) and Side Balcony (9d). In addition there was a Gallery priced at 4d.[10:29]

When the theatre re-opened on Monday, 30th August, 'an imposing porch' had been erected at the

138   *Royal Albion Theatre, Ashby: Playbill for 1869. (Courtesy of E. Arthur Crane)*

front of the building housing the pay offices. From here

> 'to the right and left the back seats in the auditorium are approached, ... opposite is the entrance to the balcony ... reached by two wide staircases ... The orchestra stalls and chairs and other high class parts are gained by a private approach, a separate corridor being provided. ... With the provision of new entrances, the removal of the old staircase at the back of the pit'

made space for an additional 50 seats. The building was now lined with match-boarding to prevent draughts. There were new plush seats with arms to the balcony, while the stalls had tip-up seats. The partition separating pit from stalls was now lowered to improve sight lines, and the stage was increased to a depth of 42 feet, with eight 'commodious dressing rooms' at the rear.

Plays were still performed at the Town Hall, but the New Theatre was obviously stealing their bookings, as there were problems regarding the re-licensing of the newly adapted theatre, which the local newspaper ascribed 'to the existence of the green-eyed monster.'[10:30]

On Thursday afternoon, 31st July 1901, the theatre was burnt to the ground during the first week of the new season, and Mr G.F. Kimberley's *A Sister's Sin* company lost all their scenery and effects, in addition to the theatre's stock scenery and that of *The God of War* company which was stored ready for the following week. As a result the Corn Exchange Theatre was once again pressed into use. W. Payne Seddon and George Robertson, the lessees, presenting weekly entertainment similar to that provided by George Willmot. In 1904, however, they decided that the amenities of the Town Hall were not sufficiently up to date, and they set about building a theatre of their own.[10:31]

In September it was announced that 'The contract for the erection of the new Theatre in Packe-street, to be known by the name of "The New Theatre Royal", has been secured by Mr A. Faulks' (figs.139-41). It was designed by the Loughborough architect, A.E. King, to have accommodation for some 800. The stage was some '57ft by 31ft, the proscenium opening being 26ft by 20ft.' There were two rows of stalls, in front of a gradually rising pit. Above was a dress circle with an upper circle behind. There were also two boxes, and 'the usual adjuncts in the form of cloak rooms.' The main entrance was in Mill Street which was 'connected with the theatre by means of a long corridor and smoking lounge about one hundred feet long with pay box at end.' The theatre was lighted by electricity, with electrically driven fans

139   *The Theatre Royal, Loughborough, 1905. Entrance in Mill Street. (Loughborough Library)*

providing ventilation, and hot water pipes for heating. Dressing rooms were provided beneath the stage, the height of which 'has been so arranged that the scenery can be hoisted into the "flies", thus obviating the necessity of shifting from the stage.'[10:32]

The theatre opened on Thursday, 26th January 1905, with Norman Macowan's company presenting *Monsieur Beaucaire.* After which the pattern followed that previously set by this management at the Town Hall. In 1910 the theatre passed into the hands of Leon Vint who re-opened the building at Whitsun as 'Vint's Electric Hippodrome' for the presentation of films. By 1912 the Hippodrome was presenting variety, when Charles Coburn was one of the performers. In 1915 it was once again known as the Theatre Royal, but it now had a chequered career, suffering from financial ups and downs. The amateurs were always able to fill the house, but by 1951

140   *The Theatre Royal, Loughborough. Interior*

141   *The Theatre Royal, Loughborough, Elevation to Packe Street. (Loughborough Library)*

revue and vaudeville, with an occasional play, was the order of the day, and in 1953 the building was sold. It was specially opened for the presentation of The Poole Academy production of *Cinderella* in January, and the Loughborough Amateur Operatic Society presented *Merrie England* during the last week of February, when the theatre finally closed.[10:33]

Theatregoers deprived of live theatre in the town had to journey to Leicester or Nottingham, or to the fully equipped little theatre at Stanford Hall (fig.142). This had been built in 1938 by Sir Julien Cahn, an expert conjurer, for the entertainment of his visitors. The estate had been taken over by the Co-operative Movement of Great Britain in 1945. The Midland Theatre Company, who had been presenting plays at the Theatre Royal in 1950, moved here in 1952, and the theatre was also used for a time by the Lincoln Repertory Company. The Festival Players, set up in 1954, successfully filled the void in the town, performing first at Martin Hall, but in 1957 moving out to Stanford. Today, the theatre is used for all the year round for amateur and other performances.[10:34]

At Ashby in 1889 a theatrical licence was taken out for the Market Hall, where 'Ramsdale's high class company' presented *Aladdin* 'on three nights ... to very large audiences.' At the time the Market Hall 'was not wholly completed,' and it was found that the 'stage, as built, would answer admirably for a concert' but would 'never admit of any large quantity of scenery being erected therein.' Ramsdale, in fact, had to build his stage within the hall. In the following year performances were given in the hall by the local amateurs, together with a visit from Miss Maggie Morton's dramatic company, who presented *Ours, Caste, Silver Queen, School for Scandal* and *Romeo and Juliet* before leaving Ashby for Swadlincote. The Hall continued as the major theatrical venue until the opening of the Venture Theatre in 1981.[10:35]

In 1904 Swadlincote was also the site for a temporary structure known as the Alexandra Theatre, which then moved to the rear of the Queen's Inn in Ashby for three months. In Coalville a 'Public Hall' was built in Belvoir Road in 1876, which was described as 'a spacious building of red brick, fitted with a stage, and retiring rooms' which seated some 500 persons. In 1901 it was renamed the Theatre Royal (fig.143). Seasons of weekly programmes by touring companies were presented, on and off, until 1911 when it became the Electric Theatre, showing films.[10:36]

In 1910 the Olympia Theatre in Jackson Street, erected at a cost of £2,500 and seating 1,000 people, was presenting variety and dramatic shows. In 1911 it was decided to improve the building which 'lacked accommodation for the scenery' by 'raising the roof over the stage.' The theatre was originally built as a skating rink, but 'when the rinking craze waned somewhat, the directors decided to turn the building

142   *Julien Cahn's private theatre at Stanford Hall. (Courtesy of the Co-operative Union Ltd)*

into a theatre.' 1912 was to see the directors let the Olympia to a London firm of theatrical agents on a long lease. Electric lighting plant was installed and further internal improvements were made. The bioscope was also set up and a programme of films ran through the summer, drama being renewed in the autumn.

The amateurs made use of the theatre, in 1924, for example, they had a great triumph with the *Pirates of Penzance*. Variety, a circus, revues and films occupied the house in 1926 until the autumn, when Ivy Maurice's Repertory Company took over for a short season. A typical programme was that of the week of September 20th when *Two Little Vagabonds* was presented on Monday and Tuesday. *A Royal Divorce* on Wednesday and Thursday, *East Lynne* on Friday, and *Sweeny Todd* on Saturday at 6.30 and 8.30. Programmes of revues followed with weekly episodes of films, a pantomime was presented at Christmas, followed by a season of weekly touring drama. Presentations at this theatre continued in this manner until 1930 when films took over.[10:37]

By 1893 Hinckley could not 'boast of even a Theatre or Palace of Varieties.' Entertainment had to be given in the Parish Schools or in St George's Hall. The Palladium Cinema was converted from a school hall in 1920, and later served for a while as a theatre. Nor was there now any theatre at Melton Mowbray. From 1912 to 1921 variety turns were being put on between films at the Picture Palace. The amateurs performed, as in the past, at the Corn Exchange; in 1926 they produced *H.M.S. Pinafore* with Dr Malcolm Sargent as Musical Director and Producer. Leicestershire has always been a stronghold of amateur players, and it is to their credit that a theatre has returned to Hinckley, when, in 1972, a derelict factory was converted into the Concordia Theatre.[10:38]

143   *The Theatre Royal, Belvoir Road, Coalville, 1876 (T. Bottle)*

Curtains, or the end of an era

In Leicester weekly touring companies were visiting the Theatre Royal at the beginning of the century. The presentations that were really successful were of the 'blood and thunder' type, for example, in 1903, *The King of Terror* was described as a 'terrifying dish' full of gruesome details but the audience loved it, and *The Face at the Window* which delighted them.[11:1]

By 1905, however, the proprietors were asking for payment of rent which was four months in arrears, and requesting that it be paid on time in future. Business cannot have been good for at the beginning of the following year, Winstanley asked to transfer his interest in the lease to Mr Milton Bode and Mr Edward Compton. This was agreed to, and in September a new lease was granted to the partners. They were soon to ask the proprietors for permission to reduce the prices of the pit and gallery, to compete with the music halls. The request was refused several times, but in 1907 the proprietors agreed to a price of 8d in the pit and 4d for the gallery, providing the lessees would agree to take the theatre for a further three years.[11:2]

The local papers do not carry regular advertisements for performances at the Royal after February 1906 until 1924; presumably to save money by relying solely on their bills to inform the public (fig.133).

From the Minute and Account books of the proprietors, it is obvious that the building was in use as a theatre throughout this period, for the rent was being paid and in 1915 the lessees asked to be allowed to perform twice nightly, new prices being agreed. A programme for July 10 1916, shows that *The Vicar's Sin* was being performed twice nightly throughout that week. Smoking was to be permitted during performances in 1917. A lease was granted to Milton Bode in 1921 and renewed in 1924, when weekly companies continued to visit. In 1925 Harry Foxwell's company stayed for four weeks, and was followed by a three week season presented by Frank H. Fortescue's Company. In October Fred Clement's Skegness Entertainers stayed for an eight week season, returning in 1926 for a further six weeks.[11:3]

From 1927 revue was the order of the day until 1932, in which year Florrie Forde appeared. At that time the manager of the house was Mr Loach. The attendants, who wore black dresses (at the posher Opera House they also had white aprons), were responsible for putting out reserved tickets, showing people to their seats and selling programmes, for which they were paid 12s a week. During the interval they sold chocolates and ice cream, receiving 1d for every shilling's worth they sold. The theatre was shut in 1933 but in 1934, by which time Prince Littler had

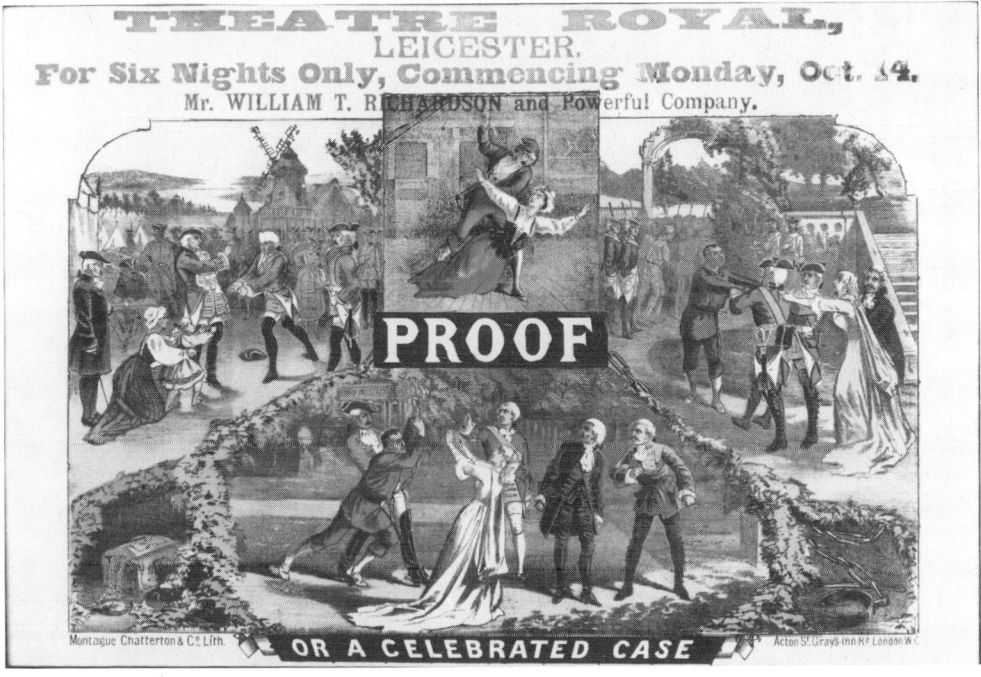

*144   Theatre Royal, Leicester.
Playbill for* Proof. *(R L C)*

145   *Theatre Royal, Leicester, November 1940. The Regency
Players in* The Wandering Jew. *(Painting by R L)*

become lessee, repertory came to the theatre and was to remain until it closed in 1957. The house was re-decorated and re-seated in 1934, with further redecoration in 1948 when new central heating was installed.[11:4]

Amateurs continued to present lively programmes. As early as 1901 the Leicester Banks Cricket Club Amateur Society had presented *Dandy Dick* at the YMCA New Hall in East Street. By 1921 there was much activity by the leading amateurs to set up a repertory movement in the town. Walter Martin spoke of the possibility at a Rotary Club luncheon. He advocated a 'resident company ... They should be

able to produce a series of clean, bright and human plays by such writers as Barrie, Bennett, Shaw, Galsworthy, Vachell and Shakespeare.' He thought there would be no difficulty in finding local artists for 'acting, dressing and mounting', but he felt that they should be paid.[11:5]

A meeting was held at the County Rooms in October 1921 to discuss the possibility of forming a committee to run a repertory season at the Opera House by arrangement with Mr Milton Bode. Mr Lionel Harris stated his views that Leicester was 'a likely place' for a repertory theatre and that if they could not have a theatre of their own the Opera

House was a possibility. By the end of November subscriptions were coming in steadily, and Milton Bode had made arrangements for the Birmingham Repertory Company to appear at the Opera House, which they did in May 1922, when they presented Eden Philpott's *Carrier Pigeon, The Importance of Being Earnest, The Romantic Young Lady*, Shaw's *Getting Married* and *The Rivals* in a single week to 'a fair-sized audience.'

In the same month the Leicester Repertory Theatre Scheme presented a three week season at the Association (YMCA) Hall, commencing on May 1st with *Twelfth Night*, when the hall was 'transformed ... into a "little" theatre with extended stage.' The smallness of the available space was found to be 'rather a handicap', but there was something to be said for 'the feeling of intimacy produced in the audience by the nearness to the scene of action.'[11:6]

In November 1921, Frank Clewlow spoke on 'The English Theatre, as it is today', and Dr Rattray suggested the setting up of 'a large amateur dramatic society'. Herbert Pochin — president of the West End Adult School, which had produced excellent amateur performances — Walter Martin and Frank Clewlow — who had worked at Birmingham Repertory Theatre — met to discuss the matter. This led to a further meeting when it was proposed that The Leicester Drama Society should be set up. At first the society played at the Opera House and at the Association Hall, eventually having their own Little Theatre in 1930. The history of the Little Theatre, which was to become one of the foremost amateur theatres in the country, has been well documented by John Graham in his book *Before My Time*.[11:7]

In 1931 Maurice Chevalier had been booked to appear at the De Montfort Hall, where Pavlova had danced in 1925. The Watch Committee, however, made it a condition of Chevalier's appearing that he should not sing anything in French, and that a Committee member should be present at each performance. They expressed concern that his songs might be vulgar. The artiste was very angry and said

THE AVERAGE PROVINCIAL REPERTORY COMPANY rents its theatre on a sharing basis from a management which owns the place. This front of house management runs the theatre while the repertory company is concerned only with the production of the play. Staffs and expenses are divided as shown. The theatre must run to capacity to cover both sets of expenses and also provide a profit to be shared between the company and the management. The margin of profit is too narrow to allow risks being taken, and the eye of the management is fixed on commercial rather than dramatic success. Approximately 1/3 gross takings must be added to the Expenses as Entertainment Tax.

FRONT OF HOUSE	Salary £ s d
1. Manager	8 0 0
2. Box Office Clerk	2 10 0
3. Box Office Asst.	1 10 0
4. Resident Stage Manager	4 10 0
5. Electrician	4 0 0
6. Property Man	3 10 0
7. Night Staff (Stagehands)	13 0 0
8. Cleaners (3)	4 10 0
9. Attendants (6) (Usual rate of pay 3/ per performance)	9 12 0
10. Barmaids (2)	3 0 0
11. Night Watchman	3 10 0
	£57 12 0
Electricity per week	8 0 0
Rates	3 0 0
Electric fittings (bulbs, etc., per week) ...	1 10 0
Orchestra—Trio	12 0 0
Expenses (Purchase of Ropes, etc.)	1 0 0
Stamps	5 0
Programmes and printing	2 0 0
Insurance	1 0 0
Insurance (Staff)	10 0
	£86 17 0

THE REPERTORY COMPANY	Salary £ s d
1. Manager	10 0 0
2. Producer	10 0 0
3. Leading Man	10 0 0
4. Leading Lady	8 0 0
5. Character Man	8 0 0
6. Character Lady	6 0 0
7. Juvenile Man	8 0 0
8. Juvenile Lady	7 0 0
9. 2nd Man	5 0 0
10. 2nd Lady	5 0 0
11. Stage Manager	7 0 0
12. Assistant Stage Manager	4 0 0
13. Student	2 10 0
14. Student	2 10 0
15. Utility Man	7 0 0
16. Utility Lady	5 0 0
17. Boy	3 0 0
18. Girl	3 0 0
19. Scenic Designer	8 0 0
	£119 0 0

	£ s d
	119 0 0
Printing (Day Bill Double Crown per week)	3 0 0
Furniture (Hire Contract per week)	3 0 0
Carriage (On Costumes, etc., average per week/year) ...	0 10 0
Production. S.M. A/C (Props, Small purchases)	3 10 0
Production. Managers A/C (Post, Stationery petty cash)	15 0
Production. Carpenters A/C (Screws, Canvas, etc.) ...	1 10 0
Production. Designers A/C (Paint, etc.)	1 5 0
Production. Extra Furniutre	2 0 0
Scripts, Average per week over year	7 0
Gratuities. Stage Staff	1 10 0
Postage	5 0
Purchase (Curtains, Covers, Small Furniture)	1 10 0
Insurances (Health, Fire, etc.)	2 0 0
	£140 2 0
Authors Fees (10% of takings pay £400)	40 0 0
Costumes (Average of full play and small costumes) ...	3 0 0
	£183 2 0
TOTAL WEEKLY EXPENSE	
Company	£183 2 0
Front of House	£ 86 17 0
	£269 19 0

146 The Staff and Expenses of a typical Repertory Theatre in 1945. (A.B.C.A. M.E. Pamphlet, no.110. Feb.15, 1946)

that 'it was an insult to him and his country.' The performances were cancelled and some 1,300 people had their money returned.[11:8]

In August 1931, Gabrielle De Wilden — the principal of a Drama School in Leicester — brought a professional repertory company to the Corn Exchange. This ran for ten weeks. There was great activity in the city in 1932 when the Leicester Pageant was staged in Abbey Park in June. It was directed and organised by Frank Lascelles with the leading citizens taking an active part. The opening was on June 18th, and long queues formed for each performance. On Saturday, June 25th there was an ox-roasting in Charles Street, and a procession of fire engines, together with a hundred vehicles with tableaux from the pageant: about a thousand performers took part. A service was held in the Abbey Park to bring the proceedings to a close.[11:9]

Terence Byron's Leicester Repertory Company opened at the Theatre Royal on August 27th 1934, with Hal Osmond in *Lord Richard in the Pantry*. Performances were twice nightly at 6.40 and 8.50.[11:10] In the '30s going to the 'rep' was a popular evening's entertainment (fig.145). Many patrons had permanent bookings for the same seat every week. They enjoyed, not only the fare provided, but seeing the same actors playing many differing parts. The repertory theatres became the training grounds for the profession; the majority of today's leading players starting their careers in 'rep'. The work was hard but enjoyable. Many young actors, nowadays, who have several weeks of rehearsals, cannot conceive that companies could produce a worthwhile production in

a week, or that the results could be acceptable to the patrons, but many performances and settings (figs.77, 147-53) compare well with modern day productions.

The timetable of a weekly rep was: Tuesday, a.m. read through the play and block in the movements. Wednesday, rehearse Act I without a script; read Act II. Thursday, rehearse Acts I and II without scripts. Friday, rehearse Act III without a script, followed by Acts I and II. Saturday, rehearse the whole play. The actors had been playing each night as well, and had

147   *The Regency Players (below)* : in Saloon Bar, *July 1940. (right). The author, Helen Beal, as Nora. (Photos: R L)*

All these settings made use of stock units of scenery, repainted from week to week to suit each production; note the use of the same window flat on the left of figs.148-9. As flats reached the end of their lives, they could be cut up to form odd-shaped pieces such as those seen in the ceiling of fig.148, and in figs.152-3. Good and interesting designs were possible even on limited funds.

148   *The Regency Players in* Bird in Hand, *October 1940. (Photo: R L)*

149   *New Leicester Theatre Co. in* Wishing Well, *May 1947*

150   *New Leicester Theatre Co. in* Devonshire Cream, *January 1947*

151   *New Leicester Theatre Co. in* Anna Christie, *February 1947*

152   *Design for* Desire under the Elms (compare with fig.31)

153   *New Leicester Theatre Co. in* Desire under the Elms, *November 1946. (149-51, 153 Photos: R. Hunt)*

learnt their lines in their spare time during the day and after the show. Occasionally it was necessary to call a rehearsal on Sunday, but Monday was the Dress Rehearsal, which usually started about 11.00 o'clock and continued possibly to within half an hour of the curtain going up.

During the rehearsal week the Stage Manager had been getting together the furniture and properties required for the production. The Scenic Designer, having settled upon the design earlier, now picked out the required flats from the stock of scenery, and painted out the previous setting before commencing work on the new one. The play might be a single set — such as *Saloon Bar* (fig.147) — or like *Great Expectations* have eighteen scenes. On Saturday evening when the curtain came down, the stage staff moved in to strike the set. Early Monday morning saw the Designer, Stage Manager, ASMs and scene shifters setting up the scenery for the new play and dressing the set. The producer discussed the lighting with the electrician, and everything had to be in readiness for the Dress Rehearsal. When the curtain fell at the end of Monday night's performance the scripts for next week were handed out and the process started over again.

After three years Terence Byron's Company terminated their engagement. Hal Osmond then took on a lease with his Theatre Royal Players. They remained for six months, and the *Chronicle* said that they had 'presented some of the best staged shows we have had and generally done credit to the repertory movement.' In March 1938, the Lawrence Williamson Repertory Company moved into the theatre and stayed until October, when they were followed by the Edward Nelson Players. These players were very competent, and were also well known as they had done much work for the BBC London Region. When war was declared in 1939 all places of entertainment were closed in case of air raids, but after two weeks they were allowed to re-open. In 1940 the times of performances were changed to 6.0 and 8.0 o'clock, as the last trams from the city were timed to leave at 10.30 pm.[11:11]

The Regency Players opened on April 15th 1940, with *French Without Tears*. The producer was Francis Roberts, and the company were given a warm welcome. Performance times were again changed after the bombing of Leicester in November 1940 to 3.45 and 6.0 pm. Eventually the Regency Players were to perform once nightly, with a matinee on Thursdays and three performances on Saturdays. By February 1941, Barry Letts (carrying on the theatrical traditions of his family, his sister Pauline being already an established player) had joined the company. Barry became the producer of the BBC TV classic serials. Another actor well known for his television appearances was John Barron. Other members

of the company in the early years of the war were Helen Lacey, Diana Muirhead, Helen Beal, Georgina Cookson, Joan Rogers, Pearl Dadswell, Jane Cain — who first recorded the speaking clock of the telephone service — Penelope Keech, Sheila Burrell, Godfrey Harrison, Sydney Russell, Walter Chapman, Fred Derrick and Denys Jones, who became a BBC radio producer.[11:12]

On Sunday, July 20th 1941, the Regency Players took *The Brontes* to the Regimental Theatre of an Ordinance depot, co-operating with the Leicester Emergency Entertainments Committee. The actors gave their services and the scenery was transported in Army lorries. This was an experiment to see if there was a demand for straight plays. A director of the theatre company, J. Baxter Somerville; the chairman of the LEEC, Mr Tom Crewe, and committee members, all attended to see the forces give the production a very warm welcome, and the company were to play many times under such circumstances.[11:13]

The call-up of both young men and women for the forces created problems, but these were overcome. Young aspiring players joined the company straight from school, and many are now firmly established in the profession, as for example — Ivor Roberts. Hwfa Price was engaged in war work in Leicestershire, and came to play with the company when duty permitted. The burden on those over call-up age was heavy, but they responded magnificently and the company played to good houses. This was, in part, due to the many firms which were evacuated from London to Leicester: the employees being glad to enjoy an evening's relaxation at the theatres.

In 1945 the Regency Players were replaced by the Lyric Players, who included Donald Sinden. They stayed for a year and were followed by the Leicester Repertory Company, in which the actors were all established professionals demobilized from the services. One member of the company was Paul Hansard, better known to Leicester as Hans Freutal, who often appeared at the Little Theatre and with the Vaughan Players. The New Leicester Theatre Company took over in August 1946. Godfrey Harrison returned as Producer, and patrons were delighted to welcome back Walter Chapman and also John Barron, who had served in Leicester's adopted ship — *Renown*.[11:14]

The company gave their last performance on June 7th 1947, the proprietors having decided to sell the building. It was purchased by a Birmingham businessman, Samuel Locker. It was not re-opened until December 27th 1948, when Basil Thomas and Derek Salberg presented fortnightly shows, but the management was disappointed with the response. From 1950 to '56 repertory was provided by R.S. Theatres Ltd, the companies being under the names of the Saxon Players and the Leicester Repertory Company. Thelma Rogers, who moved from Leicester to play Peggy Archer in *The Archers,* and Billie Whitelaw were members of the Saxon Players, with Richard Jerrams as scenic designer, while Joseph Walker was the theatre manager.[11:15]

After the production of *Jackie,* during the week of October 20th 1956, the theatre closed, and there was much concern regarding its fate. A committee of supporters was formed to save it, and representations were made to the City Council asking for a yearly grant. In November an appeal was launched by the Theatre Committee, under the chairmanship of Professor A.R. Humphreys, with Philip Collins as Secretary, to raise £10,000, of which half the sum was required by December 6th, but their plans were hindered by new conditions set in the lease. Nevertheless the committee continued to negotiate 'with the owner of the building for a lease whose terms we would find acceptable.' However, the negotiations fell through when the owner reopened the theatre in February 1957, with the Leicester Repertory Company, but three months later the theatre was abruptly closed. Demolition commenced (figs.154-5), and new offices for the Leicester Permanent Building Society were erected on the site.[11:16]

155   *Demolition of the Theatre Royal, 1957. The auditorium after the collapse of the roof. (L Me)*

154   *Demolition of the Theatre Royal, 1957. Note the Royal Crest above the proscenium arch: see frontispiece. (L Me)*

At the beginning of the 20th century the Opera House was continuing its varied programme of musical comedies interspersed with melodramas, light opera and plays, and their effect on ladies' fashions was not overlooked by the newspapers. Writing of *The Price of Peace* in October, 1901 the ladies page of the *Guardian* tells us that 'the frocks at the Opera House this week are well worth seeing. The skirts particularly are quite a feature. They are all cut pretty well in the same fashion — that is to say, with a graceful sweep back from the hips. Even the ''supers'' manage to walk the stage gracefully with their well-cut trains to hide their natural awkwardness. Miss Ada Webster looks very charming in a gown of dead black, relieved by long bands of sequins, which she wears in the last act.'[11:17]

In 1903 Henry Irving played for three nights, and even before the opening all the reserved seats had been taken. The *Guardian* wrote that his performance of Corporal Brewster in *Waterloo*

'was one of the most masterly character studies ... of an old man who lives in the past, it was well nigh perfect. ... His make-up was as good as his acting, for it was hard to look upon his face and figure and believe he was anything but a nonegenarian. The Bells ... as handled by the great tragedian ... has great power to thrill and enthrall.' Irving returned the following year, again playing Brewster and Matthias, as well as Shylock and Beckett.[11:18]

1904 was to see Ellen Terry on the boards. She played Beatrice to the Benedick of Matheson Lang in *Much Ado About Nothing*. Harcourt Williams, a young actor in the cast, was noted as being particularly good; he was to become a prominent member of the Old Vic.

'A great feature of the play was its magnificent staging. It is as unstagey as it is possible for anything on the stage to be, and is a triumph of harmonious colouring. The production is in the hands of Ellen Terry's son, Gordon Craig, and the beautiful dresses are designed by her daughter Ailsa Craig.'

This was not the first connection that Gordon Craig had with the Opera House, for in 1890 he had appeared here in the role of Caleb Deecie in *The Two Roses*. It was said of his performance of the blind Caleb that his impersonation 'was almost touchingly true to nature' and 'he is certainly a finished actor in every respect.'[11:19]

By 1906 the Opera House had been taken over by Messrs Bode and Compton, so they were to run both this theatre and the Royal. In 1907 Mr and Mrs Frank Benson's Company presented a week of Shakespeare, while in 1909 Martin Harvey played in *The Breed of the Treshams*, *The Last Heir* and *The Corsican Brothers*. The performances were 'warmly greeted' and had 'a high standard of excellence'. Martin Harvey returned in 1911 when it was announced that he would also give a lecture during the week on the setting up of a National Theatre.[11:20] In 1913 Martin Harvey presented *Oedipus Rex* with a type of setting which Leicester had not seen before.

'There is no stage and no orchestra. There is nothing but the square columns of the palace facade and the great bronze door in the centre, opening on to some steps which divide on each side of an altar erected to Apollo. The players enter through the auditorium and act on the steps. What little music there is comes from the palace. But as the play proceeds the setting becomes wonderfully impressive, until one could not imagine such a tragedy being enacted anywhere else ... Martin Harvey ... whipped the audience into awed silence. They could not applaud. They hardly breathed ... They sat still for two hours ...'[11:21]

1914 was to see productions of *Pygmalion* and *Man and Superman* by Shaw; *Joy* by Galsworthy, and *Peter Pan* and *Hindle Wakes*. Miss Penelope Wheeler's productions of Gilbert Murray's translations from the Greek of *Hippolytus*, *Electra* and *Iphigenia in Tauris*, and such musical comedies as *The Girl from Utah* and *The Arcadians*, as well as opera were presented.[11:22]

However, the war was to affect attendances, and the question of twice nightly performances was raised in an article in the *Daily Post*, where it was pointed out that theatres had been hit by the variety houses; they had stolen theatre patrons by offering shorter entertainments and filling their houses twice a night. They also had more comfortable and attractive buildings with an air of prosperity about them. In 1914 Sir Herbert Tree and His Majesty's Theatre Company were shown in a film of *Trilby* at the Picture House: yet another form of competition. By 1917 the Opera House was described as being 'ill suited for comfort' as compared with such buildings as the Palace. The following year after re-decoration, it presented a 'clean, cosy, bright appearance', with a repainted drop curtain and fresh drapes to the boxes.[11:23]

Edward Compton died in 1918 and Milton Bode continued to run the Opera on his own. Compton's

156   *Royal Opera House: Playbill of 1915, with train connections. (R O)*

association with the house had begun in 1906, but there was poor support for his Compton Comedy Company until on a visit in 1913 he played *Everywoman* with such success that regular visits were planned. His last appearance was in 1914 when *Davy Garrick*, *Lady of Lyons*, *Money* and *Richelieu* were played. The reception from the crowded houses 'showed that Leicester was removing the reproach that the town could not appreciate good plays.'[11:24]

When *Chu Chin Chow* was presented in 1920, the bookings were very heavy. 1921 saw a varied programme which included an amateur performance of Walter Martin's Players in *Dear Brutus*, with Harry Letts (Barry's father) as Lob. The year was to see a performance of Charles Doran's Shakespearean Company at the De Montfort Hall. Ralph Richardson, undertaking his first professional engagement, was playing Lorenzo in *The Merchant of Venice*, as well as being the ASM. On his own admission 'I shouted, I screamed, I rushed about the stage,' all apparently to some effect. At any rate he overcame the acoustic difficulties of this adapted hall in which Charles Doran's 'level diction sounded from time to time a little perfunctory,' with the result that the reviewer commended him as 'deserving of special mention'. It

was as Sir Ralph Richardson, that he performed the official opening of the Haymarket Theatre in 1973. Also in Doran's company was Donald Woolfitt, playing Launcelot Gobbo; later to become a leading Shakespearean actor, by which time he had changed his name to Wolfitt.[11:25]

Walter Martin's Players put on *The School for Scandal* under the direction of F.D. Clewlow in 1922, when the dresses were those used in Tree's production at His Majesty's Theatre. Harry Martin, Roy and Harold Pochin and Harry Letts were in the company. Another Leicester combination was organised by Dr Capper and Mr W.G. Orton who presented *The Builder of Bridges*.[11:26]

Bransby Williams played his characters from Dickens, including Micawber in 1922, and the papers commented that

'Among an exellent cast must be mentioned Mr Fred E. Derrick as Uriah, a remarkable incarnation of the pictures in the old Dickens books, and in personality just the viper we expected.'

Fred will be remembered by many Leicester playgoers as a member of the Regency Players at the Royal. He made his home in Birstall and became manager of several cinemas including the

157   *Leicester Choral and Dramatic Society's* Prince Igor, *at the De Montfort Hall, with the Leicester City Male Voice Choir, Miss Iris Cooke's Ballet Class and local Territorial troops. Oct. 1933. (Courtesy of the Trustees of the Theatre Museum, V & A)*

Essoldo — originally the Temperance Hall. His wife, May Edney, had topped the bill at the Pavilion in 1926.[11:27]

The following years saw many leading players of the theatre world at the Opera House: Mrs Patrick Campbell, Cicely Courtneidge and Jack Hulbert, Phyllis Neilson Terry, Violet Vanburgh, Sir Frank Benson, Julia Neilson and Fred Terry, Phyllis and Zena Dare, Sybil Thorndike and Sir Gerald du Maurier.[11:28] By 1931 the new managing director was Prince Littler. The programmes were made up of light and musical comedies. Gracie Fields appeared in *Walk This Way*. From May to October 1932 the theatre played variety with artistes of the calibre of Harry Lauder, Flotsam and Jetsam, Gertie Gitana and G.H. Elliott. When *The Good Companions* was produced the stage had to be extended. It was a large production 'with 16 scenes and only about 12 seconds wait between each of them. The Company numbers 50, in addition to 40 "supers" who had to be engaged.'[11:29]

White Horse Inn was another large production; for which a revolving stage was carried by the company. To bring the musical to the city a special train was hired; The White Horse Special, which travelled from London on December 4th 1932, was claimed to be the biggest theatrical train on record. It had five Pullman coaches together with a corridor and dining car. There were twelve large scene trucks carrying 100 tons of scenery as well as a pantechnion and van for personal luggage — which amounted to eight tons. One hundred and seventy-five members of the company travelled and a van was also provided for birds and animals.[11:30]

When it was the custom for companies to play a different town each week, the country was criss-crossed every Sunday by trains carrying 'Theatricals' and their props. Every large railway centre such as the Midland (now the London Road) Station had a special manager to deal with their requirements. Scenic artists had to design their sets so that the pieces would fit into the 8ft high vans. After the show finished on Saturday night everything had to be removed to the station and be packed into the train, so that it could leave early on Sunday morning.

When *Cavalcade* played at the Theatre Royal, Birmingham, however, as each scene was struck on Saturday night it was immediately loaded into a lorry to be brought to the Opera House here. Thirty-two lorries were needed; if the production had been brought by train it could not have been set up ready for Monday night.[11:31]

In February, 1933, Jean Forbes Robertson played Peter Pan, and Matheson Lang appeared in *Wellington*. In the summer twice nightly performances of variety were presented. It was the time of the big bands and Jack Payne and Jack Hylton both appeared. Other performers were the Houston Sisters,

Jimmy James, Sandy Powell, and Nervo and Knox — who became part of the Crazy Gang.[11:32]

A revolving stage was used again for *Wild Violets* in 1934. A critic commented 'it provides all the continuity of the "talkies" and serves as a setting for scenes at once dazzling and beautiful.' *White Horse Inn* returned and played twice nightly.[11:33] A pattern was established in this year of twice nightly variety until the autumn, followed by a season of plays until pantomime time, a scheme which was followed until 1945.

During the war playgoers were to see the personal appearance of Noel Coward in *Blithe Spirit*. John Clements and Googie Withers played in *They Came to a City*. Richard Tauber appeared in *Blossom Time* and *Old Chelsea*, Donald Wolfit brought Shakespeare, and the Americans — Alfred Lunt and Lynne Fontaine were seen in *There Shall be No Night*.[11:34]

Playing in variety at the Opera House in the late 1930s and during the war years were such performers as Tommy Handley in *ITMA*, Reginald Foorte, Henry Hall, Carol Levis and his BBC Discoveries, Elsie and Doris Waters, Mantovani, Roy Fox, Bebe Daniels and Ben Lyon, Hughie Green and his Gang and Arthur Askey.[11:35] In 1946 the Leicester Operatic Society production was *The Vagabond King* with Lilian Dunkley, the principal dancer was Elsa Groocock. First class plays were presented in the next few years. In the 1949 Christmas pantomime, *Little Red Riding Hood*, the second comedians were played by Morecombe and Wise, but they were not then sufficiently well known to warrant a mention in the reviews. In 1950 the Wilson Barrett Company presented a twelve week season of plays, and the following year a seventeen week season was performed by the Phillip Barrett Company, following the closure of the theatre for ten weeks. In 1952 the management decided to present a further season of repertory, but although the productions of Harry Hanson's Court Players and later Carl Clopet's Company were an artistic success, this was not reflected in the box office takings.[11:36]

After the pantomime of 1952-3, with Bill Fraser as Mother Goose, four impressive musicals were played: *Carousel*, *King's Rhapsody*, *Oklahoma* and *Kiss Me Kate*, but the houses were not full even for such fare. On May 18th Mari Bici's Dancing School presented *Carnival Moments*, the annual school presentation, which was followed by Hermione Baddeley and Raymond Young in a pre-London try-out, *Murder Mistaken*, and it was now that the closure of the theatre (fig.158) for two months was announced.[11:37]

In July Leicester theatregoers were told that the house would remain closed indefinitely. It had been hoped to re-open, but this had not been found possible. One reason given was the shortage of shows on tour. When Littler announced that the pantomime for 1953-4 would be presented at the Palace, it was the end. Particularly sad for all those local people who had worked in the front of house and backstage for many years. Cyril Dawkins, the resident stage manager had begun working backstage in 1921 when he was 16. However, he was able to undertake the same position at the Palace, where in 1953 *The Blue Lamp* made use of the revolving stage with 28 scenes.[11:38]

The Palace, however, in common with most halls and theatres was fighting the new entertainment provided by Television, and there was an open letter from the Editor of the *Illustrated Leicester Chronicle* to Prince Littler, complaining that the shows were poor and that Leicester deserved better. For a while it seemed as if things were looking up, but after the summer vacation in 1956 the Palace opened to nude shows. There were some people who were pleased to patronise these, but as Douglas Goodlad commented, 'if you want to see Billy Daniels, Mel Torme, Ted Heath, Lionel Hampton and other celebrities, you can see them elsewhere in Leicester, at the De Montfort Hall.[11:39]

The Palace struggled on again with some variety (fig.159), some revues and an odd performance of a play. In May 1958, Robert Atkins presented a Shakespearean week which included *Henry IV* and *Much Ado About Nothing*, but when *She Strips to Conquer* was billed in February 1959, it was announced that the theatre would close in two weeks, after a production by the Leicester Operatic Ensemble of *The King and I*. Prince Littler had sold the property to Sketchley's Ltd, and on February 21st, the curtain fell and the demolition gangs were soon at work.[11:40]

Strenuous efforts were now being made to interest the City Council in a Civic Theatre, on the lines of the Belgrade Theatre at Coventry, and schemes were drawn up to adapt various buildings, including the Pork Pie (fig.160) (used by the Ratae Players in September 1951) and Harvey Lane Chapels. The

158   Closure of the Royal Opera House in 1953. (L Me)

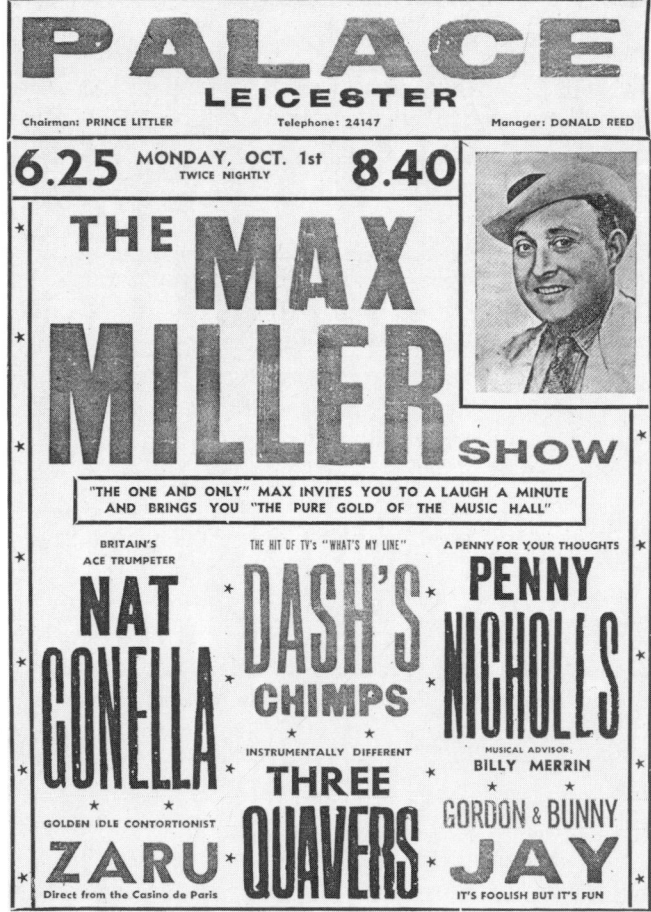

159   Palace, Leicester: Playbill of 1956. (D. Garratt)

160   Proposed adaptation of the Pork Pie Chapel, as (left) an arena stage; (right) as an end stage. (Photos: R L)

a

c

b

d

161   Proposed adaptation of the Corn Exchange, as a: an arena stage. b: a classical stage. c: an Elizabethan stage. d: a modern stage

162   *Studio Theatre production of* Phedre *at the old Vaughan College, 1958*

163   *Studio Theatre production of* Dial M for Murder *in the Hall of the then College of Art. (Photo: R L)*

Corn Exchange (fig.161) (previously used as a theatre in 1931, p.114) and the Regal Cinema, but nothing came of them. The Theatre Committee, once more in action, did, however, bring back live theatre when they invited Stephen Joseph to bring his Theatre in the Round Company to the city, and in March 1958 he presented *Phedre* with Margaret Rawlings in the title role in the old Vaughan College (fig.162). In September and October his Studio Theatre Company performed in the halls of the College of Art (fig.163) and the Wycliffe and Wyggeston Girls Schools.

Theatre in the round introduced Leicester to an even more intimate form of presentation than that earlier noted at the Association Hall (p.113). The Studio Theatre returned in March 1959, when *Ring of Roses* by David Campton, a local playwright, was produced. The Committee also arranged for the Century Theatre to play a season in De Montfort Square.[11:41] Designed and built in Hinckley, this travelling theatre was composed of trailers which fitted together to make up the stage and auditorium. Although the productions were successful, this was not the answer to Leicester's needs. The Century Theatre is now based in Cumbria.

165   *YMCA Theatre: prior to the alterations of 1980. (Courtesy of Douglas Smith Stimson Partnership)*

164   *Adaption of St. Nicholas School Hall by The Living Theatre. (L Me)*

The Opera House had remained dark and deserted, for six years. In 1959 Samuel Locker, who had earlier bought the Theatre Royal, now purchased the Opera House for £30,800. The curtain rose once more at Christmas for the pantomime *Sinbad the Sailor*. A varied programme followed, but it was no more than a weak flash in the pan and not to last. The final performance in June 1960, was *Five Finger Exercise* by Peter Shaffer.[11:42] The Opera House was demolished, and its place was taken by the Malcolm Arcade.

In December 1961, the City Council and the Theatre Committee helped the Living Theatre to set up for a limited period in St Nicholas School Rooms, which were due to be demolished in July of the following year (fig.164). The company, directed by Bill Hays and Derrick Goodwin, with Jill Gascoine in the cast, opened with Christopher Logue's *Trials*. They presented a season of plays on a fortnightly basis, which was extended beyond July, and they finally closed when their production of *Billy Liar* ended on January 12th 1963.[11:43] It was now left to the amateurs to provide for the needs of those who love to go to the theatre, and this was the situation until with the help of the City Council and the Committee, which had developed into the Theatre Trust, the Phoenix and later the Haymarket were opened; but that is the beginning of another story.

Bibliography & Abbreviations

Ashby — all the year round. Brown's Annual, 1921

AM *Architectural Magazine*

Beavin, H.A. *The Book of Hinckley,* Hinckley, 1983

Billson, C.J. *Leicester Memoirs,* Leicester, 1924

Boaden, J. *The Life of Mrs Jordan,* 2 vols, London, 1831

Booth, M.R. *Victorian Theatrical Terms,* STR, 1981

Boz, *Memoirs of Grimaldi,* Rev. ed. London, 1903

Brownlow, J. *Melton Mowbray,* MM, 1980

Burley, T.L.G. *Playhouses & Players of East Anglia,* Norwich, 1928

BC *Burton Chronicle*

Byrne, Muriel St Clare, 'Early Settings in England', *Theatre Notebook,* vol.viii, pp.81-6

CLCE *Catalogue of Leic. Commemorative Exhibition,* 1897

Cawte, E.C. *In Comes I,* London, 1972

Chambers, E.K. *Elizabethan Stage,* vol.ii, Oxford, 1923

CT *Coalville Times*

Cradock, J. *Literary and Misc. Memoirs,* vols. i-iv, 1828

Curtis, J.A. *Topographical History of the County of Leics.* W. Hextall, 1831

Deakin, J. *Loughborough in the XIX Century,* Echo Press, 1927

Deakin, W.A. *19th Century Loughborough,* Echo Press, 1974

Deakin, W.A. *The Story of Loughborough,* Echo Press, 1979

Dyer, R. *Nine Years of an Actor's Life,* Longman, 1833

Era

Egan, P., *The Life of an Actor,* London, 1892

Evans, S. *Leicester Words, Phrases & Proverbs,* 1881

Exits and Entrances, A short history of the Festival Players of Loughborough, Echo Press, nd

Francis, H.J. *A History of Hinckley,* Hinckley, 1930

Gardiner, W. *Music and Friends,* vol.iii, 1853

Graham, J. *Before My Time,* nd

Hankinson, A. *The Blue Box,* Keswick, 1983

HDF *Hinckley and District Focus*

HT *Hinckley Times*

Hillier, K. *The Book of Ashby de la Zouch,* Bucks., 1984

Horn, J.D. *Illustrated Guide to Places of Leicester,* 1905

Howell, M. & Ford, P. *The True History of the Elephant Man,* London, 1983

ILC *Illustrated Leicester Chronicle*

Johnson, T.F. *Glimpses of Ancient Leicester,* Leicester, 1906

Kelly, W. *Notes Illustrative of the Drama and other Popular Amusements,* London, 1865

Leacroft, R. *Development of the English Playhouse,* London, 1973

Leacroft, R. 'The Theatre Royal', *Trans. of the Leic. Arch. & Hist. Soc.* vol.xxxiv, 1958

Leacroft, R. 'The Remains of the Theatres at Ashby-de-la-Zouch and Loughborough', *Theatre Notebook,* vol.iv, pp.12-21

Leicester & Rutland Notes and Queries, Ed. Spencer, J.T. vol.ii, 1891-3

LA *Leicester Advertiser*

LC *Leicester Chronicle*

LDM *Leicester Daily Mercury*

LDP *Leicester Daily Post*

LEM *Leicester Evening Mail*

LMa *Leicester Mail*

LMe *Leicester Mercury*

LG *Leicester Guardian*

LRSM *Leicester Ragged School Mission,* 1866-1912

LCIC Leicestershire Collection at the Information Centre, Leicester. (Leicestershire Libraries and Information Service.)

Living Theatre, Leicester, 1962

LoE *Loughborough Echo*

LoM *Loughborough Monitor*

McCarthy, S. & Norris, H., 'J.T. Robinson,' *Theatrephile,* vol.i, no.i, pp.26-31

MJ *Midland Jackdaw*

Muskett, C. *Notices & Illustrations of the Costume, Processions, Pageantry, &c. Formerly Displayed by the Corp. of Norwich,* 1850

NHM Newarke Houses Museum, (Leicestershire Museums, Art Galleries and Records

Service).

Nichols, J. *History & Antiquities of the County of Leicester*, vol.i, pt.ii, (1815) 1971

O'Connor, G. *Ralph Richardson*, London, 1982

OCT   *Oxford Companion to the Theatre*, Hartnoll, P. Oxford, 1951

Penley, B.S. *The Bath Stage*, London, 1892

Pollock, Sir F. *Macready's Reminiscences*, 2 vols. London, 1875

Read, R. *Modern Leicester*, London, 1881

RO   Record Office, Leicestershire, (Leicestershire Museums, Art Galleries and Records Service).

RBL   *Records of the Borough of Leicester*, vol.ii, 1327-1509, Ed. Bateson, M. London, 1901: vol.iii, Ed. Bateson, 1509-1603, Cambs. 1905: vol. v, 1689-1835, Ed. Chinnery, G.A. Leicester, 1965.

RLC   Richard Leacroft Collection

Rosenfeld, S. *Temples of Thespis*, STR, 1978

Saxon, A.H. *The Life and Art of Andrew Ducrow*, London, 1978

Scott, W. *The Story of Ashby-de-la-Zouch*, 1907

Sharp, A Dissertation on the Pageants or Dramatic Mysteries, Harl. Mss. 1948, fol.48

Skillington, S.H. *History of Leics.* Leicester, 1923

STR   Society for Theatre Research

Stage

Swift, E. 'The Leicestershire Mummers Play', *Leics. & Rutland Magazine*, vol.ii, no.i, Dec. 1949, pp.34-40

TN   *Theatre Notebook*

TRA   Theatre Royal Accounts (RO)

TRMB   Theatre Royal Minute Books (RO)

Thompson, J. *Leicester in the 18th Century*, 1871

Toole, J.L. *Reminiscences*, Ed. Hatton, J. London, 1892

Torrington Diaries, 1781-1794, Ed. Andrews, C.B. 4 vols. London, 1934-38

TC   *Town Crier*

Toynbee, W. *Diaries of W.C. Macready*, 2 vols, London, 1912

Troubridge, St. V. *The Benefit System in the British Theatre*, STR, 1967

Unicome, R. *Survey Book of the Borough & Town of Leics*, 1827, RO ID 65/1

Warwick, L. *Drama that Smelled*, Northampton, 1975

Wayte, T. *A Descriptive & Historical Guide to Ashby de la Zouch*, 1831

W   *Wyvern*

References

1:1   Kelly, pp.14-19
1:2   Sharp, pp.17-18
1:3   R B L, vol.ii, 26: 3: 1478
1:4   Kelly, pp.7, 11
1:5   Kelly, pp.38, 46, 189
1:6   Muskett
1:7   Kelly, pp.191, 70. R O, DG36/288/2
1:8   Kelly, pp.51-6, Evans, p.215. Swift, pp.34-40.
      Cawte
1:9   R B L, vol.iii
1:10 Chambers, p.208
1:11 R B L, vol.iii
1:12 Wayte, pp. 62-70
1:13 Kelly, p.273

2:1   Johnson, F. p.250
2:2   L J, Nov.14, 1769
2:3   R B L, vol.v, p.169. Survey Book, R O, ID 65/1,
      pp.24-30
2:4   L J, Aug.5, 1780. March 14, 1767
2:5   L J, Feb.4, 1794
2:6   Cradock, vol.i, p.119
2:7   L J, Nov.5, 1785. Dec.21, 1776. May 15, Aug.14,
      1762. June 1, 1775, Warwick, p.56
2:8   Cradock, vol.i, p.121
2:9   L J, Nov.23, 1804. L C, Sept.26, 1835
2:10 L J, Mar.2, Apr.6, 1771. Feb.13, 1762. Mar.19, 1763
2:11 Gardiner, vol.iii, p.41. L J, Dec.10, 1790
2:12 Penley, p.24. Warwick, p.56
2:13 L J, Sept.6, 1777
2:14 L J, Oct.14, 1836, O C T, p.105
2:15 T N, vol. xv, pp.14-5
2:16 L J, July 25, 1772. Dec.25, 1773. Billson, pp.105-6
2:17 L J, Jan.28, 1774
2:18 T N, vol.vii, p.4
2:19 Troubridge, p.54. L J, Mar.29, 1783. Feb.19, 1774
2:20 L J, Feb.7, 1778. Feb.19, 1796. Nov.24, 1797
2:21 L J, Jan.24, 1778
2:22 L J, Dec.1, 1781
2:23 L J, Dec.29, 1759. Mar.8, 1760
2:24 L J, May 7, 1785. Feb.13, 1762
2:25 L J, Mar.6, 13, 1762
2:26 L J, Feb.3, 1781
2:27 L J, Oct.7, 1769. Nov.8, 1793
2:28 L J, Aug.14, 1773. Jan.8, 1763. Feb.23, 1783. Jan.1,
      1790
2:29 L J, Dec.24, 1774. June 15, 1776. Jan.29, 1790
2:30 L J, Dec.10, 17, 1790
2:31 L J, Oct. 2, 1795. Feb.26, 1796. Oct.27, 1797. May
      31, 1805. July 4, 1862
2:32 L J, Dec.17, 24, 1768. Nov.16, 1771. Nov.19, 1774.
      Feb.4, 1775
2:33 L J, Jan.24, 1778
2:34 L J, Nov.15, Dec.13, 1777
2:35 L J, June 17, 1769. Mar.14, 1794. Hillier, pp.105-6.
      R O, Misc.320/26
2:36 R O, QS3/391/7. Scott, pp.145, 232. L J, May 31,
      1822
2:37 L J, Apr.23, May 7, 1774. Torrington, p.312.
      Francis, p.111
2:38 L J, Feb.7, 1778. May 26, 1787. July 19, 1788. May
      5, 1837

3:1   L J, June 21, 1799. Unicome, p.12
3:2   L J, Mar. 14, 1800. Curtis, p.113. Nichols, p.534
3:3   L J, May 9, 1800
3:4   L C, Oct.4, 1823
3:5   L C, Sept.26, 1817
3:6   L J, May 23, 1800
3:7   L J, Jan.1, 1802. Jan.16, Sept.10, 1824. Sept.2, 1831.
      Sept.15, 1826. L C, Aug.31, 1833
3:8   L J, Mar.14, 21, 1800
3:9   L J, Nov.26, 1802. Jan.8, 22, Nov.26, 1802
3:10 L J, Oct.19, Nov.23, 1804
3:11 Pollock, vol.i, p.15. L J, Nov.23, 1804
3:12 L J, Oct.7, 1808. Oct.6, 1809
3:13 L J, Sept.8, 15, Nov.10, 1809
3:14 L J, Oct.19, Nov.16, 1810
3:15 L J, Oct.29, 1813
3:16 L J, Oct.21, 28, 1814
3:17 Pollock, p.86
3:18 L J, Sept.27, 1816
3:19 L J, Oct.25, 1816
3:20 L C, Sept.26, Oct.10, 1817
3:21 L C, Oct.30, 1818. Nov.26, 1819
3:22 L C, Sept.27, 1834. L J, June 13, Aug.15, 22, 29,
      1828. Oct.1, 1830. Nov.6, 13, 1829. Jan.2, 1824
3:23 L C, Mar.15, 1828
3:24 L C, Jan.9, Feb.6, 1830
3:25 L C, Sept. 25, Oct. 5, Nov.29, 1833. L J, Feb.28,
      1834. T N, vol.viii, pp.81-6
3:26 L C, Feb.21, Sept.12, Nov.14, 1835. L J, Nov.13,
      1835
3:27 L J, Aug.23, 1805
3:28 L J, Apr.12, 1788. Mar.14, 1794. Jan.23, 1801
3:29 L J, May 12, 1848
3:30 L J, May 23, June 6, 1823
3:31 L C, Nov.16, 1839. Oct.31, 1840. L J, Sept.7, 1840.
      L C, Aug.7, 1841. L J, Nov.25, 1842
3:32 L J, Jan.13, Feb.17, Oct.13, Nov.4, 1843
3:33 L J, Feb.14, Mar.7, 1845. Jan.9, 1846
3:34 L J, Feb.4, 25, 1848. Jan.2, 9, 16, 1852
3:35 L J, May 12, 1848. Mar.9, June 22, 1855. Apr.18,
      1856
3:36 L J, Feb.13, 1857. Feb.2, 1866
3:37 Wayte, p.137
3:38 L J, May 23, 1828
3:39 Ashby, Brown, p.vii. L J, June 19, 1835
3:40 L J, July 14, 1837
3:41 L J, July 28, 1854. Aug.17, 1860
3:42 Playbill of 1862. T N, vol.iv, pp.12-21
3:43 L J, Apr.25, 1890

4:1   L J, Dec.14, 1771. Dec.18, 1772. Cradock, vol.iv,
      p.221
4:2   L J, Sept.18, 1773. Cradock, vol.iv, pp.253, 258-9.
      L J, Dec.4, 1793. Billson, pp.107-8
4:3   Cradock, vol.iv, p.393
4:4   Rosenfeld, pp.145-50. L J, Aug.16, 1799
4:5   L J, July 31, 1801
4:6   Rosenfeld, pp.152-3
4:7   L J, Apr.16, 1847
4:8   L J, Jan.18, 1850
4:9   L J, Jan.31, 1851. Jan.28, Feb.4, 1853. Mar.3, 1854
4:10 L J, Jan.12, 1877

4:11   L J, Jan.21, 1887
4:12   L J, Feb.11, 1859
4:13   L J, Sept.11, 1874. Jan.14, 1887. W, Jan.26, Apr.6, 1894
4:14   L J, Mar.28, 1767
4:15   L J, Jan.11, 1867. Jan.10, 1868. W. Dec.16, 1892
4:16   L J, May 23, 1858
4:17   L J, Jan.18, 1867
4:18   L J, July 7, 1854. Apr.16, 1858
4:19   W, Feb.17, 24, Mar.3, 1893. L G, Mar.29, 1902
4:20   L J, Nov.27, 1773. Dec.12, 1862. Nov.25, Dec.23, 1864. Oct.13, 1865. Jan.2, 1863. Drama, Oct.1932, pp.6-7

5:1   L J, Mar.18, 1836
5:2   L C, Mar.19, 1836. L J, Mar.18, 1836
5:3   L C, Jan.7, 1837
5:4   L J, Aug.19, Sept.9, 1836
5:5   A M, 1836, vol.iii, pp.482, 584
5:6   L J, Sept.9, 1836
5:7   L J, Nov.23, 1855. Apr.1, 1859. T R M B, Oct.2, 1869
5:8   L J, Sept.3, 1869. L D P, Sept.12, 1873
5:9   Leacroft, 'Development', p.144, figs.112, 116. L J, Sept.9, 1836
5:10   L C, Sept.26, 1840. Boaden, vol.i, p.250
5:11   L J, Jan.20, 1850. Oct.20, Nov.3, 1854
5:12   L J, Sept.1, 1871. Sept.21, 1877
5:13   L J, Sept.9, 1836. T R M B, Feb.21, 1865
5:14   T R M B, May 24, 1850. L J, Aug.28, 1857. T R M B, Feb.8, Mar.19, 1862
5:15   L J, Jan.24, 1868
5:16   L J, Oct.4, 1850
5:17   L J, Nov.5, 1852. T R M B, Feb.9, 1853
5:18   T R M B, Feb.13, 23, 1863. Feb.21, 1865. Sept.29, 1869
5:19   L J, Sept.29, 1854. Sept.21, 1860
5:20   L J, Sept.15, 1865
5:21   L A, Oct.2, 1869. L J, Jan.12, 1872
5:22   L G, June 15, 1901. T R M B, Aug.23, 1872
5:23   L J, Sept.19, 1873
5:24   L C, Sept.13, 1873. L J, Apr.18, 1873
5:25   L D P, Sept.12, 1873
5:26   T R M B, Apr.2, 1874. L C, Sept.13, 1873
5:27   L J, Apr.18, 1873
5:28   L D P, Sept.12, 1873
5:29   L C, Oct.2, 1841. T R M B, Dec.1, 1869. L J, Sept.9, 1870
5:30   L J, Sept.19, 1873
5:31   Era, Sept.21, 1873. L D P, Sept.12, 1873
5:32   L J, Sept.4, 1874. July 29, 1881. L D P, July 23, 1881. M J, July 29, 1881
5:33   T R M B, June 10, 1881
5:34   L D P, July 23, 1881. Stage, June 18, 1881. Era, July 30, 1881
5:35   T R M B, May 11, 1881. L D P, July 23, 1881. Era, July 30, 1881. Booth, pp.31-6
5:36   T R M B, Mar.16, 1883
5:37   L J, Feb.9, 1866. Stage, Oct.19, 1886
5:38   L J, Jan.13, 1888
5:39   T R M B, Oct.18, 1887
5:40   T R M B, Sept.23, 30, 1892. Apr.25, 1887
5:41   Letter dated 19.4.83 from Irene Hubbard
5:42   R O, 19244 (1888), 21206 (Oct.16, 1891). T R M B, Dec.18, 1883
5:43   T R M B, May 21, 1897. Mar.14, 1898
5:44   T R M B, Nov.8, 1905. Sept.29, 1908. July 30, 1912. Mar.27, 1913. Aug.3, 1917. Mar.4, 1918

6:1   L C, Sept.10, 24, 1836
6:2   L J, Oct.7, 1836
6:3   L C, Oct.15, 1836. L J, Oct.14, 1836
6:4   L C, Oct.29, Dec.31, 1836
6:5   L C, Dec.31, 1836. Nov.4, 25, Dec.9, 1837
6:6   L C, June 2, 1838
6:7   L J, Oct.12, 1838
6:8   L J, Jan.4, 1839. L C, Apr.4, 1840
6:9   R O, 8D58. L C, Nov.28, 1840
6:10   L C, Oct.16, 1841. Read, p.214
6:11   L J, Oct.27, 1843
6:12   L J, Sept.20, 1844
6:13   L J, Oct.3, 1845. June 11, 1847
6:14   L J, Sept.17, Oct.1, 15, Dec.31, 1847
6:15   L J, Oct.15, 22, 1847. Jan.7, 1848
6:16   L J, Mar.17, 1848. Sept.28, 1849
6:17   L J, Jan.20, Mar.1, 16, 1850
6:18   L J, Jan.3, 10, 1851
6:19   L J, Jan.2, 9, 16, 23, 1852
6:20   L J, Feb.13, Nov.5, 19, 26, Dec.3, 10, 24 1852
6:21   T R M B, Mar.17, 1853. L J, Sept.16, 1853
6:22   L J, Oct.7, 14, 21, Nov.4, 1853. Burley, p.167
6:23   L J, Dec.30, 1853. L C, Jan.28, 1854
6:24   L C, Apr.1, 29, 1854
6:25   T R M B, April-June, 1855
6:26   L J, Sept.7, 1855. Aug.1, 15, Sept.12, 1856
6:27   L J, Dec.12, 1856. Feb.20, Mar.27, 1857
6:28   T R M B, Dec.15, 17, 1857. Jan.12, 1858
6:29   L J, Apr.9, May 28, 1858
6:30   L J, Sept.17, Oct.15, Nov.12, 26, Dec.3, 1858. Apr.1, July 8, 1859
6:31   L J, Sept.2, Oct.28, Nov.4, 1859. T R M B, Feb.7, 1860
6:32   L J, Sept.7, Nov.2, 9, 1860
6:33   L J, Dec.21, 28, 1860. Jan.18, Mar.1, Apr.26, May 3, 1861
6:34   L J, Sept.13, Oct.4, Dec.20, 27, 1861
6:35   L J, Jan.16, 1863. Jan.29, 1864
6:36   L J, July 1, Sept.23, 1864. Jan.13, 1865
6:37   L J, Apr.21, 1865
6:38   L J, Aug.30, Sept.13, 1867. Toole, pp.28-30. L J, Jan.10, 1868
6:39   C L C E, 1897, pp.89-90
6:40   L J, May 28, Aug.13, 27, Sept.3, 24, 1869
6:41   L J, Oct.16, 1868
6:42   L J, Aug.18, 25, 1871
6:43   L J, Aug.25, 1871
6:44   L J, Oct.18, Nov.1, 1872
6:45   W, Feb.19, 1897
6:46   L J, Sept.5, 19, 1873. L D P, Sept.16, 23, 1873
6:47   L J, Oct.3, 10, 24, 1873
6:48   L J, Nov.7, 28, Dec.5, 12, 1873. Jan.2, 9, 30, 1874
6:49   L J, May 22, July 10, 17, 1874
6:50   L J, Sept.11, Oct.23, 30, 1874. L D M, Nov.2, 1874
6:51   L J, Jan.1, Feb.5, 1875
6:52   L J, Apr.9, May 7, 1875

7:1   L J, Dec.9, 1870
7:2   L J, Apr.30, 1869
7:3   L J, Sept.14, 1877
7:4   L J, Aug.4, Sept.29, Dec.16, 1876. R O, 12091 (1876), (Filed under R). L C, Feb.17, 1877
7:5   L A, Aug.25, 1877. L D P, Sept.7, 1877
7:6   L C, June 16, Aug.25, 1877. L J, Aug.31, 1877. L D P, Aug.25, 1877. L A, Aug.25, 1877. Era, Sept.9, 1877.
7:7   I L C, Apr.25, 1952
7:8   W, June 29, 1894

7:9   L J, May 2, 1879
7:10   R O, 10778 (1903), attached to 13011 (1906)
7:11   L C I C, Programme, July 28, 1879. L J, Mar. 5, 1880
7:12   Era, Sept.9, 1877
7:13   W, Jan.25, 1895
7:14   L A, Aug.25, 1877
7:15   L C, Sept.8, 1877
7:16   L J, Sept.7, Oct.12, 1877. Jan.1, 1878
7:17   L J, Aug.31, 1877
7:18   L J, Apr.26, May 3, Aug.16, Sept.13, 1878
7:19   L J, Jan.3, Feb.14, 1879
7:20   L J, Aug.22, Oct.3, 1879. Jan.23, 1880
7:21   L J, May 6, June 3, Sept.16, Nov.4, 1881. Feb.2, 1883
7:22   L J, Feb. 15, 1884. Feb.18, 1885
7:23   L D P, Jan.24, 1888. Stage, Feb.27, 1888. Era, Oct.19, 1862
7:24   L D P, Apr.17, 1888. W, June 15, 1901
7:25   L J, Sept.20, 1889. W, Sept. 2, Aug.19, Nov.18, 1892. Sept.1, 1893. Apr.6, Dec.14, 1894. Sept.9, 1898. ILC, Dec.25, 1926. L Ma, June 13, 1922
7:26   L A, Sept.1, 1888. L C, Sept.1, 1888. Stage, Aug.27, 1888
7:27   W, Aug.7, 1896. L J, Oct.30, 1896
7:28   Era, June 27, Aug.8, 1903. R O, see 7:10. L D P, Aug.4, 1903
7:29   L G, Aug.26, 1905
7:30   L G, Aug.6, 1904. R O, 13011 (1906). L C, Sept.1, 1888
7:31   L J, Aug.23, Sept.6, 1878. Apr.25, May.2, Nov.14, 1879. Feb.20, 27, Dec.24, 1880
7:32   L J, Oct.21, 28, Dec.9, 1881. Feb.3, May 5, 1882. Aug.31, 1883
7:33   L J, Sept.5, 1884. T R A, Feb.12-Dec.31, 1884, (L C I C). L J, Jan.16, 23, Feb.20, 1885
7:34   L J, Apr.15, 22, June 3, 1887
7:35   L J, July 13, 1888
7:36   T R M B, Aug.30, 1888. Sept.6, 1889. W, Jan.22, 1892
7:37   L J, Aug.26, 1892

8:1   L J, Oct.25, 1793. Sept.16, 1796
8:2   L J, Sept.12, 1806. Sept.11, 1812. Sept.24, 1813. Sept.15, 1815. Sept.15, 1820
8:3   L J, Apr.3, 1818. Dec.22, 1838
8:4   L J, Sept.15, 1825. Sept.8, 1832. Sept.11, Oct.9, 16, 1835
8:5   L C, Apr.7, 1839. Saxon, pp.275, 455, ftn.10. McCarthy. L J, Apr.26, May 10, 1839
8:6   L C, Oct.24, 1840. May 15, 1841
8:7   L J, Dec.30, 1842. Aug.23, 1848. Oct.30, 1840
8:8   L C, Oct.9, Nov.13, 1841
8:9   L J, Nov.26, 1841
8:10   L J, Mar.31, 1843
8:11   L J, Mar.19, June 4, 1852. Oct.24, 1862. Aug.12, 1853. L C, Sept.24, 1853. L J, Oct.29, 1858. Jan.11, Apr.26, 1867. Jan.1, 1869. Feb.6, 1863. Nov.28, Dec.5, 1862
8:12   L J, Sept.29, Oct.27, 1843. M J, Oct.31, 1870
8:13   L J, Oct.6, 1843
8:14   L J, Feb.9, 16, 1844. Feb.28, 1845
8:15   L J, Sept.20, 1844. Nov.24, 1848
8:16   L J, Feb.9, 1849. Feb.14, 1890
8:17   L J, Jan.23, Oct.9, 1863. Nov.9, 1866. May 28, 1869
8:18   L J, Dec.24, 1875. Sept.1, Nov.10, 1882
8:19   L J, Sept.4, Oct.30, Nov.6, 1885. R O, 16759 (1885)
8:20   L J, Oct.4, 18, 1889

8:21   R O, 20102 (1889). W, Feb.10, 1893
8:22   L J, Aug.1840. May 19, 1843. Jan.24, 1845
8:23   L C, Oct.22, 1836
8:24   L C, May 16, 23, 1840. L J, May 19, 1854. May 21, 1858. L Me, Nov.29, 1924
8:25   L J, May 16, 1862. M J, Oct.31, 1870. L J, May 17, 1889
8:26   L C, Jan.19, 1839
8:27   Information from Miller
8:28   Information from Swift and Fletcher
8:29   L J, Mar.31, 1876. L C, Dec.16, 1876. L J, Dec.8, 15, 29, 1876
8:30   L J, Apr.6, 27, May 18, 1877. Feb.1, Mar.8, Apr.5, May 3, Sept.20, 1878
8:31   L J, Sept.26, Oct.10, 1879. July 9, 1880. Feb.29, Mar.7, 21, 1884. W, Oct.13, 1899
8:32   L A, Aug.18, 1888. W, Sept.28, Oct.17, 1890. Jan.11, Apr.12, 1895. L G, Jan.13, 1900

9:1   L D P, Aug.1, 1890. L J, Sept.12, 1862
9:2   L J, Oct.18, 1861. L Ma, Oct.5, 1912. L J, Sept.6, 1861
9:3   L J, May 9, 1862. Sept.19, 26, 1873
9:4   L J, Sept.19, 1862
9:5   R O, 238 (1864). Harrod's Dir. 1870. L J, Dec.2, 1870
9:6   Era, Sept.19, 26, 1869. L Me, Nov.3, Dec.26, 1924. L J, Sept.17, 1869
9:7   L J, Mar.5, 1875
9:8   L A, Oct.28, Nov.18, 1876. R O, 12107 (1876). L J, Nov.29, 1878
9:9   L J, Feb.10, May 5, July 7, 14, 28, 1882
9:10   L J, Sept.29, July 21, 1882
9:11   L J, Apr.29, Aug.12, 1881. Mar.3, Sept.29, Oct.7, 1882. Feb.1, 1878. May 5, 1882
9:12   L J, Oct.21, 1881. Jan.8, 1886
9:13   L J, Nov.24, Dec.8, 1882. Dec.25, 1885
9:14   L J, May 18, June 8, 1888
9:15   L J, Oct.5, 1888. R O, 19488 (1888)
9:16   L J, Mar.1, 1889. L A, Mar.2, 1889. L D P, Mar.1, 1889. L Me, Sept.21, 1956
9:17   R O, 1547 (1862). L Me, Nov.20, 1924. L J, Nov.23, 1866
9:18   L J, Aug.2, 1867. L Me, Nov.3, 1924. L J, Aug.27, 1869. Mar.20, 1874. L Me, Nov.15, 1924. L R S M. Era, July 18, 1880. M J, July 9, 1880
9:19   M J, May 13, 1881. T C, Oct.7, 1881
9:20   L D P, Sept.3, 1883
9:21   L J, Apr.17, May 8, 1885. Howell and Ford, p.86f. L J, Dec.10, 1886
9:22   T C, Oct.7, 1881. L G, Mar.3, 1906. M J, Feb.18, 1881. L J, Feb.12, 1886. Sept.30, 1887. W, Mar.13, 1896
9:23   R O, 18095 (1887). L J, Sept.28, 1888. Aug.15, Sept.5, Oct.10, 1890. Stage, May 7, 1891
9:24   R O, 358 (1892). Kelly, Dir. 1895. L G, Mar.30, Apr.13, May 18, 1901
9:25   L A, Aug.9, 1890. L D P, Aug.1, 1890. L J, Aug.8, 1890
9:26   Era, May 27, 1893. R O, 3621 (1896). 15409 (1910)
9:27   I L C, Nov.15, 1930
9:28   L G, May 25, 1901
9:29   L D P, June 18, 1901. Era, June 22, 1901. L J, June 21, 1901. L C, June 22, 1901. L A, June 22, 1901. R O, OC1, 936/51. L G, June 15, 22, 1901
9:30   L Ma, June 12, 1915
9:31   L Ma, Oct.29, 1918. L C, June 27, 1908
9:32   R O, 10831 (1903), 18085 (1913), 18505 (1913), 57504

(1938). L G, June 15, 1901

10:1 W, Dec.18, 1896. Jan.22, 1897. L J, Dec.24, 1897.
L D P, Jan.11, 1898
10:2 W, Sept.21, 1894. Nov.8, 1895. Oct.15, 1897. L D
P, Nov.1, 1898. Programmes, L C I C, Mar.6-11,
1899. Oct.22-5, 1894. L D P, Aug.30, 1898
10:3 W, Aug.6, 1897. L D P, Jan.31, Mar.22, Aug.16,
Dec.13, 1898
10:4 L J, Jan.3, 1896. L D P, Jan.25, Dec.27, 1898
10:5 T R M B, Feb.14, Mar.21, May 18, 1900. Oct.18,
1901. L G, Oct.14, 1901
10:6 L G, Feb.10, 1900
10:7 L G, Dec.8, 1900
10:8 L Ma, Jan.25, 1916. R O, 23967 (1921). 24463 (1922).
33147 (1927)
10:9 L J, Oct.24, Dec.5, 1890
10:10 L D P, June 30, 1896. L J, Mar.11, 1898. Horn,
p.200. N H M, Letter from G. Field's manager.
L Me, July 1, 1929. June 21, 1930
10:11 I L C, Dec.6, 1930
10:12 L G, June 22, 1901
10:13 L G, 1901-2. May 30, Apr.11, Sept.12, 1903
10:14 L C, Jan.30, 1909. L Ma, Dec.29, 1917
10:15 L G, Sept.8, 1906. L Me, Dec.3, 1951
10:16 L C, Dec.12, Oct.17, 1908
10:17 L Ma, Nov.19, 1921
10:18 L D P, May 24, Nov.1, 1909
10:19 L G, Oct.26, 1901. L D P, Jan.19, 1909. L C,
Aug.10, 1909
10:20 L D P, Feb.6, 1911. L G, Sept.10, 1904. L Ma, June
10, Mar.11, 1913
10:21 L Ma, Feb.17, 20, 24, 1912. Feb.25, 1913
10:22 L D P, Aug.15, 1914. L Ma, Apr.22, 1916. May 8,
1917
10:23 L Ma, Aug.5, 1922. June 12, 1923
10:24 I L C, July 24, Dec.4, 1926. July 2, 1927. N H M,
Programme *Merry Doll.* I L C, Dec.11, 1937. Feb.19,
1938
10:25 I L C, Feb.23, 1946. Sept.3, Dec.17, 1949. July 22,
1950. June 16, July 28, 1951. Feb.21, 1953. Mar.29,
1952
10:26 Deakin, W.A. *19th c. Lo.* p.70
10:27 L J, Sept. 11, 18, 1896. Lo M, Sept.10, 1896
10:28 L J, Oct.9, 16, 23, Nov.27, Dec.18, 1896. Lo M,
Jan.14, Apr.15, May 27, 1897
10:29 L J, Aug.27, 1897. Lo M, Aug.26, 1897
10:30 L J, Aug.6, 1897
10:31 Lo M, Aug.1, 1901
10:32 Lo M, Sept.29, 1904
10:33 Lo M, Jan.26, Feb.2, 1905. Deakin, W.A. *Story of
Lo.* p.75. L Ma, Jan.13, 1912. Kelly's Dir. 1915.
Lo E, Jan.9, Feb.13, 27, 1953
10:34 L Me, June 15, 1957. *Exits and Entrances*
10:35 L J, Dec.13, 1889. Feb.7, 21, 1890
10:36 B C, Jan.9, 1904. Kelly's Dir. 1895, 1904. C T,
Aug.30, 1901. Jan.13, 1911
10:37 Kelly's Dir. 1912. L Ma, May 29, 1911. Mar.9, 1912.
Feb.26, 1924. I L C, Aug.14, 1926. Feb.15, 1930.
C T, Jan.28, Feb.4, 1910. Feb.14, 1930
10:38 W, Jan.20, 1893. Francis, p.135. H D F, April 1977,
pp.30-1. N H M, M.M. Picture Palace Playbills.
I L C, Mar.20, 1926. H T, July 31, 1970. She,
Nov.1981, p.186

11:1 L G, July 18, Aug.29, 1903
11:2 T R M B, Dec.1, 1905. Jan.25, Apr.12, 1906. Feb.22,
Oct.23, 1907
11:3 T R M B, July 2, 1915. Mar.1, 1917. May 3, 1921.

R L C, Programme, July 10, 1916. I L C, Jan.3,
June 3, Oct.3, 1925. Oct.2, 1926
11:4 I L C, May 14, 1932. Information from Gladys
Petty. I L C, Aug.25, 1934. Sept.25, Dec.18, 1948.
Jan.1, 1949
11:5 L G, Feb.9, 1901. L Ma, Jan.10, 1921
11:6 L Ma, Oct.1, Nov.29, 1921. May 2, 9, 16, 1922
11:7 L Ma, Nov.21, 22, 1921. Graham. L Ma, June 13,
1922. May 29, 1923. L Me, June 24, 1924. I L C,
Feb.20, 1926. Mar.3, 1928
11:8 I L C, Jan.3, 1931. Oct.10, 1925
11:9 I L C, Aug.22, 1931. June 18, 25, 1932
11:10 I L C, Aug.5, 1934
11:11 I L C, Oct.9, 1937. Mar.12, 19, Oct.22, 1938. Oct.7,
1939. L Me, June 2, 1940
11:12 L Me, Apr.16, 1940. I L C, Feb.1, June 21, 1941
11:13 I L C, July 19, 1941
11:14 L Me, Jan.22, 29, 1945. I L C, Mar.2, Aug.3, 10,
31, Oct.12, 1946
11:15 I L C, June 7, 1947. Sept.25, Dec.18, 1948. Jan.7,
1950. July 14, 1956
11:16 I L C, Oct.20, 1956. Nov.10, 17, 24, Dec.1, 1956.
Feb.9, 1957. L Me, June 3, 1957
11:17 L G, Oct.26, 1901
11:18 L G, Mar.7, 14, 1903. Oct.15, 1904
11:19 L G, Oct.29, Nov.5, 1904. L J, Aug.22, 1890
11:20 L G, Oct.13, 1906. L D P, Oct.3, 1907. Feb.15, 16,
19, 1909. L Ma, Feb.6, 13, 1911
11:21 L Ma, Feb.20, 1913
11:22 L D P, Oct.13, Aug.11, Feb.24, Mar.31, Apr.7,
Feb.10, Dec.1, 1914
11:23 L D P, Dec.26, Oct.13, 1914. L Ma, Sept.29, 1917,
Aug.6, 1918
11:24 L Ma, July 17, 20, 1918
11:25 L Ma, Oct. 12, 1920. May 3, Oct.11, 12, 1921.
O'Connor, pp.37-8
11:26 L Ma, Jan.10, Feb.7, June 27, 1922
11:27 L Ma, Sept.30, 1922. I L C, Feb.13, 1926
11:28 L Ma, June 19, Mar.20, Sept.1, 1923. I L C,
Mar.14, 28, 1925. Jan.29, 1927. July 18, 1925.
Aug.7, 1926. L Me, Oct.21, 1929. I L C, Nov.14,
1931
11:29 T R M B, Sept.16, 1931. I L C, Dec.5, 1931. May
21, June 4, July 18, Oct.22, 1932
11:30 I L C, Dec.3, 1932
11:31 I L C, Apr.15, 1933
11:32 I L C, Feb.4, 25, June 3, July 29, 15, 22, Sept.16,
Aug.12, 1933
11:33 I L C, Mar. 3, 10, 1934
11:34 I L C, Feb.13, 27, 1943. Feb.7, 1942. Oct.23, 1943.
Oct.21, 1939. Nov.27, 1943. Oct.21, 1944
11:35 L Me, Oct.8, Apr.9, 1940. June 11, Sept.3, Aug.6,
1945. I L C, Apr.30, May 7, Oct.8, 1938. July 29,
1939. June 28, 1941
11:36 I L C, Nov.9, 1946. Jan.7, Sept.8, 1950. May 26,
Aug.11, 1951. Apr.19, June 19, 1952
11:37 I L C, Jan.3, Feb.28, Mar.14, 28, Apr.4, May 16,
23, 1953
11:38 I L C, July 18, Aug.29, Sept.19, June 27, 1953
11:39 I L C, Mar.12, 1955. Aug.4, 1956
11:40 I L C, May 3, 1958. Feb.7, 21, 1959
11:41 I L C, Jan.10, 1959. Sept.29, 1951. L Me, Feb.23,
1959. L E M, July 3, 1959. L Ma, Nov.27, 1959.
I L C, Sept.27, Oct.4, 1958. L Ma, Feb.6, 1959.
Hankinson. Tabs, vol.xvii, Sept.1959, pp.9-17
11:42 I L C, Nov.14, 1959. L Ma, Nov.2, 1959. I L C,
Dec.5, 1959. June 4, 1960
11:43 L Me, Jan.9, 1962. Jan.3, 1963. *Living Theatre*

General Index and Index of Plays